DICKENS AND THE TRIALS OF IMAGINATION

Dickens

and the Trials

of Imagination

GARRETT STEWART

HARVARD UNIVERSITY PRESS

Cambridge, Massachusetts 1974

Library of Congress Catalog Card Number 74–77086

ISBN 0–674–20440–9

Printed in the United States of America

Publication of this book has been aided by a grant
from the Andrew W. Mellon Foundation

FOR MY PARENTS

who first taught me
to love Dickens

Acknowledgments

Muses ought rightly to be ladies, and in this respect my fortunes, and those of this book, have been durable and very good. In order of their assistance to me first as an undergraduate, then a doctoral candidate, and now as a colleague and fellow critic, and for the wonderful order of their minds, my deepest thanks to Virginia Tufte of the University of Southern California, who first taught me to love with understanding a writer for his words; to Marie Borroff, who, both as my teacher and thesis director at Yale University, kept the love alive and deepened the understanding; and to Helen Vendler of Boston University, who brings this instinct and insight to such impassioned clarity in her own writing, for her invaluable help at various times and seasons in the preparation of this book for publication.

A commentator on the life of imagination in fiction who has been graced in life with the kind of imaginative mentors and friends I have had would come forward with far flimsier credentials for the task than I am willing to acknowledge if he did not realize that such personal associations provide not only inspiration but also example for his theme. Special thanks, then, for their countless enlivening conversations over the last seven years, both corrective and otherwise, to William Carroll, Ann Dailey, and Richard Westphal, whose gifts (as Dickens might pun) were just that to me. My appreciation also for the time they repeatedly gave to the reading and rereading of these and earlier pages; for their dauntless display of wit and good spirits, often a recuperative spectacle for me when the going was less than good; and for that generosity matched with humor which I can now count upon to leave them satisfied, as a meager reward for their kindnesses, with only my affection, my gratitude, and the memory of the many follies they have saved me from.

This long-term redemptive labor has been heroically continued by my keen yet compassionate editor at Harvard University Press, Miss Kathleen Ahern, whose ear for tone and eye for shades of meaning, and needless shadows, would have pleased Dickens himself.

A version of the seventh chapter appeared under the same title in the Spring 1973 issue of *ELH*, Vol. 40, No. 1, pp. 105–130, and the Johns Hopkins University Press has given kind permission for the use of this material.

A grant-in-aid from the Graduate School of Boston University eased the burden of preparing the manuscript, as did the expert and critical typing, amounting almost to editorial service, of Mrs. E. P. Goodwin.

I wish to enter here, too, a large debt of gratitude to the remarkable graduate students at Boston University who have studied Dickens with me and from whom, again and again, I have taken such lively instruction in his wonders.

And finally to Deborah Dentler—who came quite late to this project, with advice and sympathy, and who, even in the midst of the long proofreading ordeal which her own fine eye and patience helped to expedite, still found it in her heart to marry me—my thanks and my love.

Contents

Prologue: The Parable of The "Rosy Wine"

Seven chapters into Dickens's fourth novel, *The Old Curiosity Shop*, whatever curiosity we have left over for any character after that fascinating Dickensian satirist, Daniel Quilp, begins to be repaid in the person of Mr. Richard Swiveller. It is with this chapter that Dickens the light-hearted comic stylist and his tacit namesake, Dick, flamboyantly and together, come more fully into their own high styles. Such concurrent rousing of genial powers is a large point to be made about the remarkable description with which I wish to begin. The opening paragraphs of this seventh chapter could have been turned out by no other writer of English before or after Dickens. The prose declares its authorship at once. Its style is in general too finished while at the same time too brisk and effortless, the syntax too ornate yet somehow unforced, offhand, never labored, the diction too heavily ornamental yet all the while too crisp, the tone too facetious though never smug or even flippant, indeed almost delicate in its own histrionic way—all of it too gaily majestic, too self-conscious, too *much* to be the work of anyone but our greatest writer of comic prose.

'Fred,' said Mr. Swiveller, 'remember the once popular melody of "Begone dull care;" fan the sinking flame of hilarity with the wing of friendship; and pass the rosy wine!'
Mr. Richard Swiveller's apartments were in the neighbourhood of Drury Lane, and in addition to this conveniency of situation had the advantage of being over a tobacconist's shop, so that he was enabled to procure a refreshing sneeze at any time by merely stepping out on the staircase, and was saved the trouble and expense of maintaining a snuffbox. It was in these apartments that Mr. Swiveller made use of the expressions above recorded, for the consolation and encouragement of his desponding friend; and it may not be uninteresting or improper to remark that even these brief observations partook in a double sense of the figurative and poetical

character of Mr. Swiveller's mind, as the rosy wine was in fact represented by one glass of cold gin-and-water, which was replenished, as occasion required, from a bottle and jug upon the table, and was passed from one to another, in a scarcity of tumblers which, as Mr. Swiveller's was a bachelor's establishment, may be acknowledged without a blush. By a like pleasant fiction his single chamber was always mentioned in the plural number. In its disengaged times, the tobacconist had announced it in his window as 'apartments' for a single gentleman, and Mr. Swiveller, following up the hint, never failed to speak of it as his rooms, his lodgings, or his chambers: conveying to his hearers a notion of indefinite space, and leaving their imaginations to wander through long suites of lofty halls, at pleasure. (O.C.S., 7)[1]

Just as Dickens's bright comic style has asserted itself at full tilt with this description, so Dick Swiveller has here unfurled his truer colors. His first speech in the novel, five chapters earlier, had recruited that same cliché about "the wing of friendship" and had even included Dick's belief that one's "spirit" is "expanded by means of rosy wine," but there his ebullience seemed party to the mercenary tactics by which he and his friend Trent hoped to wheedle money from the latter's grandfather. There Dick's "poetical" loquacity was the vocal accomplice to hypocrisy, the smooth garrulity of a shyster. Now, in the passage just quoted, it is part of a sincere and disinterested attempt simply to cheer up his friend, and it suggests an authentic grace of temperament. Through its style the passage also suggests considerably more.

The hefty, periphrastic, deliberately inconvenient wording, "conveniency of situation," the linguistic incongruity and anticlimax of the expressions "enabled to procure a refreshing sneeze" and "maintaining a snuffbox," the obligatory twinning of phrase in "trouble and expense," "consolation and encouragement," "uninteresting or improper," "figurative and poetical"—these are all tags of the Dickensian comic rhetoric, that satiric inflation I will be taking up in some detail with the initial chapter on *Pickwick Papers.* It would seem at first glance as if those conspicuous pairings just mentioned have been carefully pared down to an emphatic redundancy for their last appearance in the phrase "figurative and poetical character of Mr. Swiveller's mind." I suspect, however, that Dickens is quietly preserving there, and in fact spelling out, the distinction implied in "double sense." Because Dick says "pass the rosy wine!" knowing full well that it is only gin, he is speaking metaphorically, "figuratively," as it were; and because he is willing by his very nature to believe in the gin as "rosy wine," he is, in that second sense, dealing "poetically" with his environ-

ment, revising the prosaic facts of his inhospitable world. Like all
his other lofty catch phrases, his poetic snippets, borrowings,
popular allusions, and clichés, the "figurative" reference to "rosy
wine" is Dick's way of paying homage to the happier version of
things that fancy can conjure up, to the "poetry of existence"
which, in a defiled and ironic context, will appear in the epigraph
to my sixth chapter.

Dick is the high priest at the altar of conviviality, where the
license of poetry has the authority of holy writ, and the consecration of his would-be wine is the transubstantiation at which he
presides. Mr. Swiveller finds an early place among Dickens's men
of fancy and in the larger tradition of ginned-up imaginations
carrying through to our own day in the inebriate poetry and pipe
dreams of Eugene O'Neill's derelicts and fogbound souls. Drinking
and phrase-making are vitally linked for Dick Swiveller, and these
two phases of his entertainment actually merge when the gin sub-
mits to imaginative revision and is trans*figured* into "rosy wine."
With this frivolous comedy, a major Dickensian allegory is visited
upon us. For what happens to the gin is what happens to anything
when the "poetical" spirit restyles it. The gin is both raw material
and emotional catalyst for the drunken poetizer, but the change
that is wrought comes to symbolize the miracle worked by all
imagination, both in art and in daydream, on the stuff of reality.

The next paragraph extends and enriches the parable. The
"flight of fancy" elaborated upon here is again the plurality of
Dick's "apartments":

In this flight of fancy, Mr. Swiveller was assisted by a deceptive piece of
furniture, in reality a bedstead, but in semblance a bookcase, which
occupied a prominent situation in his chamber and seemed to defy suspicion and challenge inquiry. There is no doubt that, by day, Mr. Swiveller
firmly believed this secret convenience to be a bookcase and nothing more;
that he closed his eyes to the bed, resolutely denied the existence of the
blankets, and spurned the bolster from his thoughts. No word of its real
use, no hint of its nightly service, no allusion to its peculiar properties, had
ever passed between him and his most intimate friends. Implicit faith in
the deception was the first article of his creed. To be the friend of
Swiveller you must reject all circumstantial evidence, all reason, observation, and experience, and repose a blind belief in the bookcase. It was his
pet weakness, and he cherished it.

The "deceptive" is here no lie, but a salutary fiction, part of that
effort of mind by which Dick's single room is multiplied into
"chambers," his imagination thereby more generously and spa-
ciously quartered. During that scene in the second chapter when

Dick's allusion to the "rosy wine" seemed a mere fraudulent gambit in his and Trent's con-game, Trent urged circumspection and Dick replied that "caution is the word, and caution is the act." It is only later that we find this formula transported into the region of honest fancy, with Dick ordained as a true believer in those miracles of imagination where word does guarantee act, where beauty translates as truth, where any such expression as "no sooner said than done" reflects an almost religious confidence in the power of saying to make good its own promises: rosy wine is the word, and rosy wine is the actuality.

With the transmutation of bedstead into bookcase, that "first article" of Dick's fanciful "creed," practical "reality" again gives willing way to poetic "semblance." Dickens has found here an uncannily neat symbol for the functional reciprocity of the real and the ideal. The seeming bookcase pulls down at night into a bed; the actual lies just on the other side of the imagined, perfectly hinged for the daily changeover from one to the other. In the description of Dick's waking denial of the bed, Dickens's own "figurative" language informs us at unusual depth about the full "poetical" significance of this bookcase/bedstead. For the metaphor "closed his eyes to the bed" hints at a dreaming-away of the domestic appliance designed in part for dreaming. And what replaces it is that item of household furniture devoted in its turn to transcribed daydreams and recorded fancies. These convertible symbols are astonishingly good, the imaginary bookcase as well as the ignored bed. Like the majority of the fanciful men in Dickens's novels, we do not see Mr. Swiveller as a conscious student of imaginative literature. His poetry has come miscellaneously, through a popular oral tradition of sprightly formulas, aphorisms, epithets, ballad lyrics, elegant clichés, high-sounding phrases of all sorts. What Dick has from books he probably has indirectly, and all of his poetry he carries in his head. It is only and wonderfully right that the books in his room should be *all in his mind* as well.

The expansiveness and profusion of phrase, with concision flouted in sentences terraced crazily with surplus detail, the constant foraging after metaphor, all the tireless flights and flourishes of Dickens's prose become occasions for a symbolic economy unknown to more chiseled and lapidary, less broadly spontaneous styles. With the scene in Dick's room, the glib effusions of Dickens's style become also a kind of prose empathy with his voluble character. Near the end of that second long paragraph I have quoted, Dickens unobtrusively addresses his audience with a direct use of the second person pronoun. It is "you," reader, who "must reject all circumstantial evidence, all reason, observation, and experience"—all rational ways of knowing—and "repose a blind belief in the bookcase," taking up for yourself the cause of "pleasant fictions." Blind to facts, we are asked to see only the idealized alternatives. Dickens's own style has already given witness to this fanciful "creed" even before its mysteries are expounded for us. For in his first reference to Dick's lodging, he twice mentioned "apartments" in the "plural number." As usual, Dickens's style asks of "you" no more than it gives.

What we have so far sampled is only Dickens's high comic style. What we will see beginning with the first paragraph of *Pickwick Papers* is the more thoroughly satiric style of linguistic parody. And there are at least two other major varieties of prose in Dickens —what I will call for now the lyric and the neurotic styles. Any one of these stylistic modes, with surprising frequency, is likely to take as its subject, whether in genuine, despoiled, or bewildered form, those same energies that drive it and give it life: the energies of an adventurous and versatile imagination. However fused or sundered in the expressive life of his characters themselves, it is the potent union of Dickens's style and motive imagination that sends us back time and again to the inevitable comparison with Shakespeare, subscribed to early in Dickens's career by Walter Savage Landor and David Masson,[2] and ringingly renewed by Steven Marcus for the 1970 Centennial: "What one feels and senses in reading Dickens is that the central genius of the English language— the genius embodied and developed in Shakespeare and the great English poets out of the changing and developing life of the language, spoken as well as written—is flowing directly through him, and that this living prose is inseparable from the higher values and achievements of our civilization, is indeed one of the chief instruments of their transmission and preservation."[3]

The "living prose" of Dickens's novels is of course—and Marcus's criticism is as quick as anyone's to acknowledge this— inseparable too from the "higher values and achievements" of Dickens's own personal greatness as a writer, the range and resource of his intuitive symbolism. The small moments of almost impossible insight and rightness, the sudden illuminations that take our breath away no matter how many times we have moved through them—these more than anything else he shares with the handful of our finest poets. Such unpredictable symbolic flashes, regularly ignored or gone round by Dickens's casual appreciators or his more vigorous apologists, have little to do with what these critics customarily take up, with Dickens's steady growth as a builder of sophisticated fictions, an engineer of massive symbolic structures, little to do with the dedicated increments of craft. These surprising moments are instead the divinations, so to say, of his poetic genius. They do not come with mastery, they simply come, and technique merely facilitates their arrival. A function of his "living prose," they appear in the native dominion of Dickens's style from the outset of his career. Style may be the last refinement of a writer's craft, the most disciplined level of a novelist's or a poet's art. Yet the greatest styles, and Dickens's is indisputably among them, bring with them as they are brought to their perfection something of the first intuitive flush of inspiration, that initial and spontaneous knowing.

Here I have worked round again to the inescapable comparison with Shakespeare, an analogy whose challenge criticism has never entirely met, despite some ground-breaking studies. The most brilliant of Shakespeare's own recent expositors, the late Sigurd Burckhardt, revealed, in the last essay written before his death, what he had come to feel was the underlying reality of Shakespeare's art. What he says also applies with full force, I believe, to the symbolic intuitions of Dickens: "It pleases our rationalist vanity to think that 'meanings' must be prior to the symbols in which they are 'clothed.' But meanings may well be—and often demonstrably are —*ex post facto*. It is the mark of Shakespeare—I am tempted almost to call it the secret of his genius—that he accepted such coincidences as somehow binding and revelatory, as belonging to the realm of dumb significants which, though initially and in themselves they seemed to mean nothing, had the most extraordinary way of acquiring meaning."[4] The description of Dick Swiveller's "apartments" in *The Old Curiosity Shop* would seem to house such *ex post facto* significance, and I will be talking about dozens of "figurative and poetical" occasions like this in the seven chapters that follow, junctures where Dickens is bound by the startling revelations of his own prose. An alertness to these symbolic nodes—and whether in dialogue or description they are often Dickens's most extraordinary realizations—is the only "methodology" I claim, a watchful interest in those scenes that become invested with meanings beyond their own advance scenarios, beyond plan or plotting.

What is more, these nerve centers of Dickens's prose frequently collapse into a single disclosure the largest themes of their books.

Most readers soon sense what recent critics tend to play down: that the whole of a Dickens novel is seldom greater than the sum of its parts. What makes Dickens our greatest novelist is not this characteristic achievement of our next best writers at all. Rather, Dickens's incomparable power often resides in those moments which summon up for us—and which tend to sum up—the complex surrounding drama which they so unsuspectingly mirror. Seeking another metaphor for the microcosmic completeness of these symbols, we might call them "monads," products of a fictional system so organic that entirety can be writ small in the least entity. Perhaps there is an analogy closer to home. Dickens does not so relentlessly call the Coketown workers in *Hard Times* "the Hands" without first explaining that they constitute "a race who would have found more favour with some people, if Providence had seen fit to make them only hands, or, like the lower creatures of the seashore, only hands and stomachs" (*H.T.* I, 10). The idiomatic synecdoche here indexes the dehumanizing exploitation of the entire social machine in *Hard Times.* For Dickens repeatedly to call the factory laborers "the Hands" is to participate with at times almost inaudible irony in the economic view which sees men as nothing but manpower, living instruments, without soul, without imagination. And so with that single recurring phrase the novel's panoramic satire is condensed and held tight. To borrow a term from this minor instance of the phenomenon, we might say that all such points of focal concentration in Dickens are acts of *symbolic synecdoche,* the part standing for and even amplifying the whole. To locate these moments in a given novel is often to take its deepest pulse, to find not only clues to meaning, but compacted versions of it.

For such interpretation, an analysis of style is the natural method, just as style was Dickens's habitual means of analyzing his own fictive material. When Dickens entered upon that Shakespearean covenant with the accidental, the intuitive, he knew, and he asked us to learn as we go, that the most profound symbolic meanings must be discovered as they are fashioned: word by word. Style inducts us into the odd realities of the Dickens world and induces our belief. But it has other business there as well. Dickens's verbal manipulation can be every bit as self-referential, as closed and introspective, as anything in Sterne's word-willed, logo-motive universe, yet Dickens's style accomplishes what Sterne's does not attempt. It is able to "verbalize" a private but credible world that is, finally, extra-linguistic, but whose hidden meanings are nevertheless self-revelatory, symbolic mysteries brought to light by a style that at one and the same time materializes and explores them.

No one, I suppose, who has ever read more than a few sentences of Dickens would argue that the choice of a stylistic focus in taking impressions of his achievement is a random or unwarranted decision. But if style provides the lens, so to speak, what is the field of vision? What sort of perspective am I seeking? Once more the passage about Dick Swiveller's "pleasant fiction" serves as example. For my large subject is the distribution of Dickens's own fluid and buoyant imagination to the tributary intelligences both of his heroes and at times of his villains, to all the people in his stories who exchange "semblance" for "reality" in various maneuvers of retreat, entrenchment, even visionary forays now and then. The irrational or "poetical" impulse is seen to be engaged in a desperate holding action against tedium and paralysis, a war against capitulation itself. From the intolerant and the intolerable around them, the beleaguered imaginations of Dickens's men and women often find no refuge but in their share of appeasing and remedial fancies. For such people of imagination, however, there is no commandingly apt term. "Irrationalist" does not quite fill the bill, and we ordinarily turn to the very circumlocution Dickens so often makes fun of, identifying Sam Weller and Dick Swiveller, say, as "men of poetic style and temperament," or noticing in Arthur Clennam "the fitful vestiges of a romantic spirit." Jane Austen recognized even earlier that there was no good categorical term to suggest those irrational mental processes that set Emma Woodhouse apart in her conjectural fancies from a "grammarian," a "linguist," or a "mathematician."[5] Austen wanted a word that would imply an activity commensurate with these professional standings, something that would connote the practiced and vocational in a way that "imaginer" would not. The word she coined was "imaginist," and it is still the best we have for that type of character whose genesis, growth, and migration I am about to trace, in both its true and its false shapes, through the novels of Dickens.

The comforts of both the "figurative" and "poetical" imagination, of both style and vision, are repeatedly falsified in the novels, on the one hand by men of rhetoric who have only words to live by, who cloak the vile hollows of their natures in opaque and elaborate language, and on the other by artificial romantics who sheathe their greed and self-indulgence in sham effusions about "the poetry of existence." A reconnaissance is made of both these

enemy camps in the fifth and sixth chapters respectively, along
with those strongholds of fancy's honest protagonists who have
fought bravely for their uneasy truce with reality. After three initial
chapters on the harmonious reign of Mr. Pickwick and his symbol
of the "servant" imagination in Sam Weller, and a fourth on the
intermediate comic "Apollo," Mr. Richard Swiveller, my fifth
chapter charts the decline of verbal imagination in the strut and
bluster of rhetoric's "naughty company," and the sixth chapter
surveys the complex romantic experiments and escapist gambles
that become necessary as verbal wit is disinherited.

When the pleasures of inventive language can no longer be
counted on to spirit us away from a minatory world, new fanciful
devices must be called into play—while by their imposture and
exploitation they are also called into question. Both sorts of imaginative fraud, the verbal and the temperamental, are pitilessly
exposed by Dickens, yet he acknowledges at the same time that
the ever-darkening world from which these self-cozening escapes
have been attempted is one in which authenticity is increasingly
difficult to achieve. Dick Swiveller says to himself in Dickens's
fourth book, "Let this gin be wine," and for the moment *would-be*
has worked its way into *is*. There is a desperation unknown to Mr.
Swiveller when Sairey Gamp later declares during *Martin Chuzzlewit*, in effect, "Let there be Mrs. Harris," thus willing into being
an imaginary suppliant who will administer, through Mrs. Gamp's
reflexive blessings, a verbal balm to her own craving fancy. It is
only by the end of his career that Dickens finds for this autonomous, self-realizing formula a more psychologically integrated, a
more internalized and personal embodiment. When Fanny Cleaver
says implicitly in *Our Mutual Friend*, "Let there be Jenny Wren,"
she has created for herself, by the act of announcing it, a new and
better presence, a personality liberated through the joint agencies
of style and vision. After the travails of a disinherited fancy, the
imagination has managed a new self-endowment. My last chapter,
on Jenny Wren, is the natural destination for a book devoted to
the numerous ways in which Dickens legitimizes the claims and
ventures of imagination, a study of that most sporadically noted
of all Dickens's major enterprises as a novelist: the drama of approximation by which certain of his characters grow into imaginative parity with their creator.

Part of what has been slighted by a commentary in this respect
is the intimate connection between such a psychological line of
development and Dickens's more often explored virtues as a social

critic. For him the two were, without question, inseparable. Though Dickens always portrays both the forfeitures and the extortions of imagination, its self-abuses as well as its external brutalizations, it is usually the case that the most damning accusations he makes in the novels about oppressive social structures have to do with their crippling effect on the human spirit, on our capacities for love and wonder. Here, from the often cited "Preliminary Word" that introduced to the public his periodical *Household Words,* is perhaps Dickens's fullest expository statement of the imagination's leverage for psychological, moral, and social improvement:

No more utilitarian spirit, no iron binding of the mind to grim realities, will give a harsh tone to our Household Words. In the bosoms of the young and old, of the well-to-do and of the poor, we would tenderly cherish that light of Fancy which is inherent in the human breast; which, according to its nurture, burns with an inspiring flame, or sinks into a sullen glare, but which (or woe betide the day!) can never be extinguished. To show to all, that in all familiar things, even in those which are repellent on the surface, there is Romance enough, if we will find it out:—to teach the hardest workers at this whirling wheel of toil, that their lot is not necessarily a moody, brutal fact, excluded from the sympathies and graces of imagination; to bring the greater and the lesser in degree, together, upon that wide field, and mutually dispose them to a better acquaintance and a kinder understanding—is one main object of our Household Words.[6]

Such a manifesto, however vague, goes far toward capitalizing the "r" in Dickens's romantic bias. Indeed, it was very much his purpose as a writer "to give the charm of novelty to things of everyday, and to excite a feeling analogous to the supernatural, by awakening the mind's attention from the lethargy of custom, and directing it to the loveliness and the wonders of the world before us." This is Coleridge, of course, in the famous fourteenth chapter of *Biographia Literaria,* writing about the part taken in the composition of the *Lyrical Ballads* by its co-author Wordsworth, that poet after Shakespeare whom Dickens seems most deeply to have assimilated.

Dickens was very much a writer in this Romantic tradition, very much a poet of the industrialized nineteenth century struggling to resist and counter its mechanizing impetus. Dickens assumes more completely his rightful stature as an original late Romantic, however, with a new contribution to the literature of fancy and imagination, mainly when he penetrates to its darker side, when he begins to examine the latencies of imagination as a maddening and destructive force. For what he calls in that *Household Words* document the "sullen glare" of a stifled "light of Fancy" can at any moment, under severe stress, flare up into fever. Through the means of what I have before mentioned as his "neurotic" style, Dickens is always ready to enter and interpret such moments. Though one of his deepest purposes as a novelist is to vindicate the honor of imagination as a force for spiritual reformation, the fancy also has a vindictive face which Dickens never flinches from exposing. And so the central noun in my title, *Dickens and The Trials of Imagination*, is—it is time to confess—a pun, to be taken in a Swiveller-like double sense. It refers not only to those "experiments" in fancy that put the irrational impulse to the proof in the fallen Dickensian world, that test its redemptive power, but also to those "ordeals" of the afflicted mind when the imagination retaliates against either its own starvation or its over-excitement, those pathological tribulations of fancy's revenge.

There is a painting by René Magritte which might be a surrealistic illustration of the industrial society's threat to imaginative privacy in Dickens. Among the major families of "imaginists" discussed in my densely populated sixth chapter are the romantic fire-gazers who seek escape from the impersonal menace of a spiritually neutralizing society, from the servitude of routine, through the visionary reading of hearth fires. It is an escape blatantly precluded in the vision of Magritte's "Time Transfixed," which pictures a drably fantastic Victorian interior with a miniature locomotive thrusting out in mid-air from the blank back wall of an empty fireplace. In the outlandish stasis of the painting, the hearth has been evacuated of its natural domestic fire, and even the candlesticks flanking a clock on the mantle are empty, a parody of decorative art giving off neither heat nor light. If we continue to read the painting as if it were a series of quotations from Dickens, the railroad engine becomes a symbol of the spirit's mechanization, an inhuman tool of industrial "progress" through time and across space. It is a machine often fueled in Dickens by the energy which should also be used to sustain, through hearth fires, the privately housed imagination, and which, in Magritte's arresting and arrested image, actually sends its noxious waste up the domestic chimney. This imagery seems especially close to the symbolic heart of *Dombey and Son* in particular, that pivotal novel for the themes of imagination where fire-gazing emerges as a central romantic motif and where one of the novel's bleakest moments has Mr. Dombey staring hopelessly into an empty fireplace (*D.S.*, 59). In *Dombey and Son*, too, the railroad first becomes a major symbol, with "time transfixed" in a violation of nature where "there was even railway time observed in clocks, as if the sun itself had given in" (15). This startling capitulation within the order of nature writes large the suicidal drift of private vision against which the imagination must try its best to hold out—and be tried.

Mostly in connection with the first exploratory sense in my title of a "tried" or "tested" imagination, I will continue to allude, as I have already done, to the High Romantic poets, loosely but I hope suggestively—in the way I believe Dickens himself to have drawn on them more often than critics have noticed. One of these poets' great contemporary heirs, Wallace Stevens, has written about the imagination in a way that should help, with some additional comment, to put our view of Dickensian "romance" into perspective before we begin to look at individual "romances." The essay is "Imagination as Value," and the crucial passage is this:

The imagination is one of the great human powers. The romantic belittles it. The imagination is the liberty of the mind. The romantic is a failure to make use of that liberty. It is to the imagination what sentimentality is to feeling. It is a failure of the imagination precisely as sentimentality is a failure of feeling. The imagination is the only genius. It is intrepid and eager and the extreme of its achievement lies in abstraction. The achievement of the romantic, on the contrary, lies in minor wish-fulfillments and it is incapable of abstraction.[7]

The comparison of the romantic and the sentimental is hardly an idle one for Dickens criticism, and no study of the Dickensian style could be so confused as not to reveal how exclusively his achievement lies in the direction of concrete and detailed reality; how far, except in parody, from abstraction. This is the drag the world had on his liberty of mind, but it was a world he loved and understood. However much Dickens's impoverished, nonconceptual "romance" and the "minor wish-fulfillments" of his characters might be thought to belittle the possibilities of imagination, still he cannot be accused of what for Stevens, in a different mood, is life's "greatest poverty"—"not to live in a physical world." In Dickens, desire is never too difficult to tell from despair, and between these two poles his characters make their way in the world, lorded over (to paraphrase "Esthetique du Mal" once again) by a gaiety of language that is the true creative source of their being and for some, in their own personal styles, an everyday gladness. In such a world false language must be sacrilege, bogus rhetoric a sin against the Word.

Only when the mind is aslant to reality, only in the revenge of imagination, is there ever repulsion from the concrete and detailed variety of the world in Dickens. It is then, too, that his versatile imitative style is equipped to portray, not the crowded, particularized life of the healthy senses, but the far side of fancy, the fevers of hysteria and hallucination. Only at such times in Dickens, when terrorized by concrete detail, would the mind ever wish it were not, as Stevens put it, "incapable of abstraction." Usually the noun "abstraction" is employed by Dickens as a comically inflated euphemism for "theft." Indeed, in its other sense as well, it is only natural that abstraction would seem to rob life of too much liveliness for a novelist who, perhaps better than any other, in his style and in the vision of the world it acts out, shows us not only the malady but also the glory of the quotidian. He shows us this glory for what it is: the way a romantic fancy can help see us through.

Sensing this demonstration in every bravura stroke, every nuance, every comic suasion of Dickens's "living prose," we may begin also to sense in the rendering of Dick Swiveller's "apartments" a final and encompassing parable. This locus of "pleasant fiction" for Mr. Swiveller becomes an image of Dickens's own house of fiction, which "you" must enter on the proprietor's own terms, as generous as they are demanding. For like Mr. Swiveller's visitors, Mr. Dickens's readers, ushered into the pages of any particular "fiction," find the host "leaving their imaginations to wander . . . at pleasure" through the "indefinite space" provided simply by being fancied, envisioned in the mind's eye of the creator. At the very least, I hope that nothing I am about to say can dim even for a second the fact that this "pleasure" in Dickens is among the largest and most continuous in our literature.

Part I

QUARANTINE OF IMAGINATION:

THE PICKWICKIAN REIGN

1 The Pickwick Case: Diagnosis

'Eruct, Sancho,' said Don Quixote, 'means belch, and
that is one of the coarsest words in the Castilian
language, though it is very expressive; and so refined
people have resorted to Latin, and instead of *belch* say
eruct and for *belches eructations* . . . for that is the
way to enrich the language.'—Cervantes, *Don Quixote*, Part II[1]

Dickens's precocious masterpiece, *The Posthumous Papers of the Pickwick Club*, is like no other novel. Its vision of innocence aside, it is in another way one of the purest books in our literature, pure because nothing has been refined or filtered off, pure precisely because nothing has been purified away. It is the essential, the instinctive Dickens, unhindered, eager, yet somehow miraculously mastered. By being in a sense all rough edges, it appears to have none. It is, at its finest times, full of those things Dickens does best and is to do better and better with the increase of his genius, but which he will never again do so freely. And the freedom of *Pickwick Papers* is not abandon, but discovery. It seems a freedom that has no second thoughts, that trumpets its own unimportance, yet, when they come, its significances can leave us gasping.

[*Pickwick* is a book with secrets; like the best moments in Dickens after it, this entire first novel seems to take itself by surprise.] Then, too, there is nothing like *Pickwick Papers* because while we are in it there seems to be nothing else. Its wholeness is not only complete but exclusive. The novel has a life of its own, a personality, the way only characters in most other books have such lives. In fact *Pickwick Papers* has a split personality, a divided nature that invites a kind of stylistic psychoanalysis. It has a nature that *speaks to us* in a rather literal sense, announcing mood and temper through its various voices. In no other Dickens novel is there quite so much dialogue, and in none is the surrounding prose so much like the talk it frames. To all this we must pay close attention, trying to catch the tone. Defined roughly for our purposes here, tone is the way style has us listen to narrative voice, and what we hear in *Pickwick Papers* we will hear over and over again in Dickens. From the intersecting and colliding styles of his first novel there results, among other things, a pervasive ironic tone discernible everywhere in that comic prose which will be his mainstay from *Pickwick* on out. There is another reason, too, for beginning at such length with *Pickwick Papers*. The primacy of tone in this first novel, with its implications about Mr. Pickwick's serene but guarded temperament, the limits imposed on his imagination, brings style and the themes of imagination into a revealing alliance.

My first chapter will explore Dickens's diagnosis, primarily in *Pickwick*, of the stylistic ills which plagued literature and public rhetoric in his day. Parody is most often his mode of analysis, and when he turns it against the Pickwickians, we begin to understand what ails the novel's opening not only in style but in implied mentality. Dickens's ironic diagnosis continues to probe the emotional make-up of Mr. Pickwick himself, discovering the symptoms of a temperamental strength that is also a peculiar kind of constitutional weakness—requiring what my second chapter will study as the quarantine of imagination. Style performs as the very means of isolation, setting the prevailing Pickwickian tone while alternately, in the interpolated tales, offering the means of experimentation for divergent forms of imaginative experience. The resolution of style and tone in the closing pages of the novel will be one subject of my third chapter, a release from quarantine which will then need comparison with the imaginations of Sam and Tony Weller—characters who have been exempt from the start of the book, and whose styles tell their stories.

There being no better place to start, let us attend (it is quite a syntactical performance!) the very first sentence, all by itself the first paragraph, of *Pickwick Papers*:

The first ray of light which illumines the gloom, and converts into a dazzling brilliancy that obscurity in which the earlier history of the public career of the immortal Pickwick would appear to be involved, is derived from the perusal of the following entry in the Transactions of the Pickwick Club, which the editor of these papers feels the highest pleasure in laying

before his readers, as a proof of the careful attention, indefatigable assi-
duity, and nice discrimination, with which his search among the multi-
farious documents confided to him has been conducted.

Whatever else this is, it is preposterous, a sodden prose in which
gravity is overheard digging its own grave. Diction and syntax
have together taken leave of at least one of their senses, and the
result is tone-deaf eloquence. Clotted by the multiple passive
forms and the five mechanical relative clauses, this is a lifeless,
colorless rhetoric which it is never dreamed any of us will spot as
verbosity. Except of course by Dickens, for it is all a joke, a parody.
I have said it is this, "whatever else" it may be, in deference to
Steven Marcus, who has deepened his own pioneering study of
Pickwick in an important revisitation of Dickens's first novel. His
interest at this homecoming is more than ever linguistic, his attention naturally drawn to that first replete sentence. "It is a parody,
which later on and at length we learn is in part not a parody," but
rather an embodiment of pure creative impulse. The novel's opening sentence "begins at the beginning, with 'creation' itself, with
the Logos appearing out of 'obscurity'—that is, the 'earlier history
... of the immortal Pickwick'—and into the light of creation. But
it also dramatizes the fundamental activity of the Logos; it dramatizes the notion of cosmic creation as a word—which is how God,
as the Logos, created the world: *fiat lux*, said God, when he was
speaking Latin, and so it was."[2] Marcus is paying tribute here to
the generative powers of Dickens's language, a just and subtle
tribute which I would want to qualify only by insisting in more
detail on the *quality* of the language in *Pickwick*, on the parody
itself which we may later manage to see beyond.

The first words of *Pickwick Papers* are poor words. If the Logos
is revealed, it is the Logos gone wrong. Dickens may well
be orienting his first sentence entirely in verbal terms. He even
appears to suggest that the antecedent chaos, the "gloom" upon
which the initial words so blindingly dawn, was itself, somehow,
a verbal disarray. There are two timid puns in the phrase "that
obscurity in which the earlier history of the immortal Pickwick
would appear to be involved," for "history," like its synonym
"life," can refer either to experience itself or to biography, to events
written down, and "involved" is a possible adjectival form not
only for "involvement" but for grammatical "involution," of
which this supposedly corrective sentence is a nasty sample.
There seem to be more hints here than Marcus has picked up;

from one angle, writing may indeed be the *only* subject of the novel's opening statement. Later in his essay, Marcus cleverly points out that with the chiseled motto "BILL STUMPS, HIS MARK," we may actually have inscribed for us a hidden truth about the novel: that it, too, like the carving on the stone, is "writing about writing."[3] There is a duplicate clue in the chapter just before the stone is found, another hint Marcus himself does not mention. Enraged at Alfred Jingle, Mr. Pickwick throws an inkstand against the wall, leaving *his* mark, and Sam Weller is on hand to interpret: "Self-acting ink, that 'ere; it's wrote your mark upon the wall, old gen'lm'n" (10). In a novel where Dickens is "undertaking to let the writing write the book,"[4] the image of "self-acting ink" may indeed be a node of unexpected meaning. Faced with all this "writing about writing," I simply wish to place my emphasis on the kind of writing it is. The topic of *Pickwick Papers* is not writing per se, not language in general. What the novel seizes as its subject by (and in) its very first words is the kind of language that is self-aware in the worst sense, words not only self-generated but self-serving. The style of *Pickwick* is a monumental satire, conceived and executed with some specific targets in mind. For Marcus's case there may be more evidence than he needed; for mine much more is now in order.

One of Gissing's few negative comments about Dickens's style —that "facetiousness is now and then to blame for an affected sentence"[5]—is a decidedly unhelpful remark, both in its understatement and in its own unfollowed lead. That more recent novelist-critic, Angus Wilson, is more specific in his distaste for what he thinks the disastrous opening of *Pickwick*, "one of the worst, most facetious chapters he [Dickens] ever wrote."[6] We may well decide that Dickens overdid his opening, but we should first decide what it was he set out to do. The trouble with Gissing's criticism, or so it appears, is his failure to recognize "affectation" as the key to what becomes an elaborate stylistic parody, perhaps overly concentrated in this first chapter but meted out in smaller doses to almost every other chapter in Dickens. Of all the moral and personal failings the novelist attacks, affectation is the best suited for immediate translation into style, and Dickens detests affectation with a vigor that communicates itself undiminished to his parodic comedy, becoming one of the hallmarks of prose. Here is a debt in theory to one of Dickens's favorite authors; at one point in *Pickwick* there is an aphoristic comment on human passion which opens with the words "Fielding tells us" (8), but any reader familiar with English fiction will have long since recognized a more widespread influence. This is Fielding from his "Preface" to *Joseph Andrews:* "I might observe that Ben Jonson, who of all men understood the Ridiculous the best, hath chiefly used the hypocritical affectation."[7] The subject of verbal hypocrisy in Dickens, of deceptive rhetoric after *Pickwick,* will get full-scale treatment in the chapter on "Naughty Company," where the Jonsonian tradition will also come in for discussion. In *Pickwick Papers,* meanwhile, it is the other phase of Fielding's "ridiculous," the affectation of "vanity," which is most often in question and which prompts the linguistic "burlesque" in Dickens's own first and purest example of the "comic epic-poem in prose."[8] In addition to Jonson, *Joseph Andrews* acknowledges a major debt to *Don Quixote* on its title page. What we are about to discover concerning Dickens's verbal satire will help place him in a tradition of linguistic comedy that dates back, as my epigraph testifies, to Cervantes, and that moves through Fielding, Smollett, and Sterne to Dickens himself, and from Dickens through Meredith to Joyce and Nabokov.

Circumlocution, the affected herding of as many words as possible into a given meaning, is one of the ways linguistic "vanity" often finds expression. Things do not amuse in *Pickwick,* they afford amusement; people do not agree, they express their concurrence. Instead of being shown a double chin, we are conducted more delicately to this observation: "his chin . . . had acquired the grave and imposing form which is generally described by prefixing the word 'double' to that expressive feature" (23). Elegant variation—in Dickens just a special case of eloquent elongation—makes a frequent appearance, with most errors into the ordinary soon valiantly set right. Jesperson cites several non-comic examples from Dickens where words of Latin or Greek derivation follow those of native origin as approximate synonyms, avoiding repetition.[9] What Jesperson notices helps us to see something characteristic about Dickens's style. While capitalizing on the wealth of synonyms at his command, Dickens never loses sight of the possible excess, the ready comedy of circumlocution and variation. As with so many of his linguistic methods, he recognizes the laughable just around the corner from the habitual. And he takes this turn into comedy as often as possible. When one moment a character cannot "believe his eyes," the next moment we can hardly believe our ears as he is forced into "the painful necessity of admitting the veracity of his optics" (2). When Dickens writes

of "the red-headed man with a grin which agitated his countenance from one auricular organ to the other" (5), he is of course
inviting this very response from us by another mock-scientific
periphrasis, one almost as ludicrous as Sterne's having Uncle Toby
whistle by "directing the buccinatory muscles along his cheeks,
and the orbicular muscles around his lips to do their duty."[10] The
satire is of course every bit as deliberate in Sterne, where the narrator Tristram at one point objects to the habit of placing "tall,
opake words, one before another, in a right line, betwixt you and
your reader's conception,"[11] and where Parson Yorick, arch-enemy
of "gravity" and "affectation" and one of the book's true heroes,
emerges as a standard-bearer for "plain *English* without any
periphrasis."[12]

Taking example from Sterne among other of his important masters, Dickens finds that epithets and honorific titles serve as an
especially good proving-ground for his verbal satire. "The fat boy,"
on one of his appearances, has his title elegantly varied a paragraph later to "the bloated lad" (8), a typical bloating of phrase
which will later be used to identify the book's main characters,
Mr. Pickwick and Sam Weller respectively, as "the illustrious man,
whose name forms the leading feature of the title of this work"
and "that eccentric functionary" (10). The difference—we sense
it at once—is that Sam, unlike his master, would get the joke, and
might well have made it. Tony Weller is at one point called Sam's
"progenitor," and on the same page Sam mocks the whole periphrastic habit by referring to his father, in direct address, as "corpi-
lence" (33). Mr. Pickwick, however, has no ear for language, no
playful spirit; and he is quite unable to savor with the proper
grain of salt those colloquial idioms that come his way. As a complete literalist, the licensed metaphors of slang have no jurisdic-
tion in his vocabulary, and when Bob Sawyer asks, "I say, old boy,
where do you hang out?", this is what we hear: "Mr. Pickwick
replied that he was at present suspended at the George and Vul-
ture" (30). Dickens answers for him, but presumably by repeating
his own words. In any case the point is made, for by now we realize that Mr. Pickwick's serious pronouncements sound alarmingly
like Dickens's parodic prose.

In *Pickwick Papers* Dickens is especially wordy and roundabout
when it comes to that communal act of ritualized significance,
the meal. At one place we find Mr. Pickwick "deeply investigating
the interior of the pigeon-pie" (4), and twice in one prandial paragraph the idea of eating is deftly circumnavigated with "yield full

justice to the meal" and "do good execution upon a decent proportion of the viands"(19). On the same page where eating is termed
"the work of destruction," we hear about the fat boy "abstracting a
veal patty" (4), and with this locution we have moved, according
to the *OED*, from circumlocution to euphemism—indirection for
propriety as well as elegance, but mocking all the while the Victorian syndrome of delicate and evasive diction. "Excisable articles
were remarkably cheap at all the public houses" (14), we are told,
facetiously asked to swallow this substitute for "alcoholic bever-
ages." Euphemism and periphrasis, of course, continually overlap
in Dickens's prose, becoming a source of laughter previously sanctioned by Fielding in his program for the "comic epic-poem in
prose." Though insisting on the differences between "the comic
and the burlesque," Fielding did make this concession for the
higher form of comedy: "In the diction, I think, burlesque itself
may be sometimes admitted."[13] Certainly both he and Dickens
avail themselves of the leeway this offers, with comic euphemism
as one of the chief forms of such "burlesque." It is interesting to
speculate about an actual debt to Fielding's description of the
sleeping Parson Adams, who "snored louder than the usual bray-
ing of the animal with long ears,"[14] when Dickens writes in the
Sketches by Boz about one Mr. Alexander, who "was deservedly
celebrated for possessing all the pertinacity of a bankruptcy-court
attorney, combined with the obstinacy of that useful animal
which browses on the thistle" ("Tales," 7).

Throughout the *Sketches*, the concept of pants is taken on
with great scrupulosity, and we hear trousers rechristened repeatedly as "inexplicables" or "unmentionables." Before the Victorian
advent, Sterne could say "breeches" but makes fun of his inability
to itemize their features, when that scabrous chestnut "fell perpen-
dicularly into that particular aperture of *Phutatorius's* breeches,
for which, to the shame and indelicacy of our language be it spoke,
there is no chaste word throughout all *Johnson's* dictionary."[15]
The last euphemism for pants in *Pickwick Papers* is "symmetrical
inexpressibles" (55), and it reminds us of the transparent farce in
all such phrases. To write about "unmentionables," for instance,
to mention them even in this way, or to express the symmetry of
"inexpressibles," is to skirt paradox rather narrowly. The logical
fallacy of such a linguistic trick is used earlier and even more
pointedly in *Pickwick*, deliberately, in fact, to point up the hypocrisy of such euphemistic sleight of hand. "Mr. Trotter smiled, and
holding his glass in his left hand, gave four distinct slaps on the

pocket of his mulberry indescribables with his right." (16). It need hardly be said that "mulberry" is itself a descriptive adjective. Self-perjured, such a phrase is its own worst indictment. We also see that it evolves from mixed rhetorical motives; Dickens is poking fun not only at false modesty but at that periphrastic high style which so often goes hand in hand with euphemism. To George Orwell, who, like Dickens, views language morally, circumlocution and euphemism are partners in essentially the same crime: "The inflated style is itself a kind of euphemism. A mass of Latin words falls upon the facts like soft snow, blurring the outlines and covering up all the details. The great enemy of clear language is insincerity. When there is a gap between one's real and one's declared aims, one turns as it were instinctively to long words and exhausted idioms, like a cuttlefish squirting out ink."[16]

That self-accusatory item, "mulberry indescribables," is a tiny instance of Dickens at his most compressed and intuitive. I would like to introduce two other related examples that bear on the verbal satire of his first novel, two sentences that put the problem of language's "insincerity" very clearly before us and that, in the process, become unexpected paradigms, reflecting from their confined surfaces an entire linguistic issue. The first of these strangely reflexive sentences, seeded with its own satiric dissent, follows a speech by Alfred Jingle, as yet unnamed:

'Come,' replied the stranger, 'stopping at Crown—Crown at Muggleton—met a party—flannel jackets—white trousers—anchovy sandwiches—devilled kidneys—splendid fellows—glorious.'
Mr. Pickwick was sufficiently versed in the stranger's system of stenography to infer from this rapid and disjointed communication that he had, somehow or other, contracted an acquaintance with the All-Muggletons, which he had converted, by a process peculiar to himself, into that extent of good fellowship on which a general invitation may be easily founded. (7)

Here the breathless and the long-winded face each other across a padded phrase, "system of stenography," which is meant to describe the telegraphic "shorthand" of the former but which in fact illustrates the circumlocution of the latter. With this minor self-critical phrase, Dickens scores against inflated prose in the very act of designating its opposite. In the chapter just before, we have already been teased into extrapolation from another loaded sentence, nominally describing a quiet evening at cards: "The rubber was conducted with all that gravity of deportment and sedateness of demeanour which befit the pursuit entitled 'whist'—a solemn observance, to which, as it appears to us, the title of 'game' has been very irreverently and ignominiously applied" (6). That first tumescent phrase, "gravity of deportment and sedateness of demeanour," borders on redundancy and then gives way to the elegant variation by which "pursuit," itself an ennobling synonym for game, is puffed up to "solemn observance." Could prose or point anywhere—either deportment of style or demeanor of meaning—possibly be rendered more grave, sedate, or solemn? Circumlocution has again located its own satire, and the sentence almost seems to take as its subject that excessive language itself by which it is drawn out. To talk in this stuffy way and be serious is to live in a closed "game" world, airless and immature, and when the satirist notices this he is of course acting "irreverently." It is his own corresponding "game," with few rules and no real restraints, in which the score is tallied against a satiric opponent embodied in the parodied style itself.

It is an irony Dickens must have enjoyed that there were critics in his day who made no objection to his satiric "game" until it was played with a mixed deck, until native diction began to spoil words "in themselves good and classical." This last is from a review in which are cited among Dickens's "various impurities of expression" and "gross offenses of the English language" such typically Dickensian transgressions, often contributing to the famous animism of his description, as "*impracticable* nightcaps . . . *inscrutable* harpsichords, *undeniable* chins, *highly geological* home-made cakes . . . and the *recesses and vacations* of a toothpick."[17] These offenders were arraigned from *Martin Chuzzlewit*, but Dickens's interest in such collocations, the nearest possible contact he can force between the high and the low styles, to the discomfiture of the former, was with him from the beginning. In the *Sketches by Boz* we hear of a gentleman with an "interrogative nose" ("Our Parish," 4), and at our first meeting with Mr. Perker in *Pickwick Papers* we find that he too has an "inquisitive nose," with which he indulges in an "argumentative pinch of snuff" (10). Later in the book, an anonymous waiter provides the occasion for such irreverent verbal coupling by having over his arm a napkin that was a fortnight old, "and coeval stockings on his legs" (22). This sort of phrasing is so inveterate with Dickens that it turns up in his last completed novel, over thirty years later, when Silas Wegg leaves *Our Mutual Friend* by being thrown into a scavenger's cart with a "prodigious splash" (O.M.F. IV, 14). Dickens never ceased to enjoy making incompatible partners within a single phrase of the two sorts of diction, invariably at the expense of the "good and classical" words. Their nearness to the native consort becomes a slight ironical jab at their own staid usage, as they somehow shed importance on the domestic or commonplace Anglo-Saxon word while continuing to look a little awkward and silly for the company they are keeping.

This is part of what happens when Nabokov takes to this sort of phrasing for *Lolita*. Charlotte Haze incarnates an earthy bourgeois grossness which she tries ceaselessly to deodorize with her "polished words."[18] It never works, and this nervous discord in her personality is captured perfectly by the narrator's Dickensian linkage of a Latinized status word and a subversive bit of homely onomatopoeia, in that "deprecatory grunt" with which Charlotte stoops to pick up a sock.[19] A sentence later, however, the narrator himself has "surreptitiously fished" a train time-table from his pocket, and the linguistic satire (as it does constantly in Dickens) has widened free of its immediate personal object. In *Lolita,* the marriage of high and low is more than phrasal; it becomes in part the theme of Humbert's union with both Haze women. More centrally yet, it is of course the theme of *Pickwick Papers* and, before it, of *Don Quixote,* where "eruct" and "belch" are abutted in the same way that Quixote and his squire, that Pickwick and his manservant later, must confront each other's opposite "styles," their divergent experience of the world. In the comic authors before Nabokov, and most strikingly in Dickens, it is both the down-to-earth vernacular and the worldly assurance it bespeaks which carry the day. The higher the style, the harder it falls.

It must not be thought that Dickens stood alone in his day as a champion of native English in all of its resource and vernacular energy. He was part of a strong nineteenth-century movement away from unquestioned deference to the classical standards of language, and he wrote a piece called "Saxon-English" for his periodical *Household Words* on the history of English, with an expressed bias toward native rather than imported diction, a preference for what we might in fact call "household words." Dickens shows his contempt for the author who makes "cavalry regiments of his sentences" and seeks abroad "for sesquipedalian words." He reminds us that we "can all read with comfort the works of Thomas Fuller, Swift, Bunyan, Defoe, Franklin, and Cobbett; there, sense is clear, feeling is homely, and the writers take care that there shall be no misunderstanding. But in Robertson, Johnson, and Gibbon, one word in every three is an alien; and so an Englishman who happens to have, like Shakespeare, 'small

Latin and less Greek,' is by no means quite at home in their society."[20] The reference to Johnson and his "alien" words is especially revealing in the light of the most important modern study of Johnson's diction.[21] William K. Wimsatt discusses Johnson's use of difficult and many-syllabled "philosophic words," words originally "scientific," as part of a long tradition of "big words in English" which "has exhibited in its successive phases a generally constant stylistic value, of pomposity, grandiloquence, or impressiveness." Such lexical choices "were stylistically the same words that became 'Johnsonese' and were given various epithets of disparagement by Macaulay and other Saxonists of the nineteenth century."[22]

Dickens, as we have seen, is of this company, and more often than not his disparagement takes the form of parody. Wimsatt observes that even for Johnson, at times, there was "a smile behind the ponderosity, a ripple beneath the grave style."[23] But when Dickens gets hold of Johnsonian words, the smile breaks into laughter, the ripple becomes a complete ironic upheaval. Wimsatt's closing section on "Philosophic Humor" is full of indirect application to Dickens's style. There is to be found in the *Rambler* a brand of humor toned down from Sterne and Smollett (authors we know to be among Dickens's favorites) but still retaining "a certain mild contrast, and at the same time a metaphorical juncture, between gravity of diction and homeliness of content, a shade of grimace at some meanness or pretense. It is humor that often involves the bigness of legal, political, or social vocabulary."[24] Change "mild contrast" to an almost grotesque disproportion and you have a fair appraisal of Dickens's prevailing ironic style. It was a comic program to which Meredith, later in the century, could not subscribe, and which he attacked along with punning in his "Essay on Comedy" (1877), though without mentioning Dickens in either regard: "The sense of the comic is much blunted by habits of punning and of using humoristic phrase, the trick of employing Johnsonian polysyllables to treat of the infinitely little."[25]

But Dickens was a Saxonist not just in his satire of Latinity. A man of words delighted by the authentic words of others, he had a deep curiosity about the intuitive metaphors of London vernacular, and he often interrupts his own narrative in the *Sketches* to offer a more colorful or engaging alternative expression, with such little-varied explanations as "to use his own appropriate and expressive description" or "to use Mr. Gattleton's expressive description" or "to use his own emphatic language" or "to adopt his own figurative expression in all its native beauty." In this way Dickens's own characters become stylists with him, and a passion for expression is diffused through every level of his writing. The same mannerisms are carried only somewhat abated into *Pickwick*, where we pause over such semantic glosses and afterthoughts as "if we may use the expression," "in the strict acceptation of the term," and "in his own expressive language." This announced preoccupation with phrase can of course accompany stale satirized language as well as vital idiom, and was perhaps cultivated in part by Dickens from his reading of Fielding, where a similar formula is used to spotlight the Latinism of the bookish Parson Adams as he "(to use his own words) replenished his pipe."[26] An even more elaborate glossing of linguistic sources occurs earlier in *Joseph Andrews*, a perfect example of "burlesque" admitted in "diction" but not in character, a mock-heroic episode in which Adams is beaten by an assailant until "he concluded (to use the language of fighting) 'that he had done his business'; or, in the language of poetry, 'that he had sent him to the shades below'; in plain English, 'that he was dead.'"[27] This is exactly the sort of thing Dickens would have picked up.

Beyond the featured "expressiveness" of borrowed figures and idioms, however, and the preening "impressiveness" of mock eloquence, there is a third kind of specialized language in *Pickwick* and in all the novels after it: the sheer verbal gymnastics of words on vacation from the chore of meaning, the stylistic fun of language at play. The enjoyment is often written right into the prose, by way of charming over-analysis. A pun, for instance, is seldom given the chance to slip by unapplauded. When in *Pickwick* we come upon Mr. Pott described as "pot-valiant," we also get a gentle hint to accept this in "a double sense" (51). In the *Sketches* we have already encountered another variety of the pun, not two senses compressed into one occurrence of the word, but two meanings adjacent in separate occurrences. Thus "we do not hear that he was advanced to any other public post on his return, than the post at the corner of the Haymarket" ("Scenes," 17). If there is any suspicion that Dickens loses interest in such word play as his artistry matures, we need only cite the description of Silas Wegg at his dusty corner years later in *Our Mutual Friend*, as it combines that "double sense" formula with the same pun on "post": "All weathers saw the man at the post. This is to be accepted in a double sense, for he contrived a back to his wooden stool by placing it against the lamp post" (*O.M.F.* I, 5). Another doubling of language's expected sense takes place in those figures of speech which Dickens probably uses more often than any other English prose writer, syllepsis and zeugma. *Pickwick* offers examples in which the governing verb appears only once for both objects, as when Mr. Pickwick "fell into the barrow and fast asleep, simultaneously" (19), and also a variant form given here to Dickens's stand-in, Sam Weller, a form in which the verb appears once for each different sense: " 'This is a wery impartial country for justice,' said Sam. 'There ain't a magistrate goin' as don't commit himself; twice as often as he commits other people'" (25). Nabokov is again a disciple of Dickens in such verbal calisthenics and tells us near the end of *Lolita*, for instance, that Quilty "had half opened his mouth and the front door."[28] As already suggested, I think it is a mistake to believe with G. L. Brook that Dickens's whole fondness for puns, turns, and other playful dexterities of style is the infatuation of a distinctly young writer.[29] As in the case of Nabokov, the fondness abides from novel to novel, becoming a real insight into the surfaces and hidden recesses of language, of style itself, as it can be made to yield up parables of the ethical and imaginative life.

In his survey of "Surface Wit and Structural Rhetoric" in Dickens,[30] H. P. Sucksmith pursues distinctions between incidental linguistic antics and verbal devices employed "structurally," by which he means put to some thematic use. But inutility itself is often the point of Dickens's word play. No one can deny the importance of seeing how Dickens's language *works*, but it is also important to notice in his prose a kind of verbal "fun" that is there largely to remind us that something exists which is the exact opposite of work, an impulse utterly non-utilitarian, a spirit of truancy and trifling. No one knew better than Dickens that the devices of style and rhetoric, in proper hands, become invaluable instruments for the probing of character and psychology. The countless appearances of "surface wit" as treated by Sucksmith—such as malapropism, cliché, hyperbole, syllepsis, pun, polysyllabic humor, personification, mock heroics, bathos, anticlimax—are not, however, thematically negligible when they are not directly analytic. For style itself has its own independent character, its own implicit psychology. This, too, no one knew better than Dickens, and this we must also watch for as we go.

But fun with words is a rarity, and except for such very rare creatures as Sam Weller, it is almost entirely in the charge of the narrative voice, just as it usually was in the earlier comic writers to whose linguistic satire I have been alluding. Too many characters in Dickens speak a language that is stiff, spent, joyless, a language anesthetizing rather than enlivening—and, what is worse, deliberately so. A travesty on this calculated inhibiting of the word, this deliberate abdication of the power of language, is of course the reason for those thick forests of woodenness with which, at intervals, Dickens landscapes his comic narrative. And when all traces of verbal restraint and integrity have been uprooted, Dickens's prose settles down into direct, unequivocal satire, with the abuse of language its acknowledged and only subject. It is my argument that this is essentially what happens in the opening chapter of Dickens's first novel, and there are other moments in *Pickwick*, as in the *Sketches* earlier, that take focus in this way. To some of these clearly marked satires I will now turn with a closer focus of my own, to see the ways in which Dickens puts under more direct fire the spoiled language of rhetoric and public address, whether its corrupt accents are heard in pulpit oratory, in Parliamentary declamation, in the written periods of the newspapers, or in the official "legalese" of the courts.

Our recent acquaintance from the *Sketches* with the "interrogative nose" happens to be a pulpit speaker of no small self-esteem who, as Dickens facetiously puts it, "prides himself, not a little, on his style of addressing the parishioners in vestry assembled" ("Our Parish," 4). In his next sentence, Dickens shows that he himself is hardly seduced by such worn, snobbish inversion as "in vestry assembled" when he destroys the orator with a crisp, tightly balanced Johnsonian announcement: "His views are more confined than extensive; his principles more narrow than liberal." The orator stands accused in a clear-cut case of rhetoric as hypocrisy. In "A Parliamentary Sketch" ("Scenes," 18) we meet a Member "deluding himself into the belief that he is thinking about something" and—here the mock grandiloquence is triggered off—providing a "splendid sample of a Member of the House of Commons concentrating in his own person the wisdom of a constituency." As usual, Dickens gets the Parliamentarian with his own style. Later still, there is a piece on "The Parlour Orator" ("Characters," 5) which lambastes oratorical flourishes at their most absurd, deprived even of the public occasion of their sins. We hear the blowhard "gradually bursting into a radiating sentence, in which such adjectives as 'dastardly,' 'oppressive,' 'violent,' and 'sanguinary,' formed the most conspicuous words." Dickens, the master of exaggeration and hyperbole, an expert in some of these same high-pitched adjectives, still manages to expose their artifice in an empty and blustering rhetoric. Once again, the habitual is re-evaluated for satire.

But something else happens here with peculiar consequence for Dickens's own style. The "parlour orator" has received high praise from the gathered listeners as a "Wonderful man!" and a "Splendid speaker!" with "Great power!" The company soon disbands, and Dickens is alone with his mind. What takes place is an unusual revelation: "If we had followed the established precedent in all such instances, we should have fallen into a fit of musing, without delay . . . and we should have gone dreaming on, until the pewter pot on the table, or the little beer-chiller on the fire, had started into life, and addressed to us a long story of days gone by. But, by some means or other, we were not in a romantic humour; and although we tried very hard to invest the furniture with vitality, it remained perfectly unmoved, obstinate, and sullen." His characteristic imaginative power, his artist's ability to animate the inanimate, is strangely incapacitated, and strains without effect. That "romantic humour" so essential to Dickens's art is now beyond his grasp. And the fatuous style of the orator appears somehow to be at fault: "Being thus reduced to the unpleasant necessity of musing about ordinary matters, our thoughts reverted to the red-faced man, and his oratorical display." Dickens's own style is unavailable, it seems, because he continues to dwell on the charlatan's. False style has not only insulted an authentic imagination, but somehow poisoned it. Portrayed in a very personal way for Dickens, this is the real threat of rhetoric as an enemy of romantic fancy.

Following the *Sketches* there is certainly no sign of a cease-fire in the parodic bombardment of oratory, Dickens's war against the mongers of false eloquence. In the chapter on the Eatanswill election in *Pickwick Papers*, we are informed that "everybody and everything then and there assembled was for the special use, behoof, honour, and renown" (13) of a candidate for the House of Commons, and these two redundant noun pairs merely typify the verbal snowballing that goes on in campaign rhetoric. When, three pages later, a man tries publicly to "nominate a fit and proper person to represent them in Parliament," this prepackaged adjectival redundancy is another such ceremonial gesture of oratory, one hardly appreciated by the rowdy assembly, however, for the speaker was "repeatedly desired by the crowd to 'send a boy home, to ask whether he hadn't left his woice under the pillow.' " Dickens has here cleverly delegated his satire to this anonymous audience, and though they are not expected to heed the resonance of what they say, the idea of disembodied speech, the dichotomy of "woice" and person, suggests the specious, self-sufficient life that oratory seems to take on. Every irony is therefore intended when Sam Weller, that artist of talk whose style and personality do beautifully coincide, is accused by Mr. Smauker of being "unparliamentary" in his use of the plural "mississes" (37). What else would we expect from Sam, whose sense of English is the exact opposite of official? His response to this accusation is, fittingly, a parody of "parliamentary" expression, as he promises to "amend the obserwation and call 'em the dear creeturs."

The orotund banalities of journalistic style also come in for Boz's early parody, and even that "Parliamentary Sketch" has subsidiary fun at the expense of the press when it records that "the mover of the address will be 'on his legs,' as the newspapers announce sometimes by way of novelty, as if the speakers were occasionally in the habit of standing on their heads" ("Scenes," 18). In the lampoon of "Public Dinners" ("Scenes," 19), Boz slips into his newspaper voice for some well-signaled parodies of the Victorian press. When "God Save the Queen" is rendered by the guests at a public banquet, we are told that they impart to the national anthem "an effect which the newspapers, with great justice, describe as 'perfectly electrical.' " And on the same page Dickens is also "compelled to adopt newspaper phraseology, and to express our regret at being 'precluded from giving even the substance of the noble Lord's observations.' " It is an invigorating historical fact that the same hack journalistic formula turns up in a newspaper review of the *Sketches* themselves: "We regret that our limits will not allow us to extract an inimitable specimen of the intense feeling he has displayed in the tale of the broker's man."[31]

Stephen C. Gill has recently made an interesting suggestion about the style of *Pickwick*, tracing it back to the "penny-a-liners," those free-lance journalists who handled everyday reporting other than Parliamentary debates and who, since they were paid by the line, had a vested interest in expansive phrasing of all kinds.[32] Gill mentions in passing the parody of these "chroniclers by the line" in the thirty-third chapter of *Bleak House*, and it is worth looking at this episode more closely here. Two of these reporters are preparing their copy on Krook's bizarre death, and they "note down . . . how the neighbourhood of Chancery Lane was yesterday, at about mid-night, thrown into a state of the most intense agitation and excitement by the following alarming and horrible discovery." In their characteristic use of "as many words as possible," their synonymous doublings of both nouns and adjectives, we have an example of those "syntactic doublets" Wimsatt mentions in his first study of Johnson's style as a special form of parallelism in the master's prose,[33] a strategy for increasing the emphasis of certain weighty words by multiplication so promiscuously borrowed by the journalists of Dickens's time. When these same reporters in *Bleak House* proudly display their Latinized alliteration, "foetid effluvia," to describe the atmosphere after Krook's spontaneous combustion, they are also exposing another Johnson-derived bad habit which shows up, along with the doublets, in *Pickwick's* own newspaper parodies.

Most frequent of such parodies are the quotations from the *Eatanswill Gazette,* and perhaps most outrageous of these is the prognostication for Mrs. Leo Hunter's party, the ornate promise that it "would present a scene of varied and delicious enchantment—a bewildering coruscation of beauty and talent—a lavish and prodigal display of hospitality—above all, a degree of splendour softened by the most exquisite taste; and adornment refined with perfect harmony and the chastest good keeping . . . " (15). And so on, and on . . . This is worse than just newspaper padding. With its deluxe syntax and showcase diction, this is in fact self-promotional prose; the very reflection of its author Mr. Pott, it is a culture-climbing style that strives after the same splendor and adornment it describes, but has forgotten all sense of "chastest good keeping" in the process. Two chapters before, Mr. Pott reads several of his "leaders" to Mr. Pickwick, and we are sarcastically assured that our hero "was perfectly enraptured with the vigour and freshness of the style," a confidence derived from "the fact that his eyes were closed, as if with excess of pleasure, during the whole time of their perusal" (13). There is, it seems, a style too overblown even for Mr. Pickwick. When the style of this same *Gazette* is again read to us near the end of the novel, a most interesting commentary is implicit. Again we are pelted with those "syntactic doublets," used to heighten both the calumny and the praise: "A reptile contemporary has recently sweltered forth his black venom in the vain and hopeless attempt of sullying the fair name of our distinguished and excellent representative" (51). This runs on for most of a page, and we learn that, like Mr. Pickwick before them, "Messrs. Bob Sawyer and Benjamin Allen ... had irreverently fallen asleep during the reading," only to be "roused" at last "by the mere whispering of the talismanic word 'Dinner' in their ears." The language at once perks up, as "to dinner they went with good digestion waiting on appetite, and health on both, and a waiter on all three." It seems that a typical Dickensian play on words has been inspired by the belated arrival, after all the ready-made palaver of newspaper rhetoric, of a word that really does have meaning. When words tend to come cheaply packaged in redundant multiples, it *is* almost a miracle, something magic or "talismanic," when a word like "Dinner" can become an act of real communication.

To be of worth, Dickens is reminding us, the word must have a final cause beyond its own marketability; it must point elsewhere, at some meaning, rather than being itself the point. Too often, and nowhere more than in the press, language degenerates into a kind of wholesale commodity. A parody of the poet's autonomous handling of verbal entities, the word falls victim to the merchandizing spirit and becomes a thing. The debased "poet"—the journalist or the orator—trades on language, bartering it, hoarding it, making of his verbal stockpiles a second-rate inventory of words, to be sold off cheaply when occasion demands. In the same year that Dickens, in *Pickwick Papers,* was mounting this attack on the squandered economies of language, Emerson, waging the same war in the American theater, found a tempting fiscal metaphor for the decline of the word: "The corruption of man is followed by the corruption of language. When simplicity of character and the sovereignty of ideas is broken up by the prevalence of secondary desires, the desire of riches, of pleasure, of power, of praise ... new imagery ceases to be created, and old words are perverted to stand for things which are not; a paper currency is employed, when there is no bullion in the vaults."[34] Both Emerson and Dickens detested the spurious coinages and indiscriminate expenditures of language which were everywhere in the public writing of their day. To prolong Emerson's analogy, the "paper currency" of expression had become so inflated and devalued that it was already a kind of counterfeit. Yet such easy metaphors, as Emerson would have admitted, are themselves accessories to the crime. They are meant only to signal their own danger, to warn of the initial mistake one makes by thinking of language in this way at all, as if the exchange of words and ideas were a commerce, not a communication.

Journalism in Dickens's day is not only a good place to look for the styles he apes and parodies, but also for commentary on his style that is more likely than twentieth-century criticism to report the topical, contemporary nature of the satire. *The Saturday Review of Politics, Literature, Science, and Art,* for instance, not only offers samples of Victorian journalese in its own pages, but also tells us, in a review of Dickens, that his writing is "the apotheosis of what has been called newspaper English."[35] Historical distance has, in this respect, done some disservice to modern commentary on Dickens's style. We are only now coming to realize the true scope of Dickens's symbolic and psychological explorations, but as verbal adventure his style has left its context behind. All too often we take it merely, gratefully, as "Dickensian." We are not well-equipped to judge its satire. For us, meretriciousness in style is a new and different thing. The chic flair of Madison Avenue copy, the pallid and platitudinous expanses of television dialogue, eighth-rate imitators of Hemingway, the ghost-written bluster of our own hustings, the stuffiness of literary scholarship itself, scientific jargon, and today's most influential brand of journalese, the contagious *Time*-style, are some of our favorite targets. Dickensian stylistic satire is another matter. Its force as parody of degenerate and popularized Johnsonian style, newspaper Gibbonese, Parliamentary rhetoric, political and domestic euphemism, and the whole cloying atmosphere of the High Style, the prose of false show and evasion, is considerably blunted for readers a century later. Here the critics of Dickens's own time provide a welcome adjustment for our updated approaches.

We have already discussed the importance as a negative standard for Dickens the Saxonist of the Johnsonian hard word. In matters of style apart from diction—in syntax, rhythm, tone—Johnson was also, even as late as the mid-nineteenth century, the acknowledged model for fine writing. Stripped of talent and sincerity, the same sort of self-assured style became Dickens's satiric model for pomp and hypocrisy. It is an interesting biographical coincidence that both Dickens and Johnson spent part of their apprenticeship in letters as notably fluent and successful Parliamentary reporters. The aura of confident eloquence aspired to in political oratory, and captured by Johnson when manufacturing whole debates out of his imagination on the basis of the scantest details,[36] was further refined and sharpened over the course of his career to become one of the outstanding formal styles in English. Dickens's career, from similar beginnings, took quite a different turn. The parliamentary style's same rhetorical aspirations, when bereft both of intelligence and of integrity, become, in Dickens's hands, the parodic basis for the most versatile, the most successful comic writing in the language. It is a style lavished disproportionately on little things and little people. The result is indirect but unmistakable: affectation stands accused.

In his article on "Saxon-English," Dickens included Gibbon with Johnson among the brandishers of "sesquipedalian" words. In a notebook entry from 1875 quoted by Miriam Allott, Thomas Hardy also seems to link Gibbon, among others, with *"Times* leaders" as promulgators of "too much style."[37] And Alice Meynell, too, stresses the influence of Gibbon on the style of the Victorian press that Dickens was forever satirizing. "The burlesque so gayly undertaken by Dickens rallies a lofty and distant Gibbon," the "wreck" of whose style "strewed the press" in Dickens's day. "It was everywhere. Dickens not only was clear of the wreckage —he saw it to be the refuse it was; he laughed at it, and even as he laughed he formed a style."[38] Once again, the press itself was not wholly unable to see what was going on, and the article already mentioned from *The Saturday Review* came very near to a full appreciation; in spite of his "intentional fallacies," the reviewer did see that Dickens was attacking the moribund standards of English which followed in the wake of Johnson and Gibbon:

Pickwick is throughout a sort of half-conscious parody of that style of writing which demanded balanced sentences, double-barrelled epithets, and a proper conception of the office and authority of semi-colons ... Whenever he can get an opportunity, Mr. Dickens rakes up the old-fashioned finery, twists it into every sort of grotesque shape, introduces it to all kinds of strange bedfellows, and contrives, with an art which is all the more ingenious because it was probably quite undesigned, to convey the impression that every one who tries to think, or to act by rule, is little more than a pompous jackass.[39]

A just conclusion, except in its withholding of credit for conscious parodic design. The style is hardly "all the more ingenious" for being "quite undesigned." It is art that tries to look artless; it is the satiric mask of naiveté, the ingenious passing itself off as the ingenuous. This is its charm, and a large part of its comedy.

Meynell tells us that Dickens laughed at journalistic style and that "even as he laughed he formed a style." His satiric prose was shaped, however, by a laughter not only at the press, but also at the pulpit, the podium, and the bench. And it is Dickens's parody of legal jargon, which I have not yet discussed, that is both most crucial for *Pickwick Papers* and most accessible for the modern reader. It is still very much with us today. Indeed, we even recognize the familiar jammed cadences of "legalese" as far back as Mrs. Shandy's marriage settlement, from which, since Sterne pretends it would be a "barbarity" to translate it into other words, we get reproduced for us such redundant barbarisms as "doth grant, covenant, condescend, consent, conclude, bargain, and fully agree to and with," or "fall out, chance, happen, or otherwise come to pass."[40] One of Dickens's later comic tactics is to render such repetitive phrasing all the more ridiculous by divorcing it from its legal context altogether, and so we hear (with my italics) that when Sam Weller settles down before a tavern fire for a glass of brandy and water, the barmaid "carried away the poker to preclude the possibility of the fire being stirred without the *full probity and concurrence* of the Blue Boar being first *had and obtained*" (33). Dickens's satire can of course be more directly aimed, and we find what *The Saturday Review* termed "double-barrelled" locutions treated as if they were themselves (the word as weapon) among the "ingenious machines put in motion for the torture and torment of His Majesty's liege subjects, and the comfort and emolument of the practitioners of the law" (31). It is no surprise that Dickens names an "eminent counsel" in *Pickwick* "Mr. Prosee," or that the prosiest of all the lawyers, the eloquent Buzfuz, buzzes continually with the fuzzy pseudo-distinctions of the "doublet" style. Dickens's general parodic voice points out the "majesty and dignity" of Buzfuz, and then sneaks into the lawyer's own identical two-for-one diction for an indirect report of the responsibility Buzfuz feels so humbly burdened by: "—a responsibility, he would say, which he could never have supported were he not *buoyed up and sustained* by a conviction so strong that it amounted to positive certainty that the cause of *truth and justice*, or, in other words, the cause of his *much-injured* and *most oppressed* client, must prevail with the *high-minded and intelligent* dozen of men whom he now saw in that box before him" (34, my italics). It is such a rhetorical climate Pickwick will attempt, and fail, to weather in the famous trial of Bardell vs. Pickwick, where he will be, in a sense, punished by words themselves for his own misuse of language.

To show how this comes about, I must turn again to the novel's first chapter, from whose excesses there is still much to be learned. I have strayed so far in order to bring a more widely trained sense of just what style has at stake there, and of what precisely is called into question about the morality of style, the ethic of imagination. G. L. Brook, in his chapter on "Language to Suit the Occasion," does not seem to realize the implicit scope of this particular rhetorical occasion when he says merely: "The first chapter of *Pickwick Papers* contains a parody of the minutes, prolix and full of clichés, of a small debating society, and Mr. Pickwick's speech to the members of the Pickwick Club is a parody of the sort of speech that such societies encourage."[41] In *Dickens as Satirist,* Sylvia Manning sees in this opening chapter only a "satire on scientific associations and on parliamentary procedures," a "failure" that "is actually as eccentric to the whole design of the novel as the satire in the story of Prince Bladud is shown to be by its undisguised interpolation into the narrative."[42] By slighting the linguistic implications of the chapter, this critic of satire is in fact closing off one of its most interesting arenas in Dickens, interesting for *Pickwick,* for his style generally, and for the comic tradition he works within and perpetuates. When, in *The Egoist,* George Meredith distinguishes between the speech of a professed "artist in phrases" and the plainer clarities of his heroine, who at one point had "not uttered words, she had shed meanings,"[43] he is taking a leaf from Dickens's own Book of Linguistic Egoism, where false artists of phrase like the Pickwickians—as we are about to see—"shed" meanings in an opposite sense, casting them off in favor of the mere sounds of their words, discarding the proper and effective function of language for mere effect.

The climax of *Pickwick's* first chapter holds the key. The altercation between Pickwick and Blotton brings to a head tensions naturally aroused by prolonged contact with a padded prose that makes of style the mere upholstery of an overstuffed rhetoric. Chanting his own praises over his "Tittlebatian Theory," Mr. Pickwick manages twice to use the word "celebrated" about his own achievement, and then, in the same sentence with its second appearance, twice "pride" and once "proudest" about his state of mind. He is roundly cheered, and then adds, again in the report of the editor, that he "was a humble individual (No, no.]" His auditors, responding in parenthesis and apparently unanimous, mean, we must assume, that he is no ordinary or unimportant man. Only Dickens, one step beyond the editor, intends this negative response to deny Pickwick's modesty. Yet just as the word "humble" divulges two contrasted meanings, so the twin negatives of "No, no" may be found to part company, for after two more preening sentences from Pickwick, the next parenthetical record of his listeners' response is indeed sharply divided: "(Cheers—a voice: 'No')." The anomalous voice turns out to be Blotton's, and unless this is merely the implicit charge of vanity repeated—the satiric half of "No, no"—we are left without a guess as to the immediate force of its negation, suspended as it is without a referent. Finally, it would seem, the deflation can only be intended to generalize. When Pickwick is heckled with that obstreperous and entirely unfocused "No," it is as if, by a single daring monosyllable, all the windy and lavishly syllabled rhetoric has been sweepingly negated—blotted out by the matter-of-fact Blotton, who is later to puncture Mr. Pickwick's archeological reputation.

"Let that honourable Pickwickian who cried 'No' so loudly come forward and deny it if he could." Deny what? Or how? Since his vociferous exception was taken to nothing in particular, "it" will be hard to retract. On the other hand, there would seem to be no way for anyone to step forward as the confessed dissenter and, in the very process of doing so, "deny" the admitted act of dissent. Yet this, as we will see, is exactly what comes to pass through a semantic evacuation of the charge itself. First Mr. Pickwick adopts the oratorical pose of *praeteritio*—a blatant form of hypocrisy under rhetorical sanction—and proceeds on that well-worn model, "I will hardly lower and demean myself by telling you the following." Dickens devoted most of a long paragraph in the *Sketches* to this same trick of "parliamentary style" ("Our Parish," 4), and we are to laugh just as hard at Pickwick: "Who was it that cried 'No'? (Enthusiastic cheering.) Was it some vain and disappointed man—he would not say haberdasher (loud cheers)." And so we do indeed see Pickwick "come forward and deny" what, only by so doing, would he get said at all. Not only rhetoric, however, but definition itself will soon be at stake in this scene. Pickwick next fires against Blotton with the doubled barrels of his rhetoric, terming Blotton's "mode" of attack "vile and calumnious," to which Blotton retorts on the principle of an eye for an eye, adjective for adjective, that Pickwick's counterattack against his accusation is itself a "false and scurrilous accusation." The carefully paired epithets are balanced against each other in an over-armed rhetorical standoff, and the linguistic broil is further escalated when Blotton's combative language revealingly divides one of his own sentences against itself by saying of Pickwick that the "hon. gent.

was a humbug. (Immense confusion and loud cries of 'Chair' and 'Order.')" This dis-"order" is a kind of verbal anarchy, an "immense confusion" in the very idea of meaning. With it we have one of the first and clearest examples in the novel of self-incriminating rhetoric, for to call a man first "honourable" and then a "humbug" is in its own to speak duplicitously, to utter humbug. Of course "hon." is a null adjective in this context, endorsed uncritically by the Pickwickians like the title "gentle-man," voided of meaning, but then so, we find, are almost all their words. The "order" just cried for is restored only when the accusa-tory style is neutralized by a remarkable evasion. After the charge of "humbug," the chairman "felt it his imperative duty to demand of the honourable gentleman, whether he had used the expression which had just escaped him in a common sense." But there is no room for "common sense" in this rhetorical fray. Words seem to have a deceptive life of their own; they are not called forth, they "escape," and once out in the open they defy literal interpretation. Personally, he vows with yet another doublet, Mr. Blotton "held the highest regard and esteem" for Mr. Pickwick; he had only "used the word in its Pickwickian sense . . . he had merely con-sidered him a humbug in a Pickwickian point of view. (Hear, hear.)" Hear that indeed. Mr. Pickwick fast avails himself of the same shelter, explaining, of course, that his own remarks "had been merely tended to bear a Pickwickian construction. (Cheers.)" So before we learn any other meaning for "Pickwickian," we under-stand it stylistically, so to speak, as a kind of verbal nullification, a retroactive euphemism under whose aegis words are able to retreat from their own consequences.[44]

The chapter has drawn to its inevitable crisis. Here we have a vain and evasive use of language that is the final symptom of the word's degeneration, deepening the stylistic parody which began with the novel's first sentence. Characterized from the start by writing rather thoroughly inoculated against meaning, the injec-tion of the magic word "Pickwickian" into the chapter at this point simply reduces to the absurd a style that has never steered very far clear of it. And it is a perfect stroke for Dickens to choose as the word highlighted by the debate the very word which best charac-terizes it. The style of the first chapter and its culmination, in its leaden elevation and the hypocritical dodges of its semantic double standard, is indeed *humbug prose*. It is a style in which there is always more saying going on than meaning and which, when cornered, admits to meaning not even the little it seems to mean. This is language on the edge of disintegration, and only the control of comedy can hold it together. Sarcasm salvages the hypocrisy of Pickwickian double talk and makes a comic virtue out of saying the reverse of what is meant. "Mr. Pickwick felt much gratified by the fair, candid, and full explanation of his honourable friend," and Dickens, in the naive guise of editor, mocks this ploy by himself facetiously treating the conclusion of the debate as the arrival "at such a highly satisfactory and intelligible point." Early in this chapter, taking the hint from Fielding, I made a distinction between the verbal affectations of "vanity" on the one hand and "hypocrisy" on the other, a distinction it is now time to retract. The point of *Pickwick's* first chapter is that the two faults overlap. The Pickwickians' humbug prose is more than just bogus eloquence; they are looking for a sort of verbal impunity, the middle ground between saying and meaning which "Pickwickian" implies. They think that by loosening the bond between saying and meaning, for the purposes of lofty and libelous speech, they are taking a merely rhetorical liberty. But Dickens wants to show us that the bond between expression and intention is not simply stylistic, but ethical as well; and that by forgetting this, the Pickwickians become not just pompous rhetoricians but moral humbugs.

The large resonance I am suggesting for this debate in the first chapter is further argued, it seems to me, by the fact that Dickens has composed two later scenes that echo the two keynotes struck in the first chapter—first the specific use of the term "humbug" and then the general misuse of vocabulary in its Pickwickian "definition." During the ice-skating fiasco in Chapter 30, we hear an indignant Mr. Pickwick himself use the term "humbug" against a fellow Pickwickian in a "common sense" this time, capable of restatement with an unequivocal synonym. When Mr. Winkle's pretense of knowing how to skate is exposed, Pickwick "uttered in a low but distinct and emphatic tone these remarkable words: 'You're a humbug, sir' " (30)—words "remarkable" for nothing so much as the contrast with how we have heard them before. Now plain-speaking is the intention, and when Winkle asks "A what?" Pickwick offers clarification, as if remembering his own complicity in the initial meaningless use of the term: "A humbug, sir. I will speak plainer if you wish it. An impostor, sir."

This dominant chord of Pickwickian semantics then finds an

absurd comic transposition two chapters later, reminding us that we are never far from the collapse of verbal communication admonished against by the book's chaotic opening. The episode, in which Mrs. Raddle confronts Bob Sawyer about his bill, is full of Dickensian word play and implied linguistic commentary of all sorts. When a question about how long the bill has "been running" is posed, the narrator stokes the hidden metaphor until the bill becomes "the most extraordinary locomotive engine that the genius of man ever produced. It would keep on running during the longest lifetime, without ever once stopping of its own accord." (32). Mrs. Raddle herself turns the language of definition and tautology to her own advantage, though with a facile reliance on mere "calling" to corroborate character that reminds us of the questionable title "gent." in the first chapter: "every gentleman as has ever lived here, has kept his word, sir, as of course anybody as calls himself a gentleman, does." But the keeping of words in any kind of order is about to meet an impossible challenge. Ben Allen interrupts to call Mrs. Raddle an "unreasonable woman" and then at once opts for that standard "Pickwickian" dodge: "I didn't make use of the word in any invidious sense, ma'am." The honorific "ma'am" and the accusation itself are of course at odds here the way "honourable gentleman" and "humbug" were in the first debate, but this scene has gone even farther into semantic mayhem than the opening chapter. We are meant to be just as confounded as Mr. Allen when we discover that Mrs. Raddle, who has in fact recently referred to herself as "a hard-working and industrious woman," takes her objection not to the adjective "unreasonable" but, with sublime unreasonableness, to the other "invidious" word: " 'I beg your parding, young man,' demanded Mrs. Raddle in a louder and more imperative tone. 'But who do you call a woman? Did you make that remark to me, sir?' "

Long before this ironic echo of the first chapter, this parody of a parody, there is another more important extension of those linguistic themes with which the novel began. This is the famous scene in which Pickwick asks Mrs. Bardell whether it is "a much greater expense to keep two people, than to keep one?" (12), and she misreads the plans to make Mr. Weller his manservant as a proposal of marriage to herself. Steven Marcus has written that "Mr. Pickwick's use of the language is literal, abstractly symbolic, and almost entirely denotative and normative,"[45] that Pickwick "does not yet understand language, and his innocence is primarily a linguistic innocence."[46] This is what we might call his comic rather than his tragic flaw, and it drives the novel to its first major crisis. When Mr. Pickwick speaks, as he is unaccustomed to, in metaphor, fate seems to retaliate, and Mrs. Bardell, who knows his characteristic use of language, takes him literally. Envisioning Sam as his valet, he alludes to "the person I have in my eye," and catastrophe follows because of the attendant literal circumstance that he "looked very hard at Mrs. Bardell" at the time. Language itself is bested, and when Mrs. Bardell faints publicly into the hero's arms, he is "struck motionless and speechless." So Mr. Pickwick is tried and sentenced to prison for breach of promise, dramatizing in an oblique way the first revenge of imagination in Dickens outside of the interpolated tales. For this over-spoken gentleman, who from the first page of *Pickwick Papers* represented a use of language held culpable by Dickens for not meaning what it said, is here punished —in an ironic reversal of guilt and innocence—for accidentally not saying what he meant.

The adjective "Pickwickian," as brought forward by the debate, has found its way into modern usage in two senses, both the verbal and the personal. It can suggest some esoteric or eccentric sense of a word's meaning, occasionally associated with the rhetorical license of parliamentary or congressional oratory, a definition owed specifically to the first chapter of *Pickwick*, or it can refer to the qualities of simplicity and benevolence which Mr. Pickwick himself comes to embody as the novel unfolds.[47] The two meanings are simultaneous in the opening chapter; or rather, "Pickwickian" only exists for us at this point as a stylistic label, for words understood in no "common sense." Indeed, throughout *Pickwick Papers* the Pickwickian style and the Pickwickian personality remain much more closely fused than either modern vocabulary or Dickens criticism seems to have recognized. Style is the man, and helps us to understand the man. The opening chapter may be primarily a stylistic experiment, a full-dress verbal *tour de force*, but so are many things in *Pickwick*, many things in Dickens generally. His characterization only benefits from such experiments, for they are the ways mentality and imagination find portrayal.

2 Quarantine

'But, Lord bless me!...it was an uncommonly pleasant
thing being in quarantine, wasn't it? Do you know, I
have often wished myself back again?'—*Little Dorrit* (I,16)

Style is the man in *Pickwick Papers*, and finally eases out of
satire until it is actually commending the man to us. That an
attractive personal sense of "Pickwickian" ever does maneuver itself free of the novel's ironic pressures is the great success of style
and tone in Dickens's first novel. But criticism often takes us off
center and misses the subtlety of this emergence by placing what
seems to me too much emphasis on "benevolence" as the controlling "Pickwickian" meaning. Dostoevsky stressed this aspect
in 1868, writing that the "chief idea of the novel is to portray the
positively good man."[1] More true, finally, and more important for
the way the novel works, is the idea of Pickwick as the positively
cheerful man. It is not until his next novel that Dickens will give,
in Oliver, full thematic weight to "the principle of Good surviving
through every adverse circumstance, and triumphing at last" (*O.T.,*
"Preface"). There are quite different urgencies in *Pickwick,* where
the principle of Good takes second place to the principle of Good
Spirits.

Mr. Pickwick's temperament operates by radiation: he literally
beams his good cheer. The first image we get of this gentleman in
the second chapter likens him to the morning sun, the symbol of
ever renewed brightness. The novel announces itself with the
words "The first ray of light," and, combining the openings of the
first two chapters, we have a kind of trivialized and ironic version
of Milton's famous invocation to light. "The first ray of light which
illumines the gloom" (the silly chiming assonance being the per-

fect diminishing touch) of Mr. Pickwick's previous history turns out to be derived from the very entry in the posthumous papers of his club that is about to get the novel under way. And the enlightenment it provides, like the inner light of the blind bard which inspires and initiates his poem, is intimately identified with the brilliance of the subject to be treated, the divine effulgence of God in Milton, the cheerful brightness of the "immortal Pickwick" in Dickens.[2] Here is our hero at the dawn of his second chapter: "That punctual servant of all work, the sun, had just risen, and begun to strike a light . . . when Mr. Samuel Pickwick burst like another sun from his slumbers, threw open his chamber window, and looked out upon the world beneath." The mock-heroic vestiges here and the mild ironic over-writing, leveled off considerably from the facetious flights of the opening chapter, begin what will be the prevailing tone of the novel, at the same time that this description introduces to the Pickwickian mythos its archetypal scene, the hero up with the sun and as bright and refreshed as the morning itself. As if to recall this symbolism later, Dickens has his hero say to Mr. Wardle at one point: "The sun is tremendously hot, even to me" (19). Even to such "another sun." On his first morning awake in the book, we learn that Samuel Pickwick, Esq., free of the indolent self-satisfaction of some "philosophers," will make the "effort to penetrate to the hidden countries which on every side surround" his home at Goswell Street. Yet if his bright morning spirits are to go unclouded through the novel, there must be something in the novel itself to defend him against certain "hidden countries" of the mind which would jeopardize his innate and naive good cheer.

It is for just this reason that the principle of good spirits is more helpful in explaining the structure of the novel than the principle of good. The power of *Oliver Twist* resides in its polar opposition of absolute good and incarnate evil, and just as Oliver has his Fagin, Little Nell will later have her Quilp. The polar opposite of good cheer, however, is not evil itself so much as the knowledge of evil that can lead to melancholy and depression, even paranoia. Evil makes good look better, but the awareness of evil makes inveterate good cheer look a trifle shallow and heartless; beaming benevolence becomes perverse. The structure of the novel, to a large extent, guards Pickwick against this awareness, holding it at a safe distance in the interpolated stories. But a distinction must be respected between these stories, a distinction which criticism often disregards when lumping them all together as the "dark tales."

There are other awarenesses from which Pickwick is protected. Not all the interpolations are bleak gothic departures from the main narrative. There are, in fact, fewer tales of evil and dementia, of terrorized and diseased imaginations, than there are of active and potentially healthy ones. It is not darkness but imagination itself which seems to be the common denominator. And it is perhaps the novel's most original and disturbing insight that Mr. Pickwick must be excluded equally from both sorts of imagination, from the imprisonment of psychosis and the release of fancy—saved from nightmare but denied the daydream. In order that imagination bring no dark knowledge, that it never turn on Pickwick and unsettle his placid mentality, it must be withheld in any form, fenced off in the tales. Whatever we may think about the failed art of these stories, we should notice the strategic art of their inclusion. The interpolated tale is part of the novel's debt to epic, with its digressions and its drive toward inclusiveness. The comic epics of Cervantes and Fielding conveyed this formula to Dickens, but what he has done, his first time out as a novelist, is to transform a mere convention of the loosely plotted picaresque form into something new and private as it answers to the original demands of his own novel.

Criticism has not favored the interpolated tales in *Pickwick Papers,* for some very good reasons. The general consensus is that they are bad tales badly told. But Dickens was proud of them, and I think we can discover reasons for this which will tell us much about his art. The critics have in fact spent considerable time with these stories, however grudgingly, because they can be plundered for parallels to the main themes, and for biographical and psychological clues to Dickens's mind, and also because their relation to the larger story constitutes one of the few "problems" of the novel. I have found no critic who has really solved it. In tracking down terms of comparison between the major story and its digressions, commentators frequently ignore the uneasy terms on which the tales exist with the surrounding narrative. Trying for comparison, they may miss the fact that the orders of experience in each are finally incomparable, existing side by side only in mutual isolation. On the trail of relevance and integration, critics often fail to notice that the plan of interpolation is one of calculated irrelevance and total segregation. Again style clarifies, for on the large scale as well as the small what we have called "Pickwickian" rhetoric acts as a kind of softening or "euphemizing" agent to insulate Pickwick from all that would disturb or depress him, from the fanciful as well as the feverish imagination. He is often agitated, but his mind stays resilient and he is soon serene again. As we watch this happen time after time, we begin to recognize subjectivity as the very subject of the novel. *Pickwick* is about a bright and peaceful state of mind and about other moods of imagination which contradict or threaten it. In a Dickensian punning spirit, I would nominate *disposition* as the key term for an analysis of *Pickwick Papers*. It is a novel about the way a cheerful disposition and the joyous world it nourishes must be preserved by the disposition of other impulses into digressive stories. The interpolations are experiments in style, just as they are studies in imagination. They enter the novel in a format of partition and isolation continuously reinforced by an opposite impersonal style. This format goes far toward explaining Dickens's first novel, at the same time that it introduces themes and stylistic methods which will occupy him from here on. It is this format I am calling the quarantine of imagination.

"The Stroller's Tale" (3) is the first of the interpolations, a detailed account of the death from drink and the deathbed hallucinations of an itinerant pantomime clown, recited to Mr. Pickwick and friends by Dismal Jemmy. However amateur and garish by Dickens's later standards, the style of this tale strives to penetrate the fatal experience itself and to confront us, through the eerie immediacy of the narrator's own delivery, with the inner fatigues and horrors of the clown's mad "paroxysms." Satiric detachment is here only a memory. "The theatre, and the public-house, were the chief themes of the wretched man's wanderings. It was evening, he fancied; he had a part to play that night; it was late, and he must leave home instantly. Why did they hold him, and prevent his going?—he should lose the money—he must go. No! They would not let him." The most innocent terminology of imagination, the tame "he fancied," is at once violently belied in this neurotic, staccato prose. "He rose in bed, drew up his withered limbs, and rolled about in uncouth positions; he was acting—he was at the theatre... Fill up his glass. Who was that, that dashed it from his lips? It was the same persecutor that had followed him before. He fell back on his pillow and moaned aloud" (3). Such an experiment in style takes up quite literally where *Sketches by Boz* left off. The last of the *Sketches* was in fact "The Drunkard's Death"; unlike "The Stroller's Tale," it made a genuine effort at plot and characterization. Instead, the first interpolated tale in *Pickwick*, with little story to tell, attempts a dramatizing prose that includes the obliquely reported speech of *erlebte Rede* in a kind of indirect interior monologue, as the teller actually begins to inhabit the perceptions of the suffering mind. Unlike the inflated self-consciousness of Dickens's prevailing ironic style, which distances its subject matter, this unmediated style seems almost to appropriate the central consciousness within the described scene. The opposite of Dickens's *impersonal* mode, it is what I will call (to coin an adjective) the *impersonatorial* style, a technique not merely for describing experience but for simulating, for impersonating it. "The Stroller's Tale" may be only an awkward first try at this style, but it is vitally important for Dickens's development. It is also significant that the first efforts in this manner should be made to render the first feverish trauma in Dickens, the beginning of a career-long interest in such warpings of the imagination.

The immediacy of the style here is ascribed not to Dickens, of course, but to Dismal Jemmy. Yet how can he possibly have access to the clown's delirious visions? We would at once doubt the status of his tale as a true story if he did not seem somehow exempt himself from naturalistic criteria. It is Jemmy rather than his tale who seems "marvellous," who seems to have been imported into a realistic narrative from another and mysterious genre of imagination. With his eyes "unnaturally bright and piercing," his strange arresting power over his auditors, he seems akin to the gothic and ballad worlds of errant and often involuntary tale-telling, a near relative of the Wandering Jew or the Ancient Mariner—thus compelling an automatic suspension of disbelief for his narrative gifts. His tale continues with the same lurid phrasings and erratic, throttled grammar until the death of the clown, his last feverish pantomime: "He grasped my shoulder convulsively, and, striking his breast with the other hand, made a desperate attempt to articulate... There was a rattling in his throat—a glare of the eye—a short stifled groan—and he fell back—dead!" (3).

And what follows? How is the tale rerouted into the course of the narrative? How are we cued to interpret the detour? In short, what does the context offer to help us incorporate the tale? There is nothing; the entire experience is simply blanked out, its tensions gone slack in the placid banalities of the high style: "It would afford us the highest gratification to be enabled to record Mr. Pickwick's opinion of the foregoing anecdote. We have little doubt that we should have been enabled to present it to our readers, but for a most unfortunate occurrence" (3). Here we have the most important fact about the whole plan of incorporation—the deliberate lack of it. We are assured that Mr. Pickwick "had just made up his mind to speak," and that (here the ironic phrasing picks up, again with the "sun" image implicit) he was "on the point of delivering some remarks which would have enlightened the world, if not the Thames," when his friends interrupt him just in time and return him to the thoroughly comic dilemma through which the plot has been wending its way. So far from being able to enlighten us on the subject of the tale, Mr. Pickwick is incapable of dealing at all with the imaginative intensity and disorder it portrays. So he is kept from it both by the comic plot and the ironic prose, and with that timely interruption from his associates "Mr. Pickwick's equanimity was at once restored." All real emotional contact is prevented between his bright world of mental composure and the feverish world of drunkenness, anguish, and death.

As if to cement the separateness of the two worlds, to wall up for good one from the other, we get a second encounter between Mr. Pickwick and Dismal Jemmy which stresses the virtual immunity of the old gentleman to any tinge of unhappy imaginings. The fifth chapter opens with a syntactic "equanimity" typical of a Pickwickian description, the prose composed and balanced as it relaxes in the unanxious luxury of inversion: "Bright and pleasant was the sky, balmy the air, and beautiful the appearance of every object around, as Mr. Pickwick leant over the balustrades of Rochester Bridge, contemplating nature, and waiting for breakfast" (5). Jemmy appears, and the tone at once changes. "Ah! People need to rise early, to see the sun in all his splendour, for his brightness seldom lasts the day through. The morning of day and the morning of life are but too much alike." Jemmy gives the sun masculine personification as if to mock its complacent incarnation in Mr. Samuel Pickwick, and Jemmy's is a sad pessimism which would make of the novel itself an impossibility. When Mr. Pickwick says "You speak truly, sir," he either misunderstands what has been remarked or excludes himself and his bright world from its application. For it is the utopian achievement of *Pickwick Papers*, in the person of its hero, to have sustained the "morning of life" into serene old age. Jemmy now becomes suicidal: "Did it ever strike you, on such a morning as this, that drowning would be happiness and peace?" And Dickens must step in: " 'God bless me, no!' replied Mr. Pickwick, edging a little from the balustrade, as the possibility of the dismal man's tipping him over, by way of experiment, occurred to him rather forcibly." Dickens is working deliberately to make his facetious style a sort of buffer between Mr. Pickwick's equanimity and the suicidal melancholy of the stroller.

Pickwick evinces a perfunctory interest in a "romance of real life" which Jemmy offers to send him, gives the dismal man his address, and asks him to the waiting breakfast. But this invitation into the novel's happy and hospitable world is declined, and the dismal wanderer in the novel's romance world, that true and subversive "hidden country" of the book, moves slowly, silently away, dismissed by Mr. Pickwick as little more than a hale fellow well met. The surface of the novel is not even ruffled by what has passed. At a deeper level, however, the book is slightly jarred, its axis tilted a fraction too far toward an upsetting gloom. The balance must eventually be righted.

During their time together in the Fleet, Mr. Pickwick asks Jingle, for no apparent reason, about the long-lost Jemmy, of whom we have heard not one word in forty-eight chapters. Now we are told that he is not only Job's brother, but, like him, a complete charlatan and "hoaxing genius" (53). Mr. Pickwick seems instantly satisfied with this as an explanation for his not having received that promised manuscript. I doubt that we are meant to be. Job and Jingle convince us as hoaxing geniuses. Their motives are clear—self-interest, cleverly, sometimes brilliantly implemented. Would either of them ever go to the trouble of telling one long tale and promising another for no immediate remuneration or deceitful purpose, and for no conceivable long-range gain? Can we imagine Job or Jingle refusing an offer of breakfast? No, there is something very wrong with this for any naturalistic sense to be made of it. We simply cannot believe in Jemmy as Job's brother. He is a different order of being altogether, a hoaxing eccentric maybe, but also a morbidly compulsive story-teller, a gothic artist who exemplifies that very side of Dickens's own narrative genius. Expression seems, in the final analysis, to be his only motivation. His burden is a dark knowledge which it appears his driving need to share, to cast into compelling language, and he is allotted Dickens's first experiment in the impersonatorial mode. Mr. Pickwick is too eager to have this unhappy knowledge discredited: "I need not enquire whether his dismal behaviour was natural or assumed" (53). He does not even risk a straightforward question, but Job's response has unexpected import: "He could assume anything, sir . . . You may consider yourself very fortunate in having escaped him so easily." Indeed Pickwick, the man and the book, are lucky to have slipped free from the influence of such a dismal imagination, assumed or not. This is the point I am laboring. If everything Jemmy said were "made up," still his lies about his own and other lives hold profound truths about shadowed human experience. Of these, as we know, Mr. Pickwick must remain innocent.

Good spirits are again preserved by a kind of prevenient grace at Manor Farm, after the clergyman's gruesome tale of "The Convict's Return," begun as one of the "cheerful entertainments" at the fireside. It seems to make no impression at all. It happens and passes as a mere soporific, with all the "somniferous influence" (again the inflated buffer prose) of a bedtime story. Any unsettling effect the tale might have been expected to have is softened and absorbed by the stolid paragraph which follows it at the start of the next chapter, as this transitional prose climbs to a sort of mock-heroic elevation only to descend from the field of valor to the bed chamber with a precipitous afterthought: "The fatiguing adventures of the day or the somniferous influence of the clergyman's tale operated so strongly on the drowsy tendencies of Mr. Pickwick, that in less than five minutes after he had been shown to his comfortable bedroom, he fell into a sound and dreamless sleep, from which he was only awakened by the morning sun darting his bright beams reproachfully into the apartment. Mr. Pickwick was no sluggard; and he sprang like an ardent warrior from his tent—bedstead" (7). Though "dreamless sleep" here is presumably just another way of saying that Mr. Pickwick slept peacefully and undisturbed, the larger context invites speculation. Modern psychology, with which Dickens seems so often to be clairvoyantly in touch, has discovered that nightly dreaming is routine for everyone, and warns us against artificial interference with such dreams, whether through alcohol or drug abuse, or by any other means. When the ordinary functions of the nervous system are disrupted, when, for instance, subconscious energies are blocked by chronic drinking and denied their normal vent, it is now supposed that the resulting delirium tremens, like those of the dying clown in "The Stroller's Tale," may be the dream mechanisms gone berserk. Throughout his career Dickens will often portray such a revenge of the starved imagination, but in the nonrealistic world of Pickwick Papers the psychic pattern is so rearranged that the hero can be safely vaccinated against all fancy, forced to give up dreams of any sort, without danger, in order to insure against nightmare.

One of the chief services of dreaming is to suspend the pressures of time, to effect release from the normal demands of successive reality. But for the "immortal Pickwick," as we learn in a later moment of intriguing dream psychology, time itself is so soothing and beneficent that he is unable to sleep without being reminded of it. The passage begins as "Mr. Pickwick sat himself down in a chair before the fire and fell into a train of rambling meditations" (22). The successive "train" of his thought, however erratic, bears little resemblance to the romantic fancies kindled on the hearth by later "imaginists" in Dickens's novels, those dedicated fire-gazers I will be discussing in my sixth chapter. Pickwick's mind is said to have "wandered, by a natural process, to the dingy counting-house of Dodson and Fogg. From Dodson and Fogg's it flew off at a tangent to the very centre of the history of the queer client." The strayings of Pickwick's drowsy brain are not fancies, but memories; they have a "process" held within bounds of the "natural," and even the metaphor "tangent" is a geometric one. It is an orderly chaos, and at this second remove the effect of the remembered tale seems, once again, to help "convince Mr. Pickwick that he was falling asleep." Suddenly, however, he notices that his watch is missing: "The possibility of going to sleep unless it were ticking gently beneath his pillow or in the watch-pocket over his head had never entered Mr. Pickwick's brain." His "rambling" mind had allowed no real sojourn into the irrational, nothing so inventive, so insubordinate as a freely imagined fancy that might evict him from the temporal scheme of things. Diurnal time and its sunny renewals determine his world, and the absence even of their emblem in a "gently" ticked-off time is a thought too mutinous and ungovernable to be allowed "entrance" to his selective "brain." The very idea of such chaos is too chaotic to be admitted, and he at once goes off in search of his timepiece.

In the ordinary course of events, once the sound of time has lulled Mr. Pickwick to sleep his mind always refuses to brave the liabilities of sleeping fancy. After the story of "The Convict's Return," for instance, he awakens from his "dreamless sleep" into an "enchanting and delicious revery" during which he "cross-examined solitude after the most approved precedents" (7). The comic prose is there to remind us that the solitudes investigated in the main body of *Pickwick Papers* never risk being subconscious ones. The closest Mr. Pickwick comes to this danger we hear about four chapters later, when, alone in his chambers, he "fell into a train of meditation on the hurried events of the preceding days" (11). And just as the influence of a brilliant morning can inspire a bright revery, here the external night scene is shown to infiltrate an interior state of mind. "The hour and the place were both favourable to contemplation," but the very isolation begins to register as emptiness, in a kind of disturbing imaginative vacuum which brings to Pickwick for the first time in the book an unaccountable sense of loss: "The first stroke of the hour sounded solemnly in his ear, but when the bell ceased the stillness seemed insupportable;—he almost felt as if he had lost a companion." Quite unable to sleep, he tosses in his bed while "his thoughts kept reverting very uncomfortably to the grim pictures down stairs, and the old stories to which they had given rise in the course of the evening." Some stories, at least, seem to have made an impression on him. When he decides that anything is "better than lying there fancying all kinds of horrors," we realize that he is undergoing a real uneasiness of imagination. The prose now seeks its impact not in broad ironic strokes but in a blank repetitive simplicity like nothing before in the major narrative, with even the intensifiers now stark rather than hyperbolic: "He looked out of the window—it was very dark. He walked about the room—it was very lonely."

What Mr. Pickwick needs, and he knows it, is another "somniferous influence" like the clergyman's tale, and this is precisely what he comes up with when "the clergyman's manuscript for the first time entered his head. It was a good thought." He approaches it exactly as one might a bedtime story. "If it failed to interest him, it might send him to sleep." He removes the tale from his coat pocket and begins to read. The title "A Madman's Manuscript" gives him a start, and he looks anxiously about the room, but knowing that such "feelings," such nervous imaginings, are "absurdity," he plunges into the tale. With the deranged affirmation of the first words we have entered a totally different world, drawn with frantic strokes for us in a maniacal style that swerves between lucidity and frenzy: "Yes!—a madman's! How that word would have struck to my heart, many years ago! ... I like it now though. . . It's a grand thing to be mad! to be peeped at like a wild lion through the iron bars—to gnash one's teeth and howl... Harrah for the madhouse! Oh, it's a rare place!" (11). Punctuated by hysteria, end-stopped only by panic or exhaustion, this is the impersonatorial manner first tried out by Dismal Jemmy and carried here into the directness of first person. It is a style constantly driven forward by obsessive repetition, often of the cognitive forms "I know" and "I remember," in an effort, at the margin of grammatical coherence, to keep the mind moving against distraction and breakdown.

This kind of dementia is worlds apart from Mr. Pickwick's late-night fidgetings and nervous fancies. He cannot even be exposed to this "diseased imagination" in anything like its full tortured force. Rather, he must be allowed to use the manuscript as a kind of purge to rid himself of his own mild anxieties. When Miss Tomkins says of Pickwick at one point that "He must be respectable—he keeps a man-servant" (16), the governess plays on the verb "keep": "It's my opinion that his man-servant keeps him. I think he's a madman, Miss Tomkins, and the other's his keeper." She has, of course, pinpointed the ironic dependency of this inverted father-and-son relationship, yet as a psychiatric diagnosis her witty insight is no more than metaphoric. However "loony" Pickwick's bumbling innocence may seem, he has no trace of the madman's chaotic energy. And with "The Madman's Manuscript," an interpolated tale again becomes nothing more than a soporific, a good gothic shocker, after which Pickwick "soon fell fast asleep." The morbid imagination must be bled from the main body of the novel, its virulence disinfected. Pickwick becomes nervous and is, for the first and last time in the book, actually beset by "fancies," and so a tale is at once provided to dispel them. When the therapeutic story is completed, the sudden dying of Mr. Pickwick's candle "communicated a very considerable start to his excited frame," but having shaken off the last effects of his cathartic ordeal in this way, he sinks immediately to contented sleep. He awakes as expected: "The gloom which had oppressed him on the previous night, had disappeared with the dark shadows which shrouded the landscape, and his thoughts and feelings were as light and gay as the morning itself."

Style has retrieved its cheery assurance, and there is no surprise when a "hearty breakfast" is in order. But style takes over even before this to cordon off the deranged imagination, to oppose and control the two distinct moods of mind under analysis. Before the manuscript is actually finished, the prose itself has set up a tonal barrier between the lunatic's ravings and the sleepy apprehension of Mr. Pickwick. There is introduced a third consciousness, a new but familiar voice—in a fatuous moralistic gloss on the "fever and delirium" of the madman, who has just broken off his own narrative. The tale is thus completed by this new editorial voice with its aloof truisms: "The unhappy man whose ravings are recorded above, was a melancholy instance of the baneful results of energies misplaced in early life, and excesses prolonged until their consequences could never be repaired" (11). So it continues, the overwrought rhetorical style used to nullify the overwrought psychic activity of the tale—one excess trying, on Pickwick's behalf, to cancel the other out. It is the imagination of Sam Weller alone that becomes, through irony and understanding, mutually tangent to both these spheres of experience in the novel, to the verbose and the unspeakable.

The spirit of Mr. Weller presides at a curious inverse assimilation of the "somniferous narrative" motif near the middle of Ingmar Bergman's film "Cries and Whispers," when the painfully dying Agnes, relieved momentarily from the throes of her agony, is lifted out of bed, gently bathed, and then read to by her sister from an unnamed book. What we hear at once is Sam's "Hooroar for the principal, as the money-lender said ven he vouldn't renew the bill" (35). This is the "Wellerism" blurted out when Mr. Pickwick refuses for a second time to pay damages in the Bardell suit, thus committing himself to a prison term during which he will have to deal with the realities of death and pain for the first time. Grief for him will soon become more than an ingredient in a gothic story, no longer to be gotten round by going off to sleep, and so Sam's remark is a comic signpost for the major turn the plot is about to take. Ironically for Bergman's exhausted heroine, who has been forced to face death unrelievedly in her waking world— itself a gothic nightmare come true—the brief reading from *Pickwick Papers* serves her now as a soporific, a merciful interpolation, and immediately after hearing it, in her last moment of peace in the film, she drops away to sleep.

Sam Weller's protean fancy is as much at home with the gothic sensibility as it is with the frivolous tall tale that is about to take over the interpolated stage in *Pickwick*. The novel's double vision has been sustained by a quarantine of imagination which, until now, has kept apart in grotesque stories all trace of the "diseased imagination." Most of the inserted tales to come, like the next one, the bagman's story of Tom Smart and the talking chair (14), will isolate other hypersensitive, but lighter and more fanciful mentalities, and, in so doing, extend our sense of the "romance of life." We know that the chair's transformation into an instructive old man is not the work of the ordinary "waking imagination," that it in fact occurs while Tom is under stimulation by "hot punch." We are therefore invited to discount the miracle. In the sober light of day, "it must have been a remarkably ingenious and lively imagination, that could have discovered any resemblance between it and an old man." Dickens himself, of course, has just such an imagination, and the whole tale seems to have unrolled from a simple instance of his typical descriptive trick—the animation of lifeless objects. To believe in the plot so derived, how the chair *qua* old gentleman helps Tom win the widow of his eye, we must believe in the imagination turning into magic and realizing its own daydreams. But we are encouraged not to believe it, even for a moment. Everywhere in *Pickwick* fantasy and drink are too close together to leave room for magic, and this particular case in point is further sabotaged with some skeptical cross-examination by the bagman's audience when the tale is through. But just as this brand of tall story is plainly "marvellous," so, obviously, the first three dark tales were not. That both kinds of experience, the deranged and the fantastic, the too real and the unreal, must be kept with equal watchfulness from impinging on the main narrative, must be either ignored and forgotten or seriously undermined, tells us much about the unusual priorities of the novel.

It is the style, again, that helps define the isolated vision of the tale, style as a fairly direct and sensitive register of the controlling imagination, which in the story of Tom Smart is more "ingenious and lively" than most of the prose so far, more concrete and variously responsive—in short, more "Dickensian" as we will come to know it. This is all the more true of the fifth tale, "The Parish Clerk: A Tale of True Love." It is the only interpolation of the nine which is not weird or demented in some way, which does not dip into fantasy or dive into some psychic abyss. At the same time, hardly by accident, it is the only tale with which Mr. Pickwick is at all engaged. He has "edited" it from a story recited to him on his sickbed by Sam Weller, and he reads it to Mr. Wardle and Mr. Trundle after the illness from which Sam's "anecdote and conversation" have helped him recover. Sam's imagination shines through the story at many points, here in a punning play on words laminated with Pickwickian over-expression: "I repeat it, to be matter of profound astonishment and intense wonder, that Nathaniel Pipkin should have had the temerity to cast his eyes in this direction. But love is blind: and Nathaniel had a cast in his eye: and perhaps these two circumstances, taken together, prevented his seeing the matter in its proper light" (17). What this overlapping of the two styles, the high and the humorous, reads most like is the mottled and multidimensional comic prose which Dickens commands in his best narrative. Here it is a style in which we can hear, now and then, Sam's fresh and irrepressible comic spirit rising through the blanket of Pickwickian formality and tinging it with good-natured sarcasm, a style in which dead-pan circumlocution becomes comic delight: "Nathaniel Pipkin could make no reply, so old Lobbs shook him backwards and forwards, for two or three minutes, by way of arranging his ideas for him."

The next chapter will deal in part with the remarkable Mr. Weller and his closeness to the creative spirit of Dickens himself. For now, Sam can help us into the ethos of the sixth interpolated tale. We first meet him in the tenth chapter at the White Hart Inn, one of those old decrepit establishments in the Borough associated with "innumerable veracious legends," and providing material "enough for a hundred ghost stories, supposing that we should ever be reduced to the lamentable necessity of inventing any . . ." (10). This is Dickens talking, not the Pickwickian editor, and with the next sentence Sam Weller is introduced not only into the novel but into this same atmosphere of imaginative veracity, as if his superb credentials for getting along in the world were somehow associated at their source with these centers of legend and mystery, these proving grounds of imagination. By this time we also expect to hear from Dickens about the darker implication of these inns and their romantic heritage, and we are not surprised to find one of them as the setting for the last of the bleak interpolations. Amid a gathering at the Magpie and Stump Tavern, Mr. Pickwick proposes Gray's Inn as an amiable subject for conversation. He seems to have met with unexpected luck: "'By Jove,' said the chairman . . . 'You'll draw old Jack Bamber out; he was never heard to talk about anything else but the Inns, and he has lived alone in them till he's half crazy'" (20). With "a strange, wild slyness in his leer" reminding us of Dismal Jemmy's "unnaturally bright and piercing" stare, old Jack is another compulsive story-teller who at once "started forward, and burst into an animated torrent of words" (21). Before beginning his tales, however, Jack explodes at Mr. Pickwick's imaginative presumption in mentioning "what singular old places" the inns are: "What do *you* know of the time when young men shut themselves up in those lonely rooms . . . till their mental powers were exhausted; till morning's light brought no freshness or health to them . . . what do *you* know of the gradual sinking beneath consumption, or the quick wasting of fever . . . which men have undergone in these same rooms?" To be sure, Pickwick knows nothing of this. For him the "morning's light," which he himself symbolizes, is always salutary, and my later treatments of "the quick wasting of fever" in various characters will be an exploration into that part of Dickens's imagination which is no part of his first hero's. Pickwick has no contact with what Jack calls, as did Jemmy before him, "the romance of life, sir, the romance of life!" (21).

Like Jemmy, Jack has gone too far in this direction. His is a

potentially healthy fancy sickened into neurosis, a revenge of the
romantic imagination in which an initial openness to fanciful
possibilities becomes so exclusive that the mind closes back into
obsession. This is the feverish state which Dickens will later portray, more often, as the violent overthrow of a nearly paralyzed
rather than an over-exercised imagination. The problem with Jack
is partly a matter of indiscriminate taste. He treats fantastic,
almost whimsical, tall stories and tales of all too credible horror
with equal respect as life's weird romances. After a few grisly
anecdotes in which Mr. Pickwick expresses a token interest, Jack
launches into an unwitting travesty of the well-worn traditional
story of ghosts on the haunt, and then, as if it were the same sort
of tale, into the story of Heyling. Here is another miserable history
like the clown's or the madman's—disturbingly true even if not in
its particulars to the worst, most fearful reaches of human experience. Heyling is a debtor imprisoned in the Marshalsea, who
dreams of punishing those who have deserted him and his family,
and who finally choreographs his brutal vengeance in a series of
prolonged murderous hallucinations. During these "wildest ravings of fever" in the prison, Dickens strives once again with his
loud, darting, almost distracted prose for a stylistic impersonation
that will inhabit and act out the psychotic imagination, the very
"hurry" and "delirium" of the fever it reports. This is, of course, a
deranged imagination Pickwick cannot even be allowed to imagine, and again the contrasting impersonal style runs interference
for him: "As the gentleman with the Mosaic studs had fallen
asleep, and the major part of the company were deeply occupied
in the humorous process of dropping melted tallow-grease into his
brandy and water, Mr. Pickwick departed unnoticed" (21).

Jack Bamber, just before, had walked slowly away from the
scene "without saying another word." This is the last the novel
has to say of him, and—given its precarious and guarded atmosphere—the last it has the nerve to say about his narrative. When
Old Jack is recalled again four years later, along with Pickwick
and the Wellers, for *Master Humphrey's Clock*, his old gothic
preoccupations are still very much with him. This continuity in
his character helps expose the devastating change in Pickwick's
temperament and the complete artistic failure of his revival. Once
necessarily a stranger to Pickwick's circle and his entire world, a
chance and passing acquaintance, Jack lives again as a misplaced
satellite of the "immortal gentleman." This is, in every sense,
dead wrong. "When I retired into private life," Mr. Pickwick

explains, "I sought him out, and I do assure you that the more I see of him, the more strongly I am impressed with the strange and dreamy character of his mind" (*M.H.C.*, 4). Mr. Pickwick is here recommending Jack Bamber as an ideal member of Master Humphrey's circle. A "strange and secluded visionary" with a large store of macabre tales, Jack fills the bill to perfection. But what about Pickwick himself? He should have no place among the sequestered and indulgent imaginations gathered round the clock to savor the eerie tales deposited there. Nor should he be the man to sponsor Jack Bamber for those "fancies he has so long indulged," since the curiosity and surmise that are so often vital and elastic in Dickens are here an index to the monomaniacal imagination—fancy as fixation. In his own novel, Mr. Pickwick was never allowed even bright fancies, but he did exhibit the cheerfulness which breeds them. It is inconceivable that he should now choose, or even be permitted, an intimate association with the melancholy Jack Bamber. He is simply not the Pickwick we recognize when he listens with rapt pride to his own tale of witch-craft. How can we imagine *Pickwick's* Pickwick as a gothic author? His "extraordinary anxiety" (*M.H.C.*, 4) in this new role destroys the placid Pickwick we know, and though many critics have vaguely lamented the disaster, no one has really accounted for it, or for what it emphasizes again about the original Pickwickian temperament. At the moment of his revival in *Master Humphrey's Clock*, the immunities which made him "the immortal" are swept away, and Pickwick is killed by context.

Returning to the second half of *Pickwick Papers* and the remaining three interpolations—which become cheerier while the novel grows less so, as if by a law of the conservation of imaginative energy—we notice that the seventh tale stands in an interesting relation to the novel as a whole. Coming near the exact center of the book, it reverses the counter-stress between the bright whole-some forces of the main story and the sometimes fabulous, sometimes frightening energies of the interpolations. It is Wardle's tale of Grub and the kidnapping goblins, told at Mr. Pickwick's request. The tale inverts the emotional predominance of the novel by giving us as "hero" the precise opposite of Pickwick in every way, an "ill-conditioned, cross-grained, surly fellow—a morose and lonely man, who consorted with nobody but himself, and an old wicker bottle which fitted into his large deep waistcoat pocket" (29). Here is an alcoholic recluse in a world where the "social drink" is raised almost to the level of a sacrament, and it is only after some rough supernatural lessons that Grub comes to realize that "it was a very decent and respectable sort of world after all." The gloomy misanthrope has been effectively "Pickwickianized," and the fact that the whole reforming hallucination was attributable less to vision than to inebriation matters little. The crucial fact is that Gabriel Grub was altered more by his imaginings than Samuel Pickwick ever is by those that pass his way in the tales. Grub was a freer man than Pickwick, less hemmed in, his mind under fewer constraints. The morose imagination is allowed more spontaneity, freedom, and variety than the cheerful imagination, with more to be lost, can afford: this is the utopian paradox of the novel, the toll Eden takes for its safeguards. Only the Wellers, as we shall see—because they live in the real world too—are not made to pay this price.

The idea of drink as prime mover in an imaginative experience will return for the final tale. In the meantime, Pickwick reads the brief "Legend of Prince Bladud," another fantastic tale to which he responds just as we might expect: "Mr. Pickwick yawned several times, when he had arrived at the end of this little manuscript..." Even after such an innocuous fairy tale as this, his mind must shut down for the night. Again it seems a kind of retreat from turbulence: "'Ah!' said Dowler, 'going to bed? I wish I was. Dismal night. Windy; isn't it?'" (36). More fantastic yet is the final tale, which Dickens is careful to have Pickwick himself request and just as careful to finish, for the first time, without any mention whatever of Mr. Pickwick's reaction—or even his lack of it. The tales and the hero have finally drawn completely asunder; the quarantine has done its job. This last interpolation calls back for an encore the one-eyed bagman, celebrated for his account of Tom Smart and the talking chair. Once again his story, about his uncle's spooky nocturnal adventures, is an unmistakable drunken nightmare offered up in a delightfully earnest and witty tone: another fanciful tale about dreams and fancies. In some ways, in the feel of the descriptive prose itself, in its gusto and concrete detail, this is the most "Dickensian" of all the tales, a manifest fabrication which funnels at the end into a pun on the ghostly mail coaches carrying "dead letters." So completely a story, it even has a punch line. The fiction is now unmistakably ticketed.

Having arrived here in my discussion of the tales, I am really nine chapters ahead of myself. Mr. Pickwick is imprisoned in the fortieth chapter, beginning a term which probably no reader has

ever failed to recognize as the turning point of the book. And since
it is also the one point where the suffering and dismay subordinated until now in the tales actually begin to darken the main
story, any understanding of the format of interpolation comes to
depend on one's reading of the prison installments about which
the novel turns. Again, listening to style and the tone it sets
hastens such an understanding. But before this, a complaint.
J. Hillis Miller comes as close as one could to disregarding the
Fleet as a climactic episode by his failure to keep separate in analysis the previously isolated suffering and Pickwick's sudden
exposure to it. It is in the nature of Miller's critical method not to
respect the boundaries indicated by interpolation, but structural
distinctions must be observed in *Pickwick* for the very good reason
that they show us more than we can discover by overlooking them.
As I have said, Miller's mistake is characteristic, an error fostered
by theory. He is well known as a student of French structuralist
criticism, his method being to search fictional networks for lines
of developing consciousness which can then be independently
rearranged as a graph of an author's envisioned world. Miller
explains one instance of this system early in his chapter on
Pickwick: "When I speak in the following pages of 'Pickwick,' I
must be understood to be using the term in a Pickwickian sense,
and to be including within that term all of Pickwick's avatars in
the novel, all those characters who have analogous experiences."[3]
This may sound innocent enough, but we soon realize that among
the "avatars" or analogues of Pickwick, Miller is willing to include
even such a character as Heyling. In discussing the "phenomenal
scene"[4] of nightmarish anxiety in the novel, he quotes side by
side, without warning, a scene from the Fleet and a scene from
Heyling's tale, losing completely that sense of structural tension
which holds the first off for so long and which presents it, when
the time is right, in a very different way from the manner of an
interpolated tale.

When Pickwick is first hauled off to prison, Dickens tells us
about it in parodic "legalese" capped with a typical pleonasm:
"The usual forms having been gone through, the body of Samuel
Pickwick was soon afterward confided to the custody of the tip-
staff, to be by him taken to the Warden of the Fleet Prison, and
there detained until the amount of the damages and costs in the
action of Bardell against Pickwick was fully paid and satisfied"
(40). The irony of that jargon "body" is explicitly, bitterly medi-
tated in Dickens's voice when "the body of the Chancery prisoner

who had died the night before" awaits "the mockery of an inquest" (45). Dickens immediately blasts the reductive callousness of the "lawyer's term" with this inserted commentary: "The body! It is the lawyer's term for the restless whirling mass of cares and anxieties, affections, hopes, and griefs that make up the living man. The law *had* his body; and there it lay, clothed in grave clothes, an awful witness to its tender mercy." For the novel's hero, too, the point of the prison chapters is that far more than "the body of Samuel Pickwick" is to be locked away and mercilessly assaulted. Pickwick's *mind*, too, is about to enter the microcosm of the Fleet Prison, where for the first time in the novel it will meet the world by proxy. When Tupman, Winkle, and Snodgrass come to visit their leader in jail, they are visibly distraught, and Sam greets them cheerily, trying to lighten their spirits: "Mornin, gen'lm'n . . . Avay vith melincholly, as the little boy said ven his school-missis died" (44). I will soon be examining Sam's habit of quasi-allusive speech; here one need only mark the characteristic macabre note in this ambiguous "quotation," as well as the process of association by which Sam seems to graduate from the schoolroom setting into his next sentence: "Velcome to the College, gen'l'm'n." One of the chief uses of Sam's grotesque anecdotes and asides is to teach Pickwick about death and "melincholly." Pickwick has now unknowingly volunteered to accelerate this education by his matriculation in the Fleet "College," where Sam's darker awareness will be given concrete example.

Wholly the opposite of such legal jargon as "the body of Samuel Pickwick," the narration of his actual stay in prison begins, and at intervals is continued, in a stark adjectival style pared down to the reiteration of a few unspecific but powerful indicators, looking forward to similarly spare descriptive passages in the London scenes of *Oliver Twist*. No Dickens novel will ever, for very long at a time, desert concrete detail, but there is in *Pickwick Papers*, countervailing the sheer weight of described things, a certain generalizing bias. It is an abstract cast in the language itself that supports what I have been calling the theme of "subjectivity" in the book, lifting us above a landscaped and peopled and furnished world into the rendered idea of such a world, into the serener impressions of Pickwick's own utopian mentality. Style reinforces this theme even while it laughs at its own abstract diction. But in some of the tales and in the Fleet portion especially, the generalized diction embodies subjectivity in a slightly different way, binding it over to the disturbing perception of a world unwholesomely alive with ugly details, with an obnoxious objectivity faced everywhere and thus seen generally. We hear so often and with so little specification that the prison is "dirty and low" (41), "intolerably dirty and . . . perfectly suffocating" (41), "filthily dirty and . . . intolerably close" (42), that the repetition of this monotonous wretchedness begins to suggest an assaulted imagination. To some extent, the subjective is displacing the objective in order to render the scene as felt, as suffered. What we are to feel along our nerves is the loathsome, hopeless monotony of the place, as registered in the reiterated adjectives and in other simulations of miserable sameness.

In writing about Pickwick's world as a "dream Eden," W. H. Auden lists ten characteristics of such an ideal place. The fifth is, for *Pickwick* and for most of the later novels, perhaps the most interesting. In a dream Eden, "temporal novelty is without anxiety, temporal repetition without boredom."[5] The ticking of a watch, as we have seen, brings comfort, never annoyance. This is true for almost all of *Pickwick* before the hero's imprisonment. I say "almost" all because the episode at Bath, where the Pickwickians wait out the time until their leader's incarceration, brilliantly previews the debacle of Eden in the Fleet. The holiday world at Bath is indeed advertised as the dream Eden come true, where time includes "moments snatched from Paradise," and where nobody ever grows "fat or old" (35) because time itself is slowed by the magic elixir of the famous medicinal waters. But at Bath diversion grinds into boredom as the prose itself responds: "After this, they walked out, or drove out, or were pushed out in bath chairs, and met one another again. After this, the gentlemen went to the reading-rooms and met divisions of the mass. After this, they went home. If it were theatre night, perhaps they met at the theatre; if it were assembly night, they met at the rooms; and if it were neither, they met the next day. A very pleasing routine, with perhaps a slight tinge of sameness" (36). The bland, numbing progression and the flat tentativeness of the subjunctives connive to bore us even in the reading, and the last sarcastic understatement detonates the final explosion of this flimsy Eden.

By the time Pickwick has moved from Bath, where the hotel residents are in fact called 'inmates" (36), to the admitted prison itself, monotony has become not merely cloying but hellish, scene succeeding tormented scene without change or letup. In one of the most distressing of such scenes, Pickwick comes upon a room of prisoners whose minds have finally snapped under the strain, including a man lashing his single riding boot with a worn-out hunting whip, "riding, in imagination, some desperate steeple-chase at that moment" (42). No "imagination" at all, Pickwick would be the first to say, is better than this. In the midst of such a terrible company, there is the once irrepressible Alfred Jingle now destitute and forlorn. Yet these prison scenes are deliberately not drained of all humor; in the world of *Pickwick*, even the worst grief must find some comic relief. So when Jingle, accounting for his lack of a coat, explains that he had to eat and that he was able to live for a week off his various articles of clothing, Pickwick is horrified to understand this as meaning, not that Jingle pawned his wardrobe, but rather than he ate it (42). The comedy must draw on sadness, to be sure, but the surprise is that Dickens wants it there at all, when the darkening of his themes would seem to counsel otherwise. But the Pickwickian mentality is still under its author's protection. When one moment we seem to be watching Pickwick's demise as the creature of sanguine brightness and good spirits, when he exclaims on hearing about the death of a Chancery prisoner, "You make my blood run cold" (44), very soon he is himself again, in spite of the misery around him. After Jingle makes a second pitiful appearance "without one spark of his old animation," Mr. Pickwick's cheerful curiosity almost strikes us as callous: "'Curious scene this, is it not, Sam?' said Mr. Pickwick, looking good-humouredly round" (44). This is nothing more nor less than the observing, sightseeing spirit which motivated his travels in the first place, his search beyond Goswell Street for the "hidden countries" which lie on every side. And for the first time, in the Fleet's "diminutive World" (45), Pickwick has come into contact with a place of deprivation and terror until now well "hidden" from his consciousness. The passion for sightseeing in its most contemplative and philosophical sense, upon which the Corresponding Society of the Pickwick Club was founded, brings increased meaning to Pickwick's final decision to retreat, a decision prompted by both reason and feeling, by "head" and by "heart" alike: "'I have seen enough,' said Mr. Pickwick, as he threw himself into a chair in his little apartment. 'My head aches with these scenes, and my heart, too. Henceforth I will be a prisoner in my own room'" (45, my italics).

For this final retreat there is an arresting preparation four chapters earlier, a response on Pickwick's part which might have followed the reading of a grisly tale. After a frightening survey of the prison scene, "Mr. Pickwick's heart was really too full to bear it, and he went upstairs to bed" (41). The difference is that now his mind is engaged, his heart "full." No longer does sleepiness come when called, and so Pickwick falls to "wondering what possible temptation could have induced a dingy-looking fly that was crawling over his pantaloons, to come into a close prison, when he had the choice of so many airy situations." Though Pickwick must realize the close parallel to his own voluntary decision, he allows this "course of meditation" (that favorite honorific term for his thinking) to lead him at once to the "irresistible conclusion that the insect was mad." In spite of the still protective high style, we ourselves are led to another "irresistible conclusion" here about the first stirrings of projected madness, a "psychopathetic fallacy" as it were. Things are becoming precarious again, and by the next sentence some sort of welcome "somniferous influence" seems to have appeared just in time; once more the self-entwined, knotted prose of "Pickwickian" sensibility arrives to rope off all such undesired speculation from the cooler regions of Pickwick's mind: "After settling this point, he began to be conscious that he was getting sleepy; whereupon he took his nightcap out of the pocket in which he had the precaution to stow it in the morning, and, leisurely undressing himself, got into bed, and fell asleep." Not for long. His escape from consciousness has seemed a "protracted" oblivion, but for the first time in the novel an unpleasant reality cannot be slept off in this way, and the prison noise soon "roused Mr. Pickwick from one of those sound slumbers which, lasting in reality some half hour, seem to the sleeper to have been protracted for three weeks or a month."

As all options but awareness are being denied to Mr. Pickwick, Dickens surprises us by a shift of that gentleman's defensively brief attention span to Sam Weller, who falls asleep during the Chancery prisoner's autobiographical narrative: "The cobbler paused to ascertain what effect his story had produced on Sam, but finding that he had dropped asleep, knocked the ashes out of his pipe, sighed, put it down, drew the bed-clothes over his head, and went to sleep too" (44). He had just insisted that his pathetic tale was "God's truth," another of those claims for authenticity that we are familiar with from the interpolations. Sam is a character who hardly needs to be told this, indeed a man too familiar with the darker realities of the world to be much interested in the actual details of the story. His falling asleep seems introduced primarily to highlight by contrast Mr. Pickwick's gradual "awakening," yet the unnerving irony is that the new obtrusive reality which Pickwick must now confront appears to him like a bad dream.

The event that precipitates his ultimate retreat is that final tour of the prison and its monotonous turmoil. Dickens has found exactly the nonconcrete and repetitive prose to capture the subjective effect on Pickwick of the scene's "general characteristics." By an unstrained transference of epithets, the physical "place" becomes a generalized psychic space, itself "restless and troubled": "The great body of the prison population appeared to be Mivins, and Smangle, and the parson, and the butcher, and the leg, over and over, and over again. There was the same squalor, the same turmoil and noise, the same general characteristics, in every corner; in the best and the worst alike. The whole place seemed restless and troubled; and the people were crowding and flitting to and fro, like the shadows in an uneasy dream" (45). Style has stopped short of a real demented "impersonation" because these "shadows in an uneasy dream" are not yet fully the creatures of Pickwick's own nightmare. It is to protect his mind from further contamination that he must retreat. He has seen, in his own world, a reality more importunate than any of the interpolated "fictions" after which he had nodded off during the course of the novel. He can no longer ignore it. All he can do—though it turns out to be enough to save him—is withdraw.

There is, in one of the prison chapters, an odd stretch of social commentary couched ironically in the doublets of self-satisfied rhetoric: "we still leave unblotted in the leaves of our statute book, for the reverence and admiration of succeeding ages, the just and wholesome law which declares that the sturdy felon shall be fed and clothed, and that the penniless debtor shall be left to die of starvation and nakedness" (42). But with the next sentence the "Pickwickian" style is brought up as short as Pickwick himself is by his revelations in the Fleet: "This is no fiction," Dickens abruptly insists. You have been reading so far a fairy tale about a man named Pickwick, he is saying, but what you have now entered upon is no such fiction, and even Mr. Pickwick himself will be made to see this. Dickens is in fact suggesting something at large here about the novelist's art; in the middle of all authentic "fictions," the truth is upon us. When a version of this truth comes to Pickwick, of course, his wanderings are over, the quest for "hidden countries" cancelled by this sudden awareness. He has seen at last, and he is through. As he says in the next-to-last chapter of the novel, "New scenes have closed upon me; my rambles are at an end" (51). He will now retire into "repose and quiet" among his friends—no melancholy seclusion, but a new content, bred of discovery, with enclosure and rest. This retirement is possible only because of his strategic retreat into his own cell at the moment of crisis in the Fleet. There he met head-on the worst life has to offer, where before it had been safely stored away in "stories." But what did not happen to Pickwick, for it would have ended him as the hero of temperament, is that long, unrelieved contact with evil and fear which warps the imagination and shatters the mind. The "uneasy dream" was for the first time real, but it was still an external terror, and Pickwick chose to escape from it. He *chose*—this is all-important. Pickwick retains his will, unlike those wretched characters who have lost theirs in fever or surrendered it to obsession. Pickwick has chosen prison in the first place to avoid paying Dodson and Fogg, can at any time opt for release, and can also choose to isolate himself further within the prison walls. His story becomes a parable of elected suffering, an allegory of naiveté coming to knowledge, of willed initiation into the evils of the world. And this is something quite different—as the whole novel goes to show—from the shackled, inescapable derangement of life's real prisoners.

So we have seen that Pickwick's spirit is not permanently damaged, merely sobered, by his time in the Fleet. Here is the resiliency which has characterized him from the start, and which is given explicit portrayal the very last time in the book his good humor slips away from him. After shouting out the window a series of denunciations at Dodson and Fogg, Pickwick seems much relieved by the venting of his wrath: "When Mr. Pickwick drew in his head again, his countenance was smiling and placid, and, walking quietly back into the office, he declared that he had now removed a great weight from his mind, and that he felt perfectly comfortable and happy" (53). This is Pickwick's great blessing and, at the same time, the source of much of the comedy attaching to him: that he can always return from mental or rhetorical extremities, from inflammation or inflation, into complacency and comfort. And when this gift is tested by suffering toward the end of the novel, it becomes a real beauty of temperament allied for the first time with moral consciousness.

In the fifth chapter of *Pickwick Papers*, after a farcical episode in which the Pickwickians are suspected of horse-stealing, their leader exclaims: "It's like a dream . . . a hideous dream." He has no idea what he is talking about. He does not have dreams, hideous or jolly either, and even toward the end of the book his dawning sense of the world's misery is allowed to stop short of a full waking nightmare. The penumbral world of fears and fancies never really gives its various, unruly shadings to the Pickwickian sector of the novel. And of course Samuel Pickwick casts no shadows. His light source is within; he is the sun of his own bright universe. At his zenith in the dazzling good fellowship of Dingley Dell, however, almost dead center in the novel, Dickens uses two lines of Mr. Wardle's "Christmas Carol" to set off a delayed fuse for the eventual demolition of every surety and complacence *Pickwick Papers* represents. The subject of the carol's second stanza, the "Summer sun" that seeks its "bright home," could well be an emblem of Mr. Pickwick's own temperament, but it is a radiance, we are now told, whose "darling child is the madness wild / That sports in fierce fever's train" (28). Dickens is suggesting here that the relation between gaiety and madness is one of unrealized continuity, somehow organic, lineal, and that the strict apportioning of consciousness which Mr. Pickwick enjoys must in the long run be surrendered. In the fallen, equivocal world of all Dickens's novels after Pickwick, an inner life must be found by his people in various locales of the mind between the poles of unimagining contentment and "madness wild." Even where it might immunize them against the excesses of "fever's train," the colonizers of this psychic middle-earth cannot wisely forfeit their fancy. Too often it is all they have. Not so for *Pickwick Papers*, whose Eden, though it is and must be "fancy-free" in the negative sense, is still taken on faith to be better than anything which might supplant it.

Pickwick Papers is a novel about the schismatic mind. It dreams as innocent world so bright that there can be no such thing as a fortunate fall. Too complete a felicity makes impossible a "felix culpa," and instead—to rework the Latin phrase—along the "happy fault" that divides innocence from experience every effort must be made to coax the slightest crevice into a ravine, and to pump it full of words: the prose of camouflage and insulation. For most of the novel this is the style in which the hero himself speaks. Only when we have grown to love and admire the eccentric gentleman does he begin to sound different to us, less windy and pompous, less self-assured. It is in this sense that the prison sequence also becomes a turning point for the tone of the novel, beginning to redefine "Pickwickian" in its stylistic as well as its personal sense, and thus helping to explain the muted aptness of the book's last pages.

3 Release

> ... one likes to recall that the difference
> between the comic side of things and their cosmic
> side, depends upon one sibilant.—Nabokov[1]

To understand the conclusion of *Pickwick Papers,* the special
release it brings, is to listen for the ways in which style and tone
are altered as the novel draws to its close. *Pickwick* opens in an
unfortunate unanimity of tone. The style of the fatuous and self-
congratulatory editor, the transacted minutes he delivers into
evidence, the voices of the Pickwickians therein recorded, are all
of a heavy piece, swollen with the same fraudulent enormity of
expression. Eight hundred pages or so strive to transform this style
in two reviving directions. From one regrettable voice, distributed
with the satirist's impartiality between narrator and hero alike,
there emerge two distinct but complementary voices. On the one
hand, the voice of the comic ironist, the most typical of all Dickensian styles, jeers itself free of its own opulent nonsense, rising
above it without being forced to disown its comic possibilities. And
on the other hand, from the same verbal habits without humor,
Mr. Pickwick's private voice settles into a quiet sincerity, an earned
solemnity wrested at last from the contortions of "Pickwickian"
parody.

The former style is to become the texturing ingredient of Dickensian comic prose, developing steadily from novel to novel. Circumlocution, verbal excess and indirection of every kind, become
fertile options for Dickens, ready both for general comedy and for
direct parody, suited equally to the humorous tactic of delayed
disclosure (in simplest form, the withheld "punch line") and to the
vapid protractions of mocked grandiosity. In the most character-

istic stretches of this style, in fact, the boundary has been eroded between comedy and direct satire, yet the joke is no less funny for being "on" no one in particular.[2] Bombast, circumlocution, caviling and evasive delicacies of expression—the whole smothering atmosphere of euphemism and magniloquence Dickens is out to get. His own comic style, with its humorous circuities and overdone expressions, is a frontal assault on the very concept of style as sensibility in its most priggish advocacy. At the same time, it substitutes for the censorious and hypocritical morality of the high style, of humbug rhetoric, a new and more capacious sensibility, liberated by laughter and fancy into a truer ethic of imagination. And just as Dickens can organize his verbal fecundity as straight comic description or targeted parody, so another of his gifts as a writer can be developed in either of two stylistic directions, as we have seen in *Pickwick*. The unimpeded forward thrust of his sentences—readability raised to artistic power—can run at comic timing or at a very special kind of "dramatic" pace. For when the momentum of expression and the momentum of meaning move into real synchronization, style begins to enact meaning in the impersonatorial mode.

But I was talking about just one of the Dickensian styles in particular, the "Pickwickian" rhetorical style, and about what becomes of it as the novel grows and changes. The fact is that it too grows and changes, and is grounded finally in a solemnity no longer disproportionate to its issues or its understanding. At the same time, though at no expense now to Mr. Pickwick, the satiric flights of the high style are allowed their independent comedy. Nothing is given up. No literary artist ever had to sacrifice less of his innate passion for words and their humor to the integrity of his moral vision. Rather than surrender his indulgences in parodic style in order not to infect the transformation of our attitude toward "Pickwickian" rhetoric, Dickens capitalizes on untapped resources in his central character in order gradually to alter our perception, leaving time and room for the emergence of a reformed Pickwickian voice alongside the continuing ironic style.

These words announce the first speech in the novel: "Mr. Pickwick's oration upon this occasion, together with the debate thereon, is entered on the Transactions of the Club. Both bear a strong affinity to the discussions of other celebrated bodies." That last plural is one of Dickens's least obtrusive puns, a multiple form both of a singular and of a collective noun—referring either to the "somebody" named Samuel Pickwick or to the "body" of men for whom he is the appointed mouthpiece. The singular meaning is blurred, kept secondary—one may guess—because absorption of the individual personality into the collective "body" is typical of such consensus rhetoric. Prose like this, the style of "celebrated bodies," never intimate or candid, is personal only insofar as it is vaguely self-celebrating. And Pickwick is its exact personification, the rotund and the oratorical having merged completely into the orotund, as his first words will amply demonstrate. In much these same terms of physical "embodiment," an interesting passage early in the novel offers premature hints of a sincerity in Pickwick's talk as yet unrevealed, an earnestness hidden by the apparent shape of things, again whether physical or rhetorical. The scene has Mr. Pickwick trying to reconcile the disappointed lover Tupman with the world: "For half an hour, their forms might have been seen pacing the churchyard to and fro, while Mr. Pickwick was engaged in combatting his companion's resolution. Any repetition of his arguments would be useless; for what language could convey to them that energy and force which their great originator's manner communicated?" (11). The subject of that first passive clause is improbably abstract, abstract in the way Pickwick's speeches regularly are, and once our attention is caught by this we realize that language's self-scrutiny is again going forward on more than one track. We see only "their forms," only outlines or silhouettes, a physical equivalent for the mere "forms" of words we would expect to hear if Pickwick's "arguments" were being reported. It goes without saying that satire has entirely the upper hand here. Yet for the first time in the novel it is suggested that Pickwick's meanings may run deeper than mere language, that there may be an "energy and force" that make of words more than just wording—a language of the heart "communicated" by "manner" apart from rhetorical style, by personality itself.

Only at the end of the novel will this oblique prediction have come to pass. The massive showiness of style associated with language in its "Pickwickian sense" must be tempered by the humane, unrhetorical sense of "Pickwick" to which Sam Weller responds as to a "magic word" (24). Once when his master is incredulous over Sam's story of crooked election practices, Sam is heard to wonder: "Lord bless your heart, sir... Why where was you half baptised?" (13). Where (to recast the question) were you only half invested with the import of your magic or sacramental name? When will you have learned enough of the world and its suffering to deserve the Pickwickian title in its genuine personal sense? The final baptism in the humanizing waters of experience comes, as we have seen, in the Fleet, and only after his imprisonment has our hero earned the right to be called "the immortal Pickwick." To see, *to hear* what has changed we need only compare Pickwick's last speech to his friends with the humbug sonorities and perfunctory self-effacement of his first "oration," which was obviously fanning "the fire of self-importance" he pretended to have "effectually quenched." There we had a prose which tagged Pickwick right from the start as a comic butt. Here is his valedictory speech, in a reformed style of mellowed earnestness and humility which, of course, as predicted, owes much of its "energy and force" to Pickwick's newly matured and sympathetic "manner." Words are no longer just "forms":

'I shall never regret,' said Mr. Pickwick in a low voice, 'I shall never regret having devoted the greater part of two years to mixing with different varieties and shades of human character; frivolous as my pursuit of novelty may have appeared to many. Nearly the whole of my previous life having been devoted to business and the pursuit of wealth, numerous scenes of which I had no previous conception have dawned upon me—I hope to the enlargement of my mind, and the improvement of my understanding. If I have done but little good, I trust I have done less harm, and that none of my adventures will be other than a source of amusing and pleasant recollection to me in the decline of life. God bless you all!' (57)

This is the thoroughly felt and sincere style of a man speaking from the heart, and Northrop Frye's reading of the Fleet episode as the typical recognition and reversal scene in the New Comedy structure has an obvious stylistic bearing: "The pedant has become a man of principle, and the humor of pedantry is transferred to the law which entraps him."[3] When the style of pedantry is thus put aside by Pickwick, he is no longer a humors character. This is very much in line with Jonas Barish's comments about the traditional link between linguistic satire and fixed, end-stopped characters—or humors. To use Barish's terms, Pickwick undergoes a "character transformation" which sets off a "linguistic transformation," and verbal satire is left behind.[4]

It seems possible to locate almost the exact moment of this linguistic peripety, in that splendid scene (three chapters before his retreat into his own cell) where Pickwick gives Job Trotter money, his first act in the novel of wholly selfless philanthropy.

   'Come here, sir,' said Mr. Pickwick, trying to look stern, with four large tears running down his waistcoat. 'Take that, sir.'
   Take what? In the ordinary acceptation of such language, it should have

been a blow. As the world runs, it ought to have been a sound, hearty cuff; for Mr. Pickwick had been duped, deceived, and wronged by the destitute outcast who was now wholly in his power. Must we tell the truth? It was something from Mr. Pickwick's pocket, which chinked as it was given into Job's hand, and the giving of which, somehow or other imparted a sparkle to the eye and a swelling to the heart of our excellent old friend as he hurried away. (42)

Both meaning and money here are surprisingly "received," and the language of this "exchange" has a kind of synonymous reciprocity. To appreciate what the etymological rightness of the Pickwickian big word "acceptation" has allowed Dickens to do, we need only re-imagine the dialogue, lexically reversed. "*Accept* this, sir," Mr. Pickwick might have said. And the narrator: "Such language would ordinarily be *taken* to mean . . ." Mr. Pickwick never uses language in the "common sense," but here he has found a Pickwickian sense for "take this" which at last confirms his reputation for benevolence. So Pickwick emerges as the unwonted trustee of monosyllabic and meaningful expression, his verbal "coinage" at once validated by the chink of coin.

Pickwick has gone into training for this linguistic and ethical triumph in the preceding chapter, in another node of monetary and semantic intersection when he fails to understand Smangle's idiomatic use of "paper," mistaking the medium of financial transaction for ordinary writing paper, a surface for mere words. Smangle informs him that "paper has been my ruin" (42), and Pickwick lets the right side of this particular verbal coin fall face down and unrecognized: " 'A stationer, I presume, sir?' said Mr. Pickwick innocently." This example of his linguistic "innocence" seems particularly self-centered given the primacy of the stationer's services in transmitting the history of Pickwick's financially independent adventures to posterity. Pickwick in the Fleet is, however, in the process of surrendering some of his naiveté; Smangle denies the "Pickwickian sense" of his statement with "When I say paper, I mean bills," and so by this encounter Pickwick has learned a new "common sense" for the misunderstood noun: "Oh, you use the word in that sense, I see." Though caught off guard for a moment by the more worldly, financial meaning of a word, Pickwick himself will surprise not only Jingle but Dickens's readers as well with an unexpected monetary sense for "Take that" in his next chapter.

It is not, I think, claiming too much for the verbal precision of this subsequent scene to hear in it a condensed form of the novel's whole moral and linguistic drama. For the distance between the semantic kin "acceptation" and "take" measures the transformation from the old to the new Pickwick. Where his language has been pompously self-gratifying, now it is, to an uncommon extent, expressive and sincere. The ironic narrator has here assumed the full burden of prestigious talk, including the familiar Pickwickian Latinism, and Pickwick himself seems for the moment to have been educated free of such thoughtless finery in language, taught by his own heart's affections a nobler vocabulary. Despite his fame for tremendous ken and beneficence, Pickwick has been from his first appearance laughably self-concerned. In the first chapter he seems literally to be brought to life by the sounding in his ears of his own name, summoned into consciousness by the essential piece of Pickwickian diction, the Ur-word. The man whom we discovered "starting into full life and animation, as a simultaneous call for 'Pickwick' burst from his followers" (1) has learned that other words, too, can enliven and animate, and that only certain genuinely meant words can in fact make good his mythic name.

Pickwick's voice, in that farewell speech already quoted, is the last voice we hear in the novel, but the impersonal style which surrounds it has also undergone a change from its earlier ironies. The final scene, without dialogue, transpires in the more relaxed cadences of this newly straightforward narration. After the marriage of Mr. Snodgrass and Emily Wardle, the Pickwickians adjourn to the inauguration of their leader's new home, where everything is "so beautiful, so compact, so neat." There, in a neat and (for all its elaboration) compact sentence, we get Pickwick placed at the due center of the festivities in a simple main clause that unfolds syntactically into a full benevolent tableau:

And in the midst of all this, stood Mr. Pickwick, his countenance lighted up with smiles, which the heart of no man, woman, or child, could resist: himself the happiest of the group: shaking hands, over and over again with the same people, and when his own hands were not so employed, rubbing them with pleasure: turning round in a different direction at every fresh expression of gratification or curiosity, and inspiring everybody with his looks of gladness and delight. (57)

Time itself has been halted and enclosed, as Pickwick shakes hands "over and over again with the same people." The past tense of the stationary main clause has shaded into the kinetic suspension of absolutes and present participles to embody this quintessential, timeless moment. Pickwick is at last rendered "immortal" by grammar, as the conclusion of the novel moves into the present tense with the beginning of the very next sentence: "Breakfast is announced." This is a perfect touch. The wedding meal compounds the expected, almost sacramental significance of the morning repast in *Pickwick* with the additional hallowed associations of marriage, of living shared and perpetuated. And so we take our exit from the main narrative while the guests await this last happy breakfast, in a morning cheer which no longer seems facile or unmerited. This is the tonal serenity on which the novel deserves to end only because of its tonal accomplishment throughout in defending the lambency of Pickwick's world and making of it a brightness that lasts. The quarantine of imagination has been necessary to keep the healthy mind shielded and intact, so that when we are brought at the end of the novel "to the extreme verge of insanity," it is merely the state to which the wedding plans have "reduced three dressmakers and a tailor."

But just as Pickwick's story has two openings, the one introducing the posthumous papers themselves and the "first ray of light" derived from them, the other introducing the hero awakening just after dawn "like another sun" on the first day of his adventures, so the novel now has two conclusions, which reverse the order and round out the pattern. The one we have just discussed brings the hero to rest in a timeless present tense of joy and hospitality, drawing the entire picaresque to a satisfactory finish, while the coda which follows reverts to the opening chapter and forms with it a framing comment on the nature and source of the enclosed experience. For most of the novel, we are expected to believe, and are at intervals reminded, that what we are reading has been assiduously selected and meticulously edited for us from among the voluminous papers of the Pickwick Club, or, in the case of chapters four and five, from the private notebook of Mr. Snodgrass. This is the author-as-editor convention announced at the start of several chapters in fussy vouchers of authenticity. All of this is simply conventional filler, overturned by parody along the way and then completely discredited at the end of the novel. There we take our leave of the Pickwickians not as actual personages in a faithful history, but as the author's "visionary companions of many solitary hours," whom, as their creator, he has the right to put aside "when the brief sunshine of the world is shining full upon them" (57). The editorial masquerade is dropped completely, and we now hear the autonomous creative artist discussing the creatures of his own imagination: "It is the fate of most men who mingle with the world, and attain even the prime of life, to make many real friends, and lose them in the course of nature.

It is the fate of all authors or chroniclers to create imaginary friends, and lose them in the course of art." In a single stroke the whole idea of the realistic chronicle novel has been audaciously redefined—as the teller's private vision of an imagined world. I have said that subjectivity is, in a sense, the subject of the novel, the Pickwickian mentality which the structure of the book itself is at pains to preserve. The "visionary" or creative imagination, however, has conjured and contained not only the bright main narrative but also the interpolated tales, both of fever and of fantasy. So that when the entire novel is revealed in the coda as itself an imaginative construct, a mental world projected through language, the theme of subjectivity is given new scope and comprehension.

The closing prose is itself deeply attuned to the shift from a parodied editorial manner to the new glorification of creative vision. Completing the pattern of transfiguration which brought Mr. Pickwick's speech to such quiet eloquence, the Latinized formality of the coda is no longer fatuous and affected; it, too, has achieved a true mild beauty, nowhere more remarkable than in the last sentence of the novel. We have heard that Mr. Pickwick persists in his "former juvenility of spirit" (57), and the entire mentality which the phrase celebrates, the accumulated experience of the novel, is needed to make of the last lines not the lusterless verbosity of which they might smack in an earlier context, but now, warming beneath their measured, formal surface, a powerful and touching understatement closing out in the flat but plainly moving last dependent clause: "Every year, he [Mr. Pickwick] repairs to a large family merry-making at Mr. Wardle's; on this, as on all occasions, he is invariably attended by the faithful Sam, between whom and his master there exists a steady and reciprocal attachment which nothing but death will terminate."

It is now time to look at this "steady and reciprocal attachment" in some detail. For what Sam brings to his relation with Pickwick and, annexing an entirely new stylistic dimension to the novel, what is implied about his imaginative sympathy with Dickens's own comic voice—these things take form in *Pickwick Papers* as its most stunning achievement, and one of the best things Dickens was ever to do. I began talking about *Pickwick* with a diagnostic section on the comic style and its satiric motivations, as prepared for in the *Sketches by Boz* and centered in *Pickwick's* first chapter. The diagnosis was Dickens's own as much as mine—a dissection of verbal hypocrisy and humbug. What Dickens began to uncover there about the Pickwickian temperament not only necessitated but also provided the stylistic strategy for that rigid cleavage of imaginative experience explored in the second chapter. Style and tone began an important change after the Fleet episode, as we know, and the quarantine of imagination was finally lifted altogether in the coda of the novel, where the shaping mentality of the artist was at last acknowledged as a mind able to keep together in the same imaginative space both the bright central story and the eccentric tales. The novel was thus released from its partitioned atmosphere into the possession of a single creative mind. But there was another sort of escape-valve built right into the novel all along, in the persons of Sam Weller and his father Tony—a release from quarantine into the uninhibited imagination of comic high spirits.

Sam Weller is a glib but immaculate ironist, an intrepid verbal comedian who blends in his own Cockney patter many of the Dickensian habits, both of phrase and fancy, that were surveyed in the first chapter. When at one point Sam is trying to help Mr. Pickwick out of a scrape, there is a Mr. Grummer who shouts "Stand back" and a very tall man called Dubbley who suggests that they "Knock him down, if he don't." Sam's satiric rejoinder, with its prim deference and stilted alliteration, exhibits at once both the linguistic and the fictive imagination Dickens has jointly bestowed upon him,[5] with his mockery turning from what the Dickensian pathology of rhetoric might diagnose as "giantism" of phrase to the imaginary giants of fairy tale: " 'I'm wery much obliged to you, old gen'l'm'n,' replied Sam, 'for consulting my conwenience, and I'm still more obligated to the other gen'l'm'n, who looks as if he'd just escaped from a giant's carrywan, for his wery 'ansome suggestion' " (24). When Sam and his father Tony are reunited for the first time in the novel, Sam points out "the old 'un" to Mr. Pickwick and then elegantly varies the epithet for his actual greeting: "How are you, my ancient?" As usual, the narrator is on hand to extend Sam's comedy, and this quaint salute is at once glossed for us as a "beautiful ebullition of filial affection" (20), a monumental phrase laughing with us at its own alliteration and its polysyllabic showpiece, that favorite Johnsonian item "ebullition."[6] The effect achieved by this pocket of Latinate rhetoric and its flexible irony is, as usual, hard to be exact about. At one and the same time, it seems to encompass something of the predictable "Pickwickian" reaction to Sam's gallant vulgarism, something of a parody on the desire to paraphrase and soften it, something of a gratuitous delight in the very excess of the labored substitute, and something by way of commemoration for Sam's original greeting itself. In all this, and in countless instances like it, there is never a moment's doubt that the narrative conscious-ness and Sam's imagination are in complete accord, that they in fact coincide—a single comic spirit regaling itself before us and doubling the fun by meeting us in different stylistic shapes.

Here is Dickens putting Sam Weller through his comic paces in a discussion of the waters at Bath:

> 'Ah,' said Mr. John Smauker, 'you disliked the killibeate taste, perhaps?'
> 'I don't know much about that 'ere,' said Sam. 'I thought they'd a wery strong flavour o' warm flat irons.'
> 'That *is* the killibeate, Mr. Weller,' observed Mr. John Smauker, con-temptuously.
> 'Well, if it is, it's a wery inexpressive word, that's all,' said Sam. (37)

This is Sam in his role as a critic of expressive language, dissatisfied with the formal, scientific word and offering something concrete and metaphoric in its place. As the conversation proceeds, Sam also turns his fondness for puns and double understandings against his comic adversary, Mr. Smauker, whose arm he has been asked to take, and his facetious reply—"Thank'ee, you're wery good, but I won't deprive you of it"—gaily reverses such a sincere misappre-hension as Mr. Pickwick's concerning the idiom "hung out."[7] Sam always knows what he is saying and carries it off with a complete sarcastic deadpan, the pose of naiveté which heightens this sort of comedy and which is a characteristic of Dickens's own style.

In prison Sam refuses to submit to the perfuming rhetoric of euphemism or "delicate English," and says to the destitute cobbler he meets, "Well, perhaps . . . you bought houses, wich is delicate English for goin' mad, or took to buildin', wich is a medical term for bein' incurable" (44). Sam, like Dickens, loves to mock termin-ology, and in the same conversation, after his play with slang, he supposes that a "law term" like "in trust" must be applicable only in some kind of "Pickwickian sense," for "There's wery little trust at that shop." Earlier, in the encounter that leads directly to Pickwick's court case and subsequent imprisonment, Sam dis-misses even a standard legal term like "subpoena" with the deflect-ing question "What's that in English?" (31). This iconoclastic comedy is the product of Sam's wary good sense—and also its best support. The first time we meet Mr. Weller in the novel, the lawyer Perker, who thinks he has diagnosed some symptoms of Sam's wit, accosts him with "You're a wag, an't you?" and the "imperturbable Sam" retorts: "My eldest brother was troubled with that complaint . . . it may be catching—I used to sleep with him" (10). No quarantine then; yet with a last name that seems to suggest a comparative degree of good health, Sam Weller's lamenting his verbal gift as if it were a malady is one of the novel's paramount ironies.

Surely there can be no argument with Steven Marcus when he calls Sam "one brilliantly split off, deflected, and reorganized segment" of Dickens himself,[8] and the reader is not long in discovering how, in this respect, Sam and his father are imaginative peers, self-created and intuitive poets, the novel's only heroes of the verbal imagination. They listen and conceive like poets, and their ears and mind's eyes are flawless. Twice they debate a choice between polysyllabic alternatives, "circumscribed" versus "circumwented" (33) and "dispensation" versus "dispensary" (52). It seems only natural that Sam should slide into alliteration when praising the Saracen's Head cuisine, with its " 'taturs, tart, and tidiness" (51), or that metaphor should leap automatically to his mind when told by Pickwick to keep quiet: " 'Dumb as a drum vith a hole in it, sir,' replied Sam" (25). His father can elicit a comic aphorism from the slightest coincidence of sound, as when he advises Sam that "as you get vider, you'll get viser. Vidth and visdom, Sammy, alvays grows together" (55).

Their Cockney mispronunciations in themselves seem a kind of poetic license, and their self-assurance is the justifiable pride of creativity, free from the satire usually leveled at self-confident styles in Dickens. When Tony calls Sam a "prodigy son" and Mr. Pell misses both the fun and the tribute in this locution, correcting Tony with "Prodigal, prodigal son, sir," Tony simply replies: "I know what's o'clock, sir" (43). Though "an alibi" he calls "a alleybi," this lowbrow innovator of English usage can also make fun of the high style by trying to pass off his own home-grown slang as a foreign borrowing: "And my 'pinion is, Sammy, that if your governor don't prove a alleybi, he'll be what the Italians call reg'larly flummoxed, and that's all about it" (33). When a confusion over his wife's will arises and Tony demands "a probe," Pell insists on "Probate, my dear sir, probate." Tony, however, will not be condescended to: "Well, sir . . . probe and probe it, is wery much the same: if you don't understand wot I mean, sir, I dessay I can find them as does" (55). With his defiant poet's ear, Tony is the master of such homophonic puns (probe it for probate) and finds oblique rightness in them with startling frequency. Given the Wellers' verbal intuition and impunity, even their accidents are creative. Both father and son come up with other marvelous trans-literations of legal jargon. Sam's rewriting of *habeas corpus* as "have-his-carcase" (40) is matched by Tony's "leg-at-ease" for "legatees" (55). And in the Fleet, Sam counsels a prisoner charged with contempt of court to tender an apology to the judge "for makin' his court contemptible" (44). Perhaps best of all is Tony's phrase for cheering up his wife, an activity which he calls "adjestin' our little differences" (55). Here he has in fact hinted at a formula for his own role, and his son's, in *Pickwick Papers* as a whole, for it is precisely the "jests" of this lively pair that provide the vital comic "adjustment" the novel demands.

Yet even before Sam has come upon the scene, and long before we have met Tony, there is another character who seems to incorporate the same verbal energy and eccentricity. It is instructive to compare the fully charged current of the Weller imagination with the other high-voltage fancy in the book, that of the infamous Mr. Alfred Jingle. He bursts into the novel as the personification of humor and high spirits, and his first words seek it out: "What's the fun?" (2). Mr. Pickwick and his friends have been mistaken for informers by the cabman, a crowd has gathered, and only Jingle's intrusion saves the day. Again Dickens's mock inflated style seems to betray a real sympathy with his character, as Jingle is described "making his way through the crowd by the infallible process of elbowing the countenances of its component members." Almost at once Jingle erupts into his typical "string of broken sentences, delivered with extraordinary volubility" and sarcastically termed "coherent speech" by the narrator. In the "jaunty impudence and perfect self-possession" that "pervaded the whole man," he is the very type of Sam Weller. And here is his famous first anecdote, rendered with the frenetic spontaneity of the novel's own comic imagination and climaxed with a grotesque Dickensian pun: "Terrible place—dangerous work—other day—five children—mother—tall lady, eating sandwiches—forgot the arch—crash—knock—children look round—mother's head off—sandwich in her hand—no mouth to put it in—head of a family off—shocking, shocking." This is a prime example of that "black humour" which Angus Wilson sees in common between Jingle and Sam. Wilson observes in passing the "different and generous intent"[9] of Sam's humor but does not develop the comparison. I think Dickens means for us to. In the tenth chapter, immediately after we are introduced to Sam, we hear from him a hurried, broken, almost incoherent tale of the Old Baily Proctors that sounds oddly like

Jingle's own anecdotal style and reveals an imagination pitched at the same comic intensity. Sam is speaking *to* Jingle, in fact, and the "dash" of his verbal style is written into the punctuation itself, as in the ordinary typography of Jingle's speeches: "Down he goes to the Commons, to see the lawyer and draw the blunt—wery smart —top-boots on—nosegay in his button-hole—broad-brimmed tile —green shawl—quite the gen'l'm'n" (10). This is a comic exuberance barely contained by expression, and, even while we are beginning to distinguish between the honest and the dishonest imagination, Dickens makes Sam sound so much like Jingle in order that we will recognize such vitality as the shared asset of both men, the spontaneous and untutored poets of the street. While Sam thrives on this gift, however, Jingle capitalizes on it.

Alfred Jingle is Dickens's first major study in the unethical imagination, in the creative spirit perverted by self-interest. Passing himself off to Mr. Snodgrass as the author of an extemporaneous epic poem (2), Jingle becomes the first important embodiment of poetry as prevarication, an instance of hypocritical expression which will find its fullest example five novels later with Pecksniff, in connection with whom Steven Marcus has reminded us that "hypocrite" originally meant "actor."[10] For Jingle, indeed, there is no personality apart from role. It is right that Sam should be the first to identify him as a "strolling actor" (25), for when Sam shows himself to be no stranger to the theater and play-acting a few chapters later—as "he inflicted a little friction on his right eyelid with the sleeve of his coat, after the most approved manner of actors when they are in domestic pathetics" (31)—his intention is solely to mock and disconcert the "puzzled" representative of Dodson and Fogg. Jingle has no time for disinterested satire of this kind, and Dickens knew long before Pecksniff the fate to which the hypocrite, however amusing, condemns himself. The character who fakes his roles, who fabricates a series of alternate selves or personas for his own selfish gain, ends up exiled from selfhood altogether. The lived lie eventually liquidates personality. It is no accident that Jingle's name is withheld from us for over one hundred pages and thereafter evaded and denied at intervals. When our loquacious "stranger" and Tupman are asked for their names at the Charity Ball, Jingle (as yet unidentified) insists on "No names at all" (2). The ostensible reason is that their names are not illustrious enough to cause a stir, but a motive of disguise is also clearly at work. It is dangerous work, and worse is yet to come. When the stranger does finally declare himself as "Jingle—Alfred Jingle, Esq., of No Hall, Nowhere" (7), we are suspicious, and look beyond disguise to an anonymity eating away at identity itself, and making of Alfred Jingle a true precursor of the Beatles' "Nowhere Man." More than mere hypocrisy is surely at stake here. By his shameless extravagance Pecksniff will miss being the wordy bore he would otherwise have been, but from the first Jingle is a thorough delight, an intentional comedian *at* whom we never laugh. It is as if Dickens wanted to personify, in all of its unreined nervous energy, his own comic and creative imagination, and began to do so with Jingle until he discovered the capacities for evil and lie in his own expressive powers. Dickens then seems to have let Jingle's development follow this dark, unexpected logic, only to create Sam Weller in order to vindicate the comic spirit.

When we first encounter Sam as a boot-polisher at the White Hart Inn, he is aligned with the Dickensian imagination by his penchant for metonymy, as he identifies the guests at the Inn "by that particular article of their costume, which came under his immediate superintendence. 'There's a wooden leg in number six; there's a pair of Hessians in thirteen; there's two pair of halves in the commercial' " (10). Even earlier in this chapter, in the first words out of Sam's mouth, we sense a new presence in the book, a new attitude toward language. Sam is hailed by a chambermaid and told that the gentleman in room twenty-two wants his boots at once. " 'Ask number twenty-two, whether he'll have 'em now, or wait till he gets 'em,' was the reply." This answer strikes the maid as childish, but we are expected to know better. Sarcastically posing an alternative where none exists, Sam has doubled reality— and made ironic "poetry"—in his very first sentence. This is precisely what he will continue to do in a different key with his analogies, his allusions, his humorous "quotations." He will extend the actual by fashioning alongside the real world, in which he operates so successfully, a second more exciting world, where for most of us none exists, peopled by the figures of his own vivid and unflagging imagination.

When he is first approached by Pickwick and friends in their search for Jingle, Sam demands: "What the devil do you want with me, as the man said wen he see the ghost?" (10). Even in this, one of the first and simplest of his mock quotations, the pattern is clear; we are in the middle of one story when another story is created on the spot, this time a tiny gothic romance with two characters, a man and a ghost. Nothing is ever done with these

adjacent stories, and they are dropped at once. But for one extraneous moment, as in fantasy and daydream, the imagination has
enlarged and enlivened our experience. Like the interpolated tales,
these "Wellerisms" often gravitate toward either the macabre or
the fantastic, and they are Sam's way of insinuating into Pickwick's
consciousness such unwanted knowledge. Sam's split-second
ghost story, like all the imagined situations to which he alludes,
is a fiction in embryo, a twitch of the novelist's own imagination.
He repeatedly tells full-scale anecdotes, and sometimes his "quotations" are owed to authentic sources, like Tony. More often they
are extemporaneous, a private fancy produced on call, a triumph
of ad-libbing. Like the larger anecdotes of which they often seem a
condensed form, these improvised quotations may grow out of and
elaborate a pun.[11] When Jingle asks what the Old Baily Proctors
do, Sam is quick with "Do! You, sir" (10), and the illustrative story
follows. Several of the mock quotations begin the same way, and
seem to exist mainly to ground the pun. " 'Hooroar for the principal, as the money-lender said ven he wouldn't renew the bill,'
observed Mr. Weller" (35), and once more the linguistic and the
story-telling imaginations take their exercise together.

Sam's miniscule narrative of the man and the ghost, the first
Mr. Pickwick hears for himself, initiates a recurring pattern for
such comic asides when it hedges the dangerous with a mitigating
element of fantasy. Ghosts are not real, and so the idea of death
as a presence in life that must be dealt with is incarnated for Mr.
Pickwick, at this early stage, as an easily dismissible hallucination.
Yet this is already the second "Wellerism" the reader has heard in
the novel, and the first such abbreviated "tale" was more realistic,
with death there a matter of fact, even of historical record. We are
back with the chambermaid's demand for the boots, and with
Sam's reply: "Who's Number Twenty-two that's to put all the
others out? No, no; reg'lar rotation, as Jack Ketch said wen he tied
the men up. Sorry to keep you a-waitin', sir, but I'll attend to you
directly" (10). This allusion to the barbarous state executioner of
the seventeenth century, or by extension to any public executioner
who carries out the punitive will of the state, looks forward to Pickwick's own unfair punishment at the hands of public justice in
the Fleet, where death is forced inescapably upon Pickwick's attention for the first time. These different but complementary aspects of
Sam's first two "Wellerisms" are manipulated by Joyce in *Ulysses,*
where the effect is again partly to discharge the pompous and
importunate. We hear in the "Cyclops" section an accusation

against the Citizen's swaggering rhetoric as an unsavory breeze indeed, his "tall talk" being "all wind and piss,"[12] and a few pages later, after a dinosaurean paragraph of encrusted rhetoric in praise of a facecloth, all in a flamboyant Dickensian vein, a confusion over whose drink is whose is settled with Weller-like economy: "That's mine, says Joe, as the devil said to the dead policeman."[13] Death and injustice, those major aspects of Sam's first "Wellerisms" —death faced in the person of the executioner, and then at the safer remove of hallucination with the ghost; the misuse of constituted authority, as the law itself turns criminal—both seem to be caught in the easy cynicism of Joyce's casual joke, where the devil, worst of all apparitions from beyond the grave (and we remember that "what the devil do you want with me" is what the man said to the ghost in Sam's tiny anecdote), arrives to claim the corrupt officer of the law. What is no more than a simple aside in Joyce, however, is central to Dickens's first novel, where Sam's inventive irreverence shows itself as one of the book's deepest integrities.

At one point Sam cannot resist pouncing on the stupid tautology just launched by Mr. Peter Magnus: "Company, you see—company is—it's a very different thing from solitude—ain't it?" (22). Sam gives this remark far more than its due: " 'There's no denying that 'ere,' said Mr. Weller, joining in the conversation, with an affable smile. 'That's what I call a self-evident proposition, as the dog's-meat man said, when the housemaid told him he warn't a gentleman.' " Despite the jaunty satire, however, it appears for a moment as if Sam has slipped out of character, eluded his own best instincts. For what business has this untaught, free-wheeling virtuoso of counter-logical utterance, whose own first sentence in the novel ("Ask number twenty-two, whether he'll have 'em now, or wait till he gets 'em") is a kind of baroque cousin to tautology—what business has Sam Weller appearing as spokesman for the propositional use of language? It is of course the "illustrative" anecdote which sets things right again, for the use of "gentleman" in this elliptical fabliau is twofold and not "self-evident" at all: a kind of pun labeling both a socio-economic and a moral category, as well Sam as a "gentleman's gentleman" must know. Language has been engaged here by our semantic gymnast in ways that have left Mr. Magnus far behind, and once again Sam's powers are confirmed by his most characteristic device.

Only once in the novel is a serious effort made to curtail Sam's habitual "Wellerisms." His inventive powers must be straight-jacketed for his appearance in court, where the law demands that as a "witness" he tell what he has seen, not what he has imagined. Badgered by the prosecution in Bardell vs. Pickwick about his job as manservant—" 'Little to do and plenty to get, I suppose?' said Serjeant Buzfuz with jocularity"—Sam returns, "Oh, quite enough to get, sir, as the soldier said ven they ordered him three hundred and fifty lashes" (34)—another allusion, as with Jack Ketch, to the cruelty of corporal "justice." The judge cannot brook this returned volley of "jocularity" and insists that "You must not tell us what the soldier or any other man said, sir . . . it's not evidence." The calculated irrelevance of Sam's flippant testimony is meant, by Sam and by Dickens, merely to underscore the larger inapplicability of all fancy, whether such miniature story-telling or a more sophisticated and probing imagination, to the closed and misleading "facts" of the law, that circumstantial evidence which we are to find is every bit as fictitious as Sam's stories, and not nearly so credible. But Sam has been warned, and he makes his merry way through the proceedings of Bardell vs. Pickwick in strict accordance with "the rules." Even (and only) by playing it their way, this amateur poet beats the professional rhetoricians at their own game, a game of words fully as "solemn" as that card party in Mr. Wardle's parlor, and where once again the satirist is keeping secret score.[14]

Dickens is showing us with the trial episode what would happen to language without the Sam Wellers of the world, the roar and bluster that would become the sole province of speech. Noisily, the trial's first utterance gives itself the lie: "The judge had no sooner taken his seat than the officer on the floor of the court called out 'Silence!' in a commanding tone, upon which another officer in the gallery cried 'Silence!' in an angry manner, whereupon three or four more ushers shouted 'Silence!' in a voice of indignant remonstrance. A shout of "Silence!" is a paradox and a mockery. Everything is upside down in this comic nightmare, and when silence does later descend on the court, it is mistaken for more talk: "Serjeant Buzfuz, who had proceeded with such volubility that his face was perfectly crimson, here paused for breath." The "volubility" so much prized in the case of the Wellers is now a suffocating compulsion, and what follows is the perfect symbol for the vacuity of the whole affair: "The silence awoke Mr. Justice Stareleigh, who immediately wrote down something with a pen without any ink in it." Nothing will come of nothing.

This was also the point when Sam and his master were previously dragged before the bar of justice, there too about a sexual misunderstanding over the lady in curl-papers. At that time, also,

Sam played fast and loose with legal decorum, and after giving his name to Magistrate Nupkins as "Veller," found in a close phonetic relative an insulting rhyme, adding to the clerk: "Two L's, old feller" (25). After Nupkins has tried to use Sam's own words against him, calling him a "vagabond on his own statement," Sam responds in kind by turning the Magistrate's needless repetition of his legal judgment—"Then I'll commit him. I'll commit him as such"—into an ironic "sally": " 'This is a wery impartial country for justice,' said Sam. 'There ain't a magistrate goin' as don't commit himself twice as often as he commits other people.' " What has actually been "committed" is a series of legally sanctioned linguistic crimes, and the climax comes when Pickwick at last gets in a word and gets out the truth that "we are perfect strangers in this town. I have as little knowledge of any householders here as I have intention of fighting a duel with anybody." Nupkins's attempt at sarcasm now backfires symbolically: " 'I dare say,' replied the magistrate. 'I dare say—don't you, Mr. Jinks?' " And as if there is something to agree on: "Certainly, sir." We realize, however, that by having the magistrate repeat himself once again in this way, Dickens is emphasizing how all that is said is that he says—declaration drained of any but self-referential content, like the hermetic system of legal discourse as a whole which has closed out all true response. The humbug voice of the law, once gainsaid, does in fact not "dare say" more. So as if obsessed with his own discredited verb, Nupkins asks instead of Pickwick: "Have you anything more to say?"

The later trial scene in the case of Bardell vs. Pickwick is an even more arduous workout for the tricks of Dickensian verbal satire. The abutting of high and low diction is once more an assault on pomposity, as the judge "bobbed gravely to the bar, who bobbed gravely to him." Everywhere in this arena of legal jargon two or more words are proudly retailed for the price of one, in an attempt —again Dickens finds a neat self-accusing sample—consistently to "mislead and delude" the auditor. In context, that pleonastic doublet is applied by Buzfuz to the supposedly culpable messages sent by Pickwick to Mrs. Bardell. As the lawyer manipulates these innocent notes, external reality disappears as a touchstone and Buzfuz becomes a textual exegete obsessed with the internal evidence of his own microscopic close-readings. He becomes, for today's audience, almost a parody of the New Critic as he feigns outrage at Pickwick's vile cryptogram about "Chops and Tomato Sauce" and then probes the sexual innuendoes of "Slow Coach" and "Don't trouble yourself about the warming pan," the one a symbol of Pickwick's dilatory courting and the other "a mere cover for hidden fire." If Pickwick had not stepped out of linguistic character with Mrs. Bardell for that unwonted metaphor "the person I have in my eye," he might never have fallen victim to this mockery of justice; but once arraigned, he faces the final debasement of a poetic impulse he has never understood, in the law's ironic imputation of metaphorical language where, manifestly, there was no such intent. Only by refusing to participate in this violation of language, only by treating words literally for a change, and meaning as if it were compulsory—only, that is, by doing a complete about-face and sticking just this once to the very letter, as it were, of the law can Sam outwit the rhetoricians with their own words. His father has caused a disturbance in the gallery, and Sam's help is called upon to ferret out the culprit. "Do you see him here now?" the judge asks. " 'No, I don't my lord,' replied Sam, staring right up into the lantern in the roof of the court" (34). In this insane game of lies and indirections, the straight truth cleverly played is, ironically, the winning hand.

It may seem an insult to such original energy as Sam Weller's to claim for him predecessors other than Tony, but a pause is in order here over a lineage no one has yet surmised. The particular inherited trait I am suggesting is the very "Wellerism" which the judge would not admit as "evidence" and which, with Mr. Magnus earlier, was also subversive of propositional thinking—that habit not so much of mind as of imagination which is able to confound both the rational structures of language and the legal structures of society. Within a year or so of each other, two of the authors Dickens loved best gave the world their respective masterpieces, and in each, in the first part of *Don Quixote* (Ch. 50) and in *King Lear* (II, iv), Dickens was anticipated in the "Wellerism" by over two centuries. The italics are mine:

'I don't understand these philosophies,' replied Sancho Panza. 'I only wish I were as sure of the countship as of my ability to govern. For I've as large a soul as the next man, and as stout a body as the best of them, and I'd be as good a king of my estate as any other King; and being so, I should do as I liked; and doing as I liked, I should take my pleasure; and taking my pleasure; I should be contented; and when one's content, there's nothing more to desire; and when there's nothing more to desire, there's an end of it. So for Heaven's sake, let me have the estate, *and then we'll see, as one blind man said to the other.*'

LEAR: Oh, me, my heart, my rising heart! But down!
FOOL: Cry to it, Nuncle, *as the cockney did to the eels when she put 'em i' the paste alive.* She knapped 'em on the coxcombs with a

stick, and cried "Down wantons, down!" 'Twas her brother that, in
pure kindness to his horse, buttered his hay.

The homely incremental logic of Sancho's argument, seemingly a
repudiation of "philosophies," is itself a parody of deductive reasoning, and in this as well as in his frank, robust hedonism we can
preview Dickens's own picaresque squire. With the Fool in *Lear*,
too, the cruel insufficiency of his "as" comparison seems somehow
merely a harsh extension of the laughable inappropriateness of
buttered hay, in which again we are foreglimpsing the tireless discrepant comedy of that latter-day "cockney," Sam Weller. I am
not concerned, of course, with how precisely Dickens's memory
may or may not be at work here. Details aside, what Dickens indisputably has borrowed from Cervantes and Shakespeare is the
master and man archetype. Sancho Panza, Lear's Fool, and Sam
Weller all serve very foolish fond old men, and serve them by
teaching them the world, instructing them in its coarse ironies and
absolutes, humanizing their elitist vanities. The mundane is medi-
ated for Quixote, for Lear, and for Pickwick by the store of proverbial wisdom, balladry, aphorism, earthy wit, irreverent satire,
and simple felt experience embodied faithfully in their "men."[15]

If there is any doubt about Dickens's particular affinity with his
character on the score of these mock quotations, we need only take
note of a letter written to his illustrator Hablôt K. Browne some
dozen years after *Pickwick Papers*, in which Dickens requested a
personal copy of an illustration of "the boy in the flannel" complete with (and here Dickens is himself playing with "philosophic"
circumlocution) "the pigmental finishing of said boy." He insists
that the boy is "MINE!" and, following directly upon his inflated
language, as Joyce will do after him, he sidesteps into his own demonic, deflating "Wellerism": ". . . and, as the Demon says at the
Surrey

I CLAIM MY VICTIM.
HA! HA! HA!

at which you will imagine me going down a sulphurous trap, with the boy
in my grasp—and you will please not to imagine him merely, in my
grasp, but to hand him over.[16]

For an effect of facetious black comedy there was no better master
than his own Sam.

One of the most remarkable things to observe about the
"Wellerism," as regards the gothic knowledge it tends to encap-
sule, is what happens to it during the Fleet Prison episode, where

changes are rung on it that respond inconspicuously to the changes wrought upon Mr. Pickwick's character. Though usually designed to sketch out for Pickwick Sam's more shadowed, realistic picture of the world, even while couched in the mollifying terms of fantasy or of bald irrelevance, still the first of such facetious asides in the prison is used unexpectedly to soften the blow of sudden understanding. Sam has just explained in cogent detail the injustices rife in a debtor's prison, and for its gross inequities he has found his own comically incommensurate parallel: " 'It's unekal,' as my father used to say wen his grog worn't made half-and-half. 'It's unekal, and that's the fault on it' " (41). As an authority on the droll and frivolous, his father rather than some imagined character is quoted by Sam this time, in an attempt to check with humor the potential for major disillusionment on Pickwick's part. Want and suffering and the corrupt justice that perpetuates them are all too clearly placed before that gentleman now, and comedy is interposed by Sam to pad the shock of recognition, to moderate Pickwick's education in the world.

When Sam's motives are freed again into pure satire and invigoration, he reverts to his darker inventiveness, as when Stiggins and Mrs. Weller visit the prison and Sam offers the former a seat: "Set down, sir, ve make no extra charge for settin' down, as the king remarked wen he blowed up his ministers" (45). Yet for the last of Sam's half dozen "Wellerisms" while in the Fleet, he again turns to conscientious displacement and alleviation, a verbal beneficence modeled on Pickwick's surprising kindnesses to Jingle. The "strolling actor" is now an "invalided stroller," Job Trotter himself no longer trots very briskly (though suffering has legitimized for the first time the biblical sense of his Christian name), and Sam is frankly astonished at the reverses they have suffered. "Things has altered with me, sir" is Job's moving understatement, and, "surveying his companion's rags with undisguised wonder," Sam answers: "I should think they had ... This is rayther a change for the worse, Mr. Trotter, as the gen'lm'n said wen he got two doubtful shillin's and sixpenn'orth o' pocket-pieces for a good half crown" (45). This is Sam's gift to Job of allaying levity. The most brutal facts of life cannot, of course, be abated by comedy, yet a psychological balance is constantly sought in this precarious novel. Sam's miniature interpolations, complete with narrative and dialogue—his word-plays-within-the-play—hold the mirror up to the book's divided nature by using comic diabolism, on the one hand, to tweak thoughtless amiability and, on the other, a brighter humorous fancy to disinfect septic realities. By being conversant like no one in the novel but the narrator with the two halves of its experience, and by building that knowledge into his conversation, Sam is uniquely valuable to the book's quarantined hero.

Before the Fleet, Pickwick has only gradually begun to recognize the full range of Sam's sympathy and intelligence. Early in the novel he seems indifferent to Sam's feats of language, and at one point grudgingly admits that Mr. Weller "is in the right . . . although his mode of expressing his opinion is somewhat homely and occasionally incomprehensible" (16). A truer judgment is forthcoming, as expressed to Mr. Magnus: "I flatter myself he is an original, and I am rather proud of him" (17). Pickwick has, in fact, already made another acute observation about the Weller mentality when he congratulated Sam as "quite a philosopher" (16). Sam's reply at the time enlarges on the Sancho-like application of "philosophy" to his particular state of mind: " 'It runs in the family, I b'lieve, sir,' replied Mr. Weller. 'My father's wery much in that line, now. If my mother-in-law blows him up, he whistles. She flies in a passion, and breaks his pipe; he steps out and gets another. Then she screams wery loud, and falls into 'sterics: and he smokes wery comfortably 'till she comes to agin. That's philosophy, sir, an't it?' " Sam and Mr. Pickwick go through the novel at each other's side as if to throw one another into more dramatic relief, and it is in the next exchange of this same chapter that Sam declares "Bless your innocence, sir" and thereby names the central Pickwickian virtue, just as Pickwick has identified the Wellerian gift of "philosophy." More precisely, though, Sam's gift is an incomparable self-possession, a sublime stoic confidence born of the same health and vigor of mind that spawn the family imagination. The ironist's comic detachment, without sacrifice of warmth or humanity, has become a way of life, a practical philosophy in this sense. Imagination has made the man whole. And it has brought uncommon insight. Sam is the character in the novel who best understands Mr. Pickwick, sensing that odd double nature by which the innocent heart of a child is housed in the capacious body of a mature gentleman. "I never see such a fine creetur in my days. Blessed if I don't think his heart must ha' been born five-and-twenty year arter his body, at least!" (39). Pickwick's innocence makes his heart "at least" this immature, and yet his temperament is best thought of in cyclic terms as a daily rebirth. When Tony Weller speaks of his wife's zealous interest in "some

inwention for grown-up people being born again . . . the new birth,
I think they calls it" (22), Dickens may well have Mr. Pickwick
in mind—and be keeping before us a reminder of his hero's beaming diurnal renewals. We already know that Sam thinks of Mr.
Pickwick as being only "half baptised," and when the belated birth
of Pickwick's heart is suggested, it is as if Sam means to imply
that the body of his master has been named and initiated while
his heart still waits for the saddening consecration of reality. Once
again we are reminded that more than the mere "body of Samuel
Pickwick" (40) is to be delivered to prison. "I see some queer
sights," Sam once tells Pickwick, "Sights, sir . . . as 'ud penetrate
your benevolent heart, and come out on the other side" (16). Little
does either master or man know at this point that such "sights"
indeed await Pickwick in the Fleet, awarenesses that will alter the
entire nature of his once complacent benevolence.

Tracing out the implications of the Wellers' "philosophy," it is
time to notice that Sam and Tony share with Dickens (that is, he
shares with them) a peculiar gift of the visionary artist. Like
Dickens, the Wellers see the world symbolically. Not only are they
in full control of the poetic expressiveness of language, but they
have also seen in experience itself a sort of secret expressiveness, a
symbolic meaning waiting to be spoken. The first thing Mr. Pickwick is told upon entering the Fleet is that he must undergo the
ceremony known as "sitting for your portrait" (40), which amounts
to no more than a quartet of stares from the gawking turnkeys,
who in this way take his "likeness." But while Pickwick is waiting,
wishing that "the artists would come," he has by his side an authentic artist, Sam Weller, who summons forth a symbolic meaning from the simple furniture of the room, from a Dutch clock and
a birdcage: "Veels vithin veels, and a prison in a prison. Ain't it,
sir?" When the narrator labels this a "philosophical remark," we
are to understand it as a major extension of the good-humored
fancy associated with Sam's practical philosophy, his lifemanship;
it is that profounder insight of his imagination which can discover
unpleasant relevance in things but which is never soured by such
perception. And in this case the metaphoric intuition achieves the
status of prophecy, the symbolism coming true when Pickwick
finally retreats and makes of his own room a "prison in a prison."

It is Mr. Weller Senior, however, who gives us the crowning instance of metaphor in the novel. In a letter to Sam announcing the
death of his wife, Tony draws on the most instinctive materials of
his own life, his career as a coachman, to explain her passing:

'My dear Sammle,

'I am wery sorry to have the pleasure of bein a Bear of ill news your
Mother in law cort cold consekens of imprudently settin too long on the
damp grass in the rain ... her veels wos immedetly greased and every-
think done to set her agoin as could be inwented your father had hopes
as she vould have vorked round as usual but just as she wos a turnen the
corner my boy she took the wrong road and vent down hill vith a welocity
you never see and notvithstanding that the drag wos put on drectly by
the medikel man it wornt of no use at all for she paid the last pike at
twenty minutes afore six o'clock yesterday evenin having done the
journey wery much under the reglar time vich praps was partly owen to
her haven taken in wery little luggage.' (52)

The entire picaresque novel has been kept under way by coach
journeys, and here, in a stupendous flash of symbolic unification,
the coach becomes the vehicle in a comprehensive metaphor—a
pun it is a shame Tony would not have understood—for the
journey that is life itself. The joyous powers of language which
rout dullness in daily life here seem to bring a far larger understanding of life and last things. As Nabokov would have it, the
cosmic has succeeded to the comic. This is the apotheosis of
the everyday imagination, clarifying the archetypal pattern of the
novel in a single stroke and revealing a perspective that brushes
the divine. With Tony on hand again to do the honors, Dickens
could not resist a eulogy in the same vein for Master Humphrey
four years later. This time the spoken epitaph turns on an analogy
with the coach horse:

'And the sweet old cretur ... has bolted. Him as had no wice, and was so
free from temper that a infant might h' drove him, has been took at last
with that 'ere unavoidable fit of staggers as we all must come to ... and
now my predilictions is fatally werified, and him as I could never do
enough to serve or show my likin' for, is up the great universal spout o'
natur.' (M.H.C., 6)

Death is expected; it is man's resumption as part and parcel of
universal nature. Metaphor itself seems to have brought this consolation, with Tony's "philosophic" long view apparently gener-
ated out of the very fertility of his verbal imagination. And, as
always, we are to pay close attention to the comedy of his words.
We are to notice, for instance, besides his delight in driving the
analogy till its own last "staggers," the fun he has with his misuse
of a "Pickwickian" fine phrase like "predilictions is fatally
werified."

Father and son are indeed up to their old verbal tricks in *Master
Humphrey's Clock*. Tony's hilarious sexual paranoia, the mortal

fear of widows he again mocks the grand style to call a fear of "inadwertent captiwation" (5), is still very much with him. Once again, too, in speaking of a smelly pipe as a "flagrant weed" (5), he finds a characteristic aptness in malapropism. Such creative accidents, however, are about to stand in for startling new examination. When Tony tries to prod his son into ascertaining the marital status of Master Humphrey's housekeeper, Sam replies with one of his familiar "allusions": "Well, I'm agreeable to do it . . . but not if you go cuttin' away like that, as the bull turned round and mildly observed to the drover ven they was a goadin' him into the butcher's door" (3). We are not long on such firm, familiar ground, though, for when Sam expects his father to be satisfied with the information that the housekeeper is a "spinster," Tony wonders instead why Sam has offered the tangential news that the woman is given to puns: "Never mind vether she makes jokes or not, that's no matter. Wot I say is, is that 'ere female a widder, or is she not?" Even Sam is incredulous: "Vy now . . . would anybody believe as a man at his time o' life could be running his head agin spinsters and punsters being the same thing?" (3). We believe it, of course, as an extreme instance, for the first time really frustrating communication, of Tony's verbal effrontery, his power not only with but over words.

I have spoken already of those errors on Tony's part that seem to wander over into unpremeditated good sense, such fortuitous garblings as "probe it" and "prodigal son." In three of the authors Dickens knew best—in Cervantes and Fielding again, and in Sterne—there is some curious precedent for these lexical curveballs, word choices that veer from the expected path of meaning in order, only at last and by some surprise, to strike their way home. Where chivalric romances cause the initial friction that sparks the novel's very life, and where such fantasies continue to chafe against reality, Sancho Panza is clearly onto something central when he objects to Don Quixote that these knightly aspirations are "just wind and lies, and all friction or fiction or whatever you call it."[17] In *Joseph Andrews*, the twin affectations of vanity and hypocrisy combine in Mrs. Slipslop, that "mighty affector" of pre-Johnsonian "hard words" who speaks in stilted, unnecessary Latin *about* Latin—"And why is Latin more *necessitous* for a footman than a gentleman?"[18]—and whose famous malapropisms repeatedly backfire against her own sham sanctimonies. Exposing that whole species of hollow self-righteousness she represents, Slipslop at one point says to Lady Booby: "Really, your ladyship talks of servants as if they were not born of the Christian *spe-cious*."[19] In *Tristram Shandy*, convinced by Toby that a soldier cannot worry about time, Corporal Trim blithely disavows "*geog-raphy*," only to have Toby explain that the word he wants is "*chronology*."[20] But since, in this self-consciously experimental novel, time is often thought of merely as linguistic space, duration as an interval marking off a verbal terrain, Trim has gone unwit-tingly to the heart of things. He has reminded us that *Tristram Shandy* exists only through the intersection of geography and chronology—only, that is, through *traverse*, the getting from one point to another in that autobiographical time which is equiv-alent to verbal space. In writers of such stature who can allow themselves this verbal latitude, as preeminently in Shakespeare, words seem to be summoned, almost unconsciously, for more than scheduled meanings; the least detail can mirror the whole in phras-ings that are perhaps, at some level, as "accidental" for the authors themselves as for their characters.

If it appears that Tony has departed from this tradition with that semantic impasse in *Master Humphrey's Clock*, it should be noticed that the extraneous word "punster"—his "mistake" here—once again offers a key to the confusion by naming indirectly the very role Tony began it all by so arbitrarily taking on. It is as if the elder Weller, with his anarchic ear, has willfully misheard "punster" for "spinster"—as if the words themselves constituted a pun. He has bullied intractable linguistic material into an im-possible conjunction, and the episode becomes an embedded study in the chaos which poetry shapes but at times resembles. Puns are, like all poetry, forged from ordinary language under the pressure of imagination: a fusion of two meanings into one sound or into one spelling, or both, which the mind manages to hold together. But Tony is here asserting his right to ignore the distinc-tion between fusion and sheer confusion, between comic poetry and verbal anarchy. David Daiches has an essay on the humor of misunderstanding in which he sees the comic tradition in English darken until misunderstanding is no longer a source of laughter at all, but of tragic cross-purposes. The history of the pun is one instance of the decline from comedy to chaos, and Lewis Carroll's "portmanteau word" seems to be the turning point, beyond which there is finally the "multiple pun" in an author like Joyce, "the last refuge of relativism."[21] Though not mentioned by Daiches, Tony Weller's private network of verbal elisions and identities seems here, surprisingly enough, to push Dickens toward the near

edge of this linguistic disintegration. It is not often that we tread
this verge in Dickens. Certainly there is nothing like it in *Pickwick*,
where even the mad semantic "relativism" of the trial scene is
wholly programmed, not at all disinterested like Tony's use of
language. Even in *Master Humphrey's Clock*, in that lunatic confusion over what the narrator calls a "question of etymology,"
Tony's powers are on their own terms unassailable. His is the triumphant last word, a justification of his own language which
somehow seems to rest, however impenetrably, on his personal
experience of the world. Dismissing the entire muddle about
"punsters" and "spinsters," Tony confidently declares that "There
an't a straw's difference between 'em . . . Your father didn't drive
a coach for so many years, not to be ekal to his own langvidge as
far as *that* goes, Sammy."

There is a far more famous discussion about "langvidge" in
Pickwick itself, where Tony, counseling Sam on the phrasing of his
valentine to Mary, "delivers some Critical Sentiments respecting
Literary Composition" (33). This tutorial occurs in the chapter
immediately before the verbal farce of Bardell vs. Pickwick, and
Tony urges his son to have no truck with that "poetry" he obviously associates with the sluggish eloquence of the court and
with all such occasions of bombast: "Poetry's unnat'ral; no man
ever talked poetry 'cept a beadle on boxin' day, or Warren's
blackin', or Rowland's oil, or some o' them low fellows; never you
let yourself down to talk poetry, my boy." Tony recognizes what
he contemptuously labels "poetry" only as a public thing, an
"unnatural" frill meant to accompany ornate and persuasive language, the self-satisfied talk of the hypocrite or the publicist. For
Tony, "poetry" has become confused with rhetoric (as "prayer"
will later be for Little Jo in *Bleak House*), and this truer poet, who
knows the private pleasures of language, is right to despise it.

Sam, like Tony, knows that words should match feelings, that
there ought ideally to be an exact linguistic sign for every sincere
idea, but in struggling for the word "circumwented" in a love
letter, he is out of his native element, over his head in the tran-
quilizing rhetoric of Latinity he is elsewhere so adept at satirizing.
It is as if Tony knows that his glib son must be doing something
wrong if he cannot find a word, and he pokes superb fun at Sam's
remark "I forget what this here word is" with "Why don't you look
at it, then?" Sam is making the critical mistake of trying for a
Pickwickian high style in his letter to Mary; the effect is inevitably
forced, artificial, and there is more than a diverting foolishness

about his decision, after Tony's lecture against "poetry," still to conclude in "werse" with that rhymed signature "Your love-sick/ Pickvick." Suggested by Tony himself, this is an apt pseudonym for the dispenser of such strained language. The most blithely, brilliantly "self-composed" character in Dickens is for once caught out of character in an almost schizophrenic sense, impersonating his stylistic opposite at a moment when his own language has for the first time faltered. No irony could be nicer than "Sam . . . composed himself to write" when he first takes pen in hand for his amorous "composition"; the man whose verbal style can usually articulate his personality with unequalled fluency has his linguistic composure for once upset, his language coming the nearest it ever does to the inexpressive.

Beyond his diatribe against "poetry," there is a further twist to Tony's unpredictable sense of his own "langvidge." Late in the novel he becomes tongue-tied in front of Mr. Pickwick as he is about to sign over his inheritance, and stammers that he "ain't ekal to ex-pressin' myself ven there's anythin' partickler to be done" (56). This excuse from a genius of "ex-pression" may seem at first as ironic as his earlier disavowal of poetry, which at once compels us to a new definition of that art which will embrace the Wellers' verbal imagination. But the condition of poetry tends toward a use of language for its own sake—a tendency caught and exaggerated in Tony's insistent "pun" on "spinster" and "punster" —and expression recruited for the "partickler" is something else again.

In life's most intense moments of joy or tenderness or hilarity, even the Wellers may be found at a loss for words. We remember how often Tony is convulsed with laughter and thus incapacitated for speech, how he has developed a veritable lexicon of eloquent body English and "a perfect alphabet of winks" (43), and how there exists between father and son "a complete code of telegraphic nods and gestures" (43). Once, just before bestowing on Sam a look of "unspeakable" admiration, Tony employs one of his son's "Wellerisms" to make fun of the English alphabet itself: "Wen you're a married man, Samivel, you'll understand a good many things as you don't understand now; but vether it's worth while goin' through so much, to learn so little, as the charity-boy said ven he got to the end of the alphabet, is a matter o' taste. *I* rayther think it isn't" (27).

The exits of Sam and Tony from the novel are masterfully chosen to dramatize the emotion that goes beyond words. Tony's last "expressive" act, a response to Sam's announcement that he will stay on with Mr. Pickwick, is an exultation past articulate speech. This verbal magician, who the epilogue will tell us is "quite reverenced as an oracle" at the public-house where he takes up residence, leaves the novel proper in a burst of expression without a single word. Tony's admiration for Sam is at one point mentioned in passing as "unspeakable" (27), and when his son vows at the end of the novel to remain with Mr. Pickwick, "the elder Mr. Weller rose from his chair, and, forgetting all considerations of time, place, or property, waved his hat above his head and gave three vehement cheers" (56). Much the same point is made earlier when Mr. Pickwick has agreed to pay Dodson and Fogg and leave the Fleet at last; Sam, "on hearing this concession . . . harrahed in divers parts of the building until he lost his voice, and then quietly relapsed into his usual collected and philosophical condition" (47). And even before this Sam had involuntarily "lost his voice" in admiration of Mr. Pickwick's benevolence and in surprise at Job's and Jingle's desperate need of it, with a nonverbal "expression" on his "countenance" of "the most overwhelming and absorbing astonishment that the imagination can portray." Face to face with the stricken volubility of these onetime fast talkers, Sam himself lapses into "profound silence." Finally he "ejaculated the words, 'Well, I *am* damned!' . . . at least a score of times; after which exertion he appeared wholly bereft of speech and again cast his eyes, first upon the one and then upon the other, in mute perplexity and bewilderment" (45). Sam's actual departure from the novel, too, is at least as good as his father's, which it follows at the end of the same chapter. Joe, the almost catatonic fat boy, waxes for the first time "unusually loquacious" (46) in praise of Sam's Mary. And for the first time in the novel, Sam is silent: "Mr. Weller made no verbal remark in reply." Instead, he eyed the fat boy for a moment, "quite transfixed at his presumption," and then "led him by the collar to the corner, and dismissed him with a harmless but ceremonious kick. After which, he walked home, whistling." That last sentence is one of the shortest and one of the simplest in the entire novel, the perfect carrier for this last tranquil image of sounds composed without the need of articulation.

Weller and son inhabit Dickens's most optimistic vision of the safe and saving imagination, and Sam, of course, dwells there most prominently. His is a gift bestowed by Dickens, but within the dramatic framework of the novel, Sam's wealth of imagination is to be understood more specifically as an inheritance—his great gift from his father. Sam is, in every way, Tony's rightful son and heir; Tony, the perfect block to Sam's chip. Samuel Pickwick and Samuel Weller do have a sort of ambiguous and shifting father-son relationship, as if implicit in their shared first name. It is Tony Weller, however, who has willed upon his son, besides his last name, both maturity and imagination, and theirs is the most successful, the most beautiful filial relationship in all of Dickens. Three years after the publication of *Pickwick Papers*, Dickens's journal for February 5, 1839, records that he had met the younger son of Wordsworth at a small dinner party that evening; his judgment: "Wordsworth (fils) decidedly lumpish. Copyrights need be hereditary, for genius isn't."[22] This amusing sidelight helps to illuminate the opposite statement Dickens was making in *Pickwick* about the inheritance of genius. Here, in his first novel, is a solution to the problem which was to trouble him in many later books and to find its frequent symbol in the mystery or settlement of a will: the question of the right relation between father and son, of how generation becomes a continuity, parenthood a contribution. When the Weller family is installed again in the pages of *Master Humphrey's Clock*, everything that is wrong about the revival is more than made up for by one brilliant touch. Sam has at last redeemed his debt of life to Tony by passing on this life and by honoring Tony with "the ancient title o' grandfather vich had long laid dormouse" (3). The Weller dynasty is reaffirmed, for the precocious grandchild is another mimic and parodist, a Dickensian genius in small and one of the novelist's most delightful conceptions. Here is grandfather Tony describing his namesake: "He's alvays a playin' with a quart pot, that boy is! To see him a settin' down on the door-step pretending to drink out of it, and fetching a long breath artervards, and smoking a bit of firevood, and sayin', 'Now I'm grandfather,'—to see him a doin' that at two year old is better than any play as wos ever wrote. 'Now I'm grandfather!' He vouldn't take a pint bot if you wos to make him a present on it, but he gets his quart, and then he says, 'Now I'm grandfather!' " (3). In *Pickwick's* own utopian terms, Tony Weller was for Sam an ideal and magnificent father, a friend and advisor to a son in whom his own powers were mirrored and carried on. Now the theme of inheritance is given extension into a second novel and a third generation. It is the legacy of imagination.

Sam Weller of *Pickwick Papers*, of course, remains the most complete hero of this theme. He is a portrait of the whole man in his prime, a creature of soul and body, of imaginative and animal spirits. Where else in Dickens is there such frank and healthy sexuality as in Sam's courtship of Mary? Sam is the whole man and perhaps the only character in all of Dickens almost any man would like to be. When the sales of the first three numbers of *Pickwick* had fallen off drastically, Dickens created the figure of Sam Weller and saved the day.[23] The greatness of the improvisation lies in Dickens's ability to make this "salvation" relevant to the story itself. Both practically and thematically, Sam Weller is an antidote to the "Pickwickian" stuffiness which characterizes the novel without him. And he is released from any wariness or repression, emancipated from all dark or troubling pressures, it seems, by the sheer indomitable force of his own healthy imagination. He thus embodies throughout the novel the release from a quarantined into a creative and encompassing imagination which the coda is only at the very end to have realized in a different key. Sam is the solution to a problem which will continue to plague Dickens in different forms from now on, a problem which he is never to solve as well again, but only to find more hopelessly acute. Sam, who thrives not only by his wits but by his wit, is the answer to how the imaginative life can really be lived, and there will be no one quite like him again. It is only three novels until Dick Swiveller, and only two more until Tom Pinch, by which time too much has gone for consolation. When Dickens's first novel began to founder, he knew that it would take all of his talent to get it back on course. In creating Sam Weller, he not only did his best as a creative artist, he incarnated it, producing for the first and almost the last time in his career a character for whom the imagination suffices and fulfills.

Part II

THE REFUGE OF IMAGINATION:
A DISINHERITING

4 The Pivotal Swiveller

He has purchased at a great price the gems of elan
In some avid precinct of his personality . . .
—*Richard Eberhart*[1]

In *Pickwick Papers* good and evil are so effectively sealed off
from each other that, except for Sam Weller, not even awareness
seems to make the transit between them. The elaborate structure
of quarantine is dismantled for *Oliver Twist*, and there is a
head-on collision of black and white out of which no gray areas
emerge. This accounts for what many readers feel as myth or fable
or allegory in *Oliver*, with the forces of good and bad thoroughly
hostile and unmixed. The antipathy prevails again in *The Old
Curiosity Shop*. Just as Oliver must confront Fagin, so Nell must,
though less often, face Quilp. In the Nell fable, good and evil have
wholly repulsed and polarized each other into all but unbelievable
absolutes, and allegory is strained to the limit. But where *Oliver*
had no real bridge figure to travel between the light and the dark,
except the child hero himself, by the time we get to *The Old
Curiosity Shop* Sam Weller has been reinstated, *in proxima persona*, with a significant touch of Alfred Jingle as well: the first
emerging from the second in a complex characterization known
as Dick Swiveller, a young man who takes refuge in imagination
until he learns that he can actually make a home of it. To understand Dick's residence at the emotional hub of *The Old Curiosity
Shop*, we must consider those powerful forces which drive Daniel
Quilp and Nell Trent into diametric opposition. For Quilp and
Nell not only define each other, but also define and necessitate
what intervenes.

The Satanists have been capitalizing ever since Blake on the critical truism that evil is more interesting than good. Great writers need hardly succumb to this commonplace, however, as Spenser should have shown us once and for all. He erected his great quest romance on a foundation of psychological allegory which unfailingly supported his heroes and heroines and made them more interesting than either the villains or the witches. It must be admitted that Dickens is not as a rule very good at this, and that only rarely do his heroes—almost never his good women —manage to hold their own against his hypocrites, his sadists, his murderers. In the case of Quilp and Nell, however, it is not at all sufficient merely to lean on received ideas about virtue's inveterate handicap when compared with the fascinations of evil. In *Pickwick Papers* goodness managed to be bright and spirited, and evil was, by definition, the enemy of high spirits, an isolation from community, an alienation. *Oliver Twist* did tend to reorganize these lines of force somewhat, but it is not until Nell's narrative that goodness has become wholly joyless and alienated, and that evil has preempted an unhealthy share of life's energy and spirit. Nell's flight into the country is, in form, perhaps Dickens's truest romance quest—but the journey is now only an escape, and the goal is death. With his mangled shape, Quilp is indeed a villain out of conventional romance, where ugliness or beauty is no mere metaphor in morality, it is the thing itself. But unlike Spenser's ogres, Quilp really enjoys himself, taking an artist's pride and pleasure in his satiric equipment. In Spenser, for all the vitality of his major villains, evil itself was an invitation to an unearned rest, a passivity, a giving up. This same strain was inherited by the Victorians, and we have Tennyson's great monitory poems about a too easy rest, about duty—that great Victorian outlet for energy—forsaken, about false harbors and lotus-eating, about what Dickens has Pecksniff call, in a parodic context, "the siren-like delusions of art" (*M.C.*,4). Even the Romantics knew that thoughtless ease was the enemy of art itself; there is a kind of productive passivity, the quietness and surrender that summon vision, but the energy of art, the imagination itself, must outlive such moments or they are merely suicidal. Nell is a daring reversal of the post-Romantic work ethic, the national morality of energy and purpose. It seems almost Nell's *duty* to die. Whereas Oliver's passivity was in part a commentary on the child's dehumanization by society, Nell's is in large part a death-wish. She is not merely "half in love with easeful death"; she is, by her own frail standards, as passionately devoted to it as Quilp is to life.

We are told at one point that "Quilp was a perpetual nightmare to the child" (29). In context, this seems a casual metaphor for the disturbing emotional effect the dwarf has on the timid child. But it can also stand as a definition for the major structural relationship of the novel. Quilp is not just nightmarish in a figurative sense; he is Nell's worst nightmares given flesh to organize the entire novel, its prose and its themes, by his polar opposition to the child whose fears he embodies. The description of Nell's languid daydreams of green fields and songbirds, her unmistakable death-drifts, is pretty dull going, but the prose of her nightmares is riveting. The former has all the mistiness of wish-fulfillment, the vagueness of fantasy, while to the latter is brought the vividness and immediacy of terrorized imagination. And Quilp and Nell speak as they are spoken of by the narrator, Quilp's own prose tensed, gritty, raucously concrete, hers watery and abstract. While diffuse lyricism is nearly vaporizing Nell's narrative, Quilp stands in such tactile relation to the world of things, of concrete reality, that he actually tries to incorporate this world. What we get is almost a parody of the mimetic novelist "taking it all in" as Quilp

ate hard eggs, shell and all, devoured gigantic prawns with the heads and tails on, chewed tobacco and water-cresses at the same time with extra-ordinary greediness, drank boiling tea without winking, bit his fork and spoon till they bent again, and in short performed so many horrifying and uncommon acts that the women were nearly frightened out of their wits and began to doubt if he were really a human creature. (5)

While Nell is losing her appetite altogether as a prelude to death, Quilp is literally devouring the world she is about to leave behind. The abstract iambic prose of her departure is a stylistic low point for Dickens, and the modern reader hardly responds to the reverent threnody with the emotion asked for, but we must not too easily write off what we regret in the novel as its obvious failure and what we like—Quilp especially—as an accident. No one loved Nell more than Dickens did, but no one knew better that her life was a long weary struggle, her imagination stifled, her days joyless, and that Quilp had all the resource and gusto, however much defiled, that make life livable. This was Dickens's theme. He knew what was "wrong" with Nell, and he asked us to pity her for it. Though he did not know what had gone wrong with his conception of her, he certainly knew where he had gone right with Quilp. And to Quilp his readers respond just as Dickens intended.

I am not detecting here some secret and unacknowledged sympathy between Dickens and Satan; I am discussing instead a deep (and conscious) imaginative allegiance with the Muse of Satire. If Quilp is a sadist—and how could Dickens have been more direct than to say that the dwarf "delighted in torturing [Nell's grandfather], or indeed anybody else, when he could" (9)—then he is also very much a satirist. We soon learn to recognize him by his sarcasm and its complete lack of good humor. Connections are constantly being made, even within the parallel run of a phrase, between Quilp's wit and his malign nature. There is the time, for instance, when he resumes a conversation "with the same malice in his eye and the same sarcastic politeness on his tongue" (4). Quilp can be identified by what defunct metaphor (death by mixing) calls a "biting tongue," and Dickens seems implicitly to have reactivated this cliché for the perfect fused image of sarcastic wit and real brutality. In his first scene with his wife, Quilp delivered this ultimatum: "If ever you listen to these beldames again, I'll bite you" (4), and later, in his bout with Dick Swiveller, the impotence of his spite is revealed by his "biting the air in the fulness of his malice" (13). Quilp's eagerness in giving voice to his viciousness is directed into pure black comedy when he allays parental anxiety with this bizarre explanation: "Don't be frightened, mistress . . . I don't eat babies; I don't like 'em" (21). And there is Quilp's desperate self-assertion just before his death: "Where I hate, I bite" (67). In all of this, there can be little doubt that Dickens is invoking the root meaning of sarcasm in "to tear flesh, gnash the teeth" (*OED*, cf. "sarcophagous"). Such is the essence, in another likely etymology, of the Quilp quip.

This self-proclaimed and selective cannibalism brings Quilp an opportunity to play with language in very much the way Dickens did when he surreptitiously converted the satirist's "bite" into a form of corporal punishment. Quilp resuscitates a cliché in a similar fashion, and Dickens is alongside to alert us: " 'Oh you nice creature!' were the words with which he broke silence; smacking his lips as if this were no figure of speech, and she were actually a sweetmeat. 'Oh you precious darling! oh you de-licious charmer!' " (4). Quilp's banter is Dickens himself at work in a way that Nell's soliloquies never are. Quilp is a soured humorist, and his scathing facetiousness is Dickens's own sarcastic vitality deformed out of all proportion. Quilp uses the absurd to shock his victims. He is a satirist without the excuse of moral conviction, a comedian with only a desire to displease, and he uses the shocking "punch line" when he would much rather punch us instead. Alfred Jingle in *Pickwick Papers* was a study in comic versatility turned to deceit, a revelation of art as lie which needed Sam Weller to renew our faith in the joys of style. Quilp is also a study in comic style, an instance of satire turned to sadism, and he requires Dick Swiveller as a control. Even Quilp's facial expressions become the outward sign of his diseased inwardness. Nell's "nightmare" perspective is again the novel's own, with the dwarf producing "such horrible grimaces, as none but himself and nightmares had the power of assuming" (4). His smile is not of gaiety, but a "ghastly grin" (4) of mockery, "a smile of which a frown was part" (5). And his laugh is described as "a suppressed cackling in his throat, and a motion of his shoulders, like one who laughs heartily, but at the same time slily and by stealth" (5). His delight is stifled and rankling, not open jocularity but the cloaked and bridled pleasure of sarcasm at its most private, its most perverse. This is precisely *ill* humor, the autoerotic sickening of constructive comedy into inhuman satisfactions.

The crucial distinctions between the satirist's just power and the sadist's unwholesome energy are kept before us in the imaginative bond (but clear moral disjunction) between Dickens's facetious descriptions and the dwarf's own sly barbs and fierce delicacies of expression. Quilp's relentless brutalization of wife and mother-in-law under the sarcastic guise of courtly obeisance is paralleled in Dickens's own ironic treatment of the family. While Nell wallows in pastoral daydreams, Dickens is performing a mock pastoral in his descriptions of Mrs. Quilp in her "bower" awaiting the return of her "lord" (4). Quilp might well have made the same joke, and it is a similar subversion of pastoral yearnings that he sets in motion by praising a delightful "summer house overlooking the river" (21) and adjoining his favorite tavern. Dickens soon joins the fun to call it an "inviting spot" (21) and "choice retreat" (23); this haven, of course, turns out to be the vile dive known by the "appropriate name" of "the Wilderness" (23).

While there is no denying Quilp's evil, there is also no denying his gusto; of this Dickens's style reminds us by so often aligning itself with the dwarf's humor. As in the case of Jingle's stylistic environment, language itself is thus complicated as a standard. We are to notice the energy Dickens and Quilp have in common, as it issues in facetious humor, just as we are asked to remark at the same time the vast differences which lie beneath superficially similar tones. And they are indeed similar. The typical Dickensian narrator we heard in *Pickwick Papers* continues to mock the style of elegant honorific titles when referring to the dwarf as "that ugly worthy" (23), and in the same kind of broadly aimed verbal satire we find Quilp himself laughing at the monumental style of sentence architecture, in a rendering of Dick Swiveller's character that makes simultaneous fun of circumlocution and euphemism, as well as of Dick himself, who is said by Quilp to be "pretty well accustomed to the agricultural pursuits of sowing wild oats..." (33). This is so quintessentially Dickensian that Dickens himself uses the same inflated formula, with a perhaps unconscious debt to Quilp, over fifteen years later. He writes in his own voice of Henry Gowan in *Little Dorrit* that "his genius during his earlier manhood, was of that exclusively agricultural character which applies itself to the cultivation of wild oats" (*L.D.* I, 17). Quilp is so much a connoisseur of satiric language that he has developed a parodist's ear for the language of others, and he imitates the fatuous effusions of his personal toady, Sampson Brass, in an exhilarating stunt of mock sycophancy: " 'How precipitate that was, and yet what an earnest and vigorous measure!' said Quilp, conferring with himself, in imitation of his friend Mr. Sampson Brass" (48). In all of this overlap between the style of Quilp and his author, we are to notice a satirical common ground, not an artistic or creative one. Quilp gravitates to verbal satire not because it is verbal but because it is satiric, and can be made vicious. His demonic urges supply him with an energy so intense that it becomes a counterfeit of the creative impulse, and our realization of this simply heightens the irony of his early designation as "the small lord of the creation" (4). His energy is instead a frustrated and—here physical stature again corroborates—stunted thing, a ravaging not a making.

The contrast developed between Quilp and Sampson Brass is essential. The most fully drawn hypocrite of language so far in the novels, Brass becomes an augury of Seth Pecksniff and the entire "naughty company" of false-speakers to follow. Within *The Old Curiosity Shop* itself, the fact that Brass's motives are defined by such predominantly linguistic coordinates serves to remind us that the development of Quilp, on whom Brass entirely depends, both as an idea and as a man, is also plotted against a related verbal scale. The results are widely divergent, but the comparison is necessary, especially since it works into a three-way comparison with Dick Swiveller's very different reliance on the word. Brass's faith in legal "style" becomes a fanatical religious certainty, and, as a lawyer, Sampson stands in a kind of hierophantic relation to the deliberate mysteries and mystifications of the law. One of

Dickens's favorite punishments for the hypocrites in his stories is to show them finally taken in by their own lies. The case of Sampson Brass is a special one, for he is deluded not by his own words but by words like them, in other and official hands, words which he himself must actually purchase. Sampson's madness is to believe that his identity is vested by Parliamentary decree, taking a mere legal technicality as the warranty of his moral being: "I am styled 'gentleman' by Act of Parliament. I maintain the title by the annual payment of twelve pound sterling for a certificate. I am not one of your players of music, stage actors, writers of books, or painters of pictures, who assume a station that the laws of their country don't recognize" (60). Sampson has nothing to do with art or the private avenues of imagination. He is only what Parliament "styles" and certifies him, and he is even less than that, for time and again he surrenders his identity as "gentleman" by grotesque bootlicking.

Throughout *The Old Curiosity Shop* Brass must undergo "torments which his avaricious and grovelling nature compelled him to endure and forbade him to resent" (51). He is heard at one point to praise Quilp for a clarity which he ascribes to Parliament and which is quite foreign to that rhetorically muddled body: "He states his points so clearly that it's a treat to have 'em! I don't know any Act of Parliament that's equal to him in clearness!" (51). Quilp accuses Brass of being "slow as a tortoise, more thick-headed than a rhinocerous," and by this time the fawning has become almost hysterically misplaced: " 'He's extremely pleasant!' cried the obsequious Sampson. 'His acquaintance with Natural History too is surprising. Quite a Buffoon, quite!' " (51). Only a "superfluous vowel" here, Dickens explains, has denied Sampson the intended comparison between Quilp and Buffon. It is certainly to the point that Buffon gave us the proverbial equation, discussed already in connection with *Pickwick Papers*, "Style is the man," for in the relation between Brass and Quilp this dictum brings genine insight. Later, in the same conversation, Quilp reveals his motiveless loathing of Kit in such denunciations as "prowling prying hound" and "crouching cur," drawn, as Brass would have it, from "Natural History" and applying more to Brass himself than to the well-intentioned Kit. To this Brass's first reaction includes merely a clichéd adverb in "Fearfully eloquent," but the fearfulness itself seems to have the upper hand by the time Brass follows up with his most unlikely compliment: "Quite appalling!" Quilp's satire is indeed appalling, a savagery of language. In the case of Mr. Brass, too, style is the man and registers a corresponding psychological judgment. In Quilp's own personal sycophant, the sadist has found his perfect parasite and foil, a confirmed and unflinching masochist: " 'Ha ha ha!,' laughed Mr. Brass. 'Oh very biting! and yet it's like being tickled—there's a pleasure in it too, sir!' " (62).

This masochistic transformation of pain into pleasure is a kind of psychological euphemism, and it is matched linguistically by Brass's frequent recourse to verbal evasion and apology. This takes a very special turn when his villainy is exposed at the end of the novel. In two paragraphs of hopeless self-effacement he blubbers out, between stock formulations of put-upon goodness, verbal apologetics like "as I may say," "may I venture to say?" "as one may say," "suffer me to speak" (66). His hypocritical disguise is coming apart, and he is desperate to mend it with more words. But like Pecksniff stumbling over his own analogies later, Brass must employ one of these hedging catch phrases to save face after a misjudged rhetorical flight; Mr. Witherden has just withered Brass with denunciation, and Sampson is forced to reply: "Well! Ah! But I am a falling house, and the rats (if I may be allowed the expression in reference to a gentleman that I respect and love beyond everything) fly from me!" The persona has been rent, and all that is left are naughty maunderings of the rhetoric with which it was once glued together. It is his own language now that finally discloses the truth about him, as the very manner in which he recounts Quilp's tortures makes the point about their relationship through its reflexive grammar—with Quilp the sadist taking "a delight in looking on while I scorch, and burn, and bruise, and maim myself" (66). But perhaps the most devastating psychological idea in this scene is the way in which masochism is now unmistakably allied with sexual aberration, for we soon hear that the simpering Mr. Brass "in his deep debasement really seemed to have changed sexes with his sister, and to have made over to her any spark of manliness he might have possessed."

With Sampson Brass we have not touched upon merely an isolated psychiatric datum. *The Old Curiosity Shop* is a novel in which the masochistic pattern runs curiously deep. It is as if Nell's own unconventional martyrdom sets the tone. Her genius for spirituality is in fact a masochistic scourge, and, sacrificed finally to no principle higher than her own suicidal goodness, her angelic self-abnegation becomes its own dead end. Dying does not translate her to glory; all by itself it is the apotheosis. Perhaps this is meant as a signal for the disquieting sense one gets when reading *The Old Curiosity Shop* that all impulses are reversing their path and turning self-destructive. The vectors of action become the arrows of self-affliction. On the one hand, the most vicious miseries Quilp inflicts are those in which he forces others to witness his own gleeful self-torture. More importantly, Dick Swiveller's characteristic pleasure in drink is another kind of self-abuse, an assault on his nervous system which finally sets off a retaliatory fever, during which the unconscious mind of the novel's hero torments itself just as his body had once brought on its own punishment. The subconscious is also masochistic for the heroine of the novel. In a nightmarish revenge of "fancy," the same reflexive grammar used to suggest Brass's diseased intimacy with Quilp is here used for Nell's own relation to that dwarfish monster in her thought: "Quilp indeed was a perpetual nightmare to the child. . . She slept, for their better security, in the room where the wax-work figures were, and she never retired to this place at night but she *tortured herself*—she could not help it—with imagining a resemblance, in some one or other of their death-like faces, to the dwarf, and this fancy would sometimes so gain upon her that she would almost believe he had removed the figure and stood within the clothes" (29, italics mine). Next door to the intransitive, to isolation and eventual stasis, the emotional syntax by which human drives are articulated in *The Old Curiosity Shop* is essentially reflexive, and it will be Dick Swiveller's charge, by going outside himself through wit and sympathy, to break the mind loose from this fatal bind. The imagination, as we are soon to find, is both the agent of this liberation and its object. And so the novel's pattern of reflex psychology becomes no longer a sick turning inward, as Dick at last makes it possible for fancy, acting by and upon itself, to set itself free.

To hold back for a while longer from such broad psychological implications, we should simply note the way in which Brass's stale mechanical phrases acknowledge by contrast how well oiled and versatile Quilp's satiric language is, how Dickensian an instrument —an instrument misused as a sadistic weapon. Dickens throws a great deal of himself into Quilp, none at all into Nell. Thus he confirms their polarity. As absolutes, Nell and Quilp are in a sense each other's precondition, yet they are forever irreconcilable. Marriage between them, as proposed obscenely by Quilp, is to anyone but him unthinkable. Nell and Quilp can be billed among the large cast of Dickensian "doubles" only with a special reservation; they can never be incorporated into a single principle, a unified personality, nor can one be suppressed or killed off to save the other. Both Nell and Quilp define a limit which makes sense only in the presence of the other; they only exist so long as they coexist. And yet I have found no commentary which notices how careful Dickens is to have them die "together." Quilp drowns in a preternaturally black night at the end of the sixty-seventh chapter, the same night on which Kit is released from prison. The journey to find Nell begins the next morning, and two days later the search party arrives to find that the child has been dead for those same two days. "She died soon after daybreak" (72) on the morning (so we discover by working backward) just after Quilp's death, with the first coming of light after his black terror. I cannot believe that Dickens did not have this in mind, for it has always seemed odd that in this most deliberately pathetic of all his novels, with his most calculated and prolonged funereal episode, he should cheat us of death's real drama by showing us the child already dead and then flashing back to the last stages of her dying. There may be something to say for the shock value of finding Nell a corpse and then returning inconsolable to the account of her last hours. This has a certain impact, but throughout Nell's part of the story Dickens has not once shown a preference for the forceful over the tearful, and it would unquestionably have been sadder, more pathetic—indeed more effectively cathartic—to find ourselves at the child's bedside when she dies, hanging anxiously on her last words. I think it at least probable that Dickens sacrificed this partly in order to work out in the least jarring way his time scheme for the nearly simultaneous deaths of his villain and his heroine, the absolutes who could not possibly outlast each other.

As I have hinted, the manner of the deaths, as well as their proximity in time, is crucial for the polarization of Nell and Quilp. After the stage is set in each case, the lighting is all-important. The fragile child, willing and even glad, "faded like the light upon a summer's evening" (72). This dimming and flickering out at dawn (although compared with day's end) is in exact contrast to that "good black devil's night" on which Quilp is drowned, blinded by the hideous brilliance of "the hundred fires that danced before his eyes" (67). The energy of their comings and goings is the energy of their ends; Nell fades quietly and flickers out, while Quilp is violently extinguished. After all the boiling potations he has downed in the course of the novel in order to sustain himself, how else could his fiery nature be quenched than by the first water he

is made to take? Nell's death is the apotheosis of all her faint
quiescence throughout the book, just as Quilp's death, for all its
surprise and horror, is a kind of epitomizing moment, almost a
sarcastic triumph. Dickens makes part of this explicit, for he allows Quilp actually to mock his own death. When his wretched
corpse is finally washed ashore, his "hair, stirred by the damp
breeze, played in a kind of mockery of death—such a mockery as
the dead man himself would have delighted in when alive—about
its head" (67). By means of this macabre image, Dickens enables
Quilp to wrench from death itself the last grotesque laugh—or
rather, the last laugh but one. The final joke is on Quilp's survivors
at the inquest when they assume that he has killed himself. It is
true that his primordial energy is finally self-destructive, but his
will is to keep going forever. We must remember that his death is
technically an accident; he has locked out those who might have
helped him, but he dies screaming for their help—in anything but
the "willed death" James R. Kincaid describes.[2] The joke is indeed
on us if we misunderstand his demonic impulses so far as to believe
him capable of giving them up by choice, of ending his sadistic
fun without a fight. Nell's wished peace *is* a suicide, and Quilp
would have given anything to live the few more hours needed to
laugh at it.

Kincaid argues that Quilp exists in the first place in order to
neutralize our laughter at Nell, that his "witty sadism checks our
possible impatience with gentleness and drains off our mischievous
impulses."[3] What Kincaid is suggesting is that humor supports
rather than undercuts the pathos, that it "cleanses our reactions
and makes possible an unqualified response to Nell."[4] This thesis
seems itself strangely "unqualified," and, though interesting, it
might well baffle the modern readers who feel all the more "mischievous" because of the humor. We are never more impatient
with Nell than when we stop to think that, with luck, we will have
Quilp back in the next chapter. Here is Kincaid's overall claim:
"Providing for the pathetic is one of the two main rhetorical functions of laughter in this novel. The other is to provide for the final
comic solution centered in Dick and the Marchioness."[5] Laughter's
"rhetorical function," the large subject of Kincaid's book, is certainly a useful idea, but the trouble with it as a mode of approach
to *The Old Curiosity Shop* is that Kincaid has it depend too much
on intention, on Dickens's great but dated expectations. The unavoidable fact is that *The Old Curiosity Shop* is a rhetorical
anachronism, a rhetorical failure for modern readers. The pathos

no longer moves us, and the laughter cannot help it to. Naturally we still respond to the humor, and not, I think, simply because we still like jokes, but because we sense a significance in the laughter quite apart from its rhetorical deployment. It becomes thematic.

When we laugh with Quilp, we are in part responding to a comic style—and we forget Nell altogether. When we respond to style in this way, we begin to question and measure it, judging it against the idiosyncratic voices of other characters and against the stylistic capacities of the narrative voice itself. We can say all we want about Sam Weller's comedy being present in *Pickwick Papers* so that we will not laugh too long at the title character, but in the last analysis Sam and his comic style are there for their own sakes —as Sam would be the first to insist. His style, the various voices of his comic poetry, tell us something about laughter and delight and the proper channeling of imagination. So does Jingle's style, in a negative way, and so does Quilp's—and in a more complex and developing way, so will Dick Swiveller's. It is important that the styles of these characters are variously framed and confronted by the Dickensian comic prose itself; humor is cross-bred between the author and his characters, the styles exchanging and parodying each other's materials, alluding to one another and conspiring in a relentless study of the humorous imagination, its connections with psychology and moral action. This stylistic complexity, as it played across the surface of Dickens's first novel, was examined at length in the last three chapters, because it is that quality of Dickensian verbal comedy which lends laughter such resonance in his novels. It is far more than rhetorical strategy. Verbal humor, of course, is only one connection language makes with theme; styles other than comic imply other sorts of imagination, as we saw in *Pickwick*. But humor remains the most widespread, and I would propose that Kincaid's *rhetoric* of laughter be supplemented (if not superseded) by an *ethic* of laughter and a *psychology* of laughter.

When Alfred Jingle caps his speeches with an emphatic and irrepressible "very" he is giving vent to the same sort of hyperbolic verbal energy which sent him forth from Dickens's imagination in the first place. He misuses his powers and wastes himself in petty villainy, and Sam must appear on the scene to redeem the comic style. Quilp's sarcastic style is the satirist's proper energy abused and perverted, and Quilp is a major villain. The redemption of style and imagination is performed with greater struggle and against greater odds in *The Old Curiosity Shop* by Mr. Richard

Swiveller. Once we notice that both Quilp and Dick are humorists supported and qualified by the surrounding Dickensian style, we must begin to distinguish between them, between the satanic bitterness of the one and the blithe irresponsibility of the other, between a love of sarcasm for its own sake and a love of high-sounding poetic phrase, between motiveless malignity and motiveless jollity. Three ironic encounters between Quilp and Dick cut these distinctions very clearly.

There is a point in the novel where Dick's own gaiety, a natural if sometimes truant virtue with him, is the very quality he ascribes to Quilp: "Well . . . you're a jolly fellow, but of all the jolly fellows I ever saw or heard of, you have the queerest and most extraordinary way with you, upon my life you have" (21). Like Sam Weller, Dick Swiveller is a Cockney street wit addicted to all sorts of good-natured verbal play, and like Mark Tapley after him in *Martin Chuzzlewit,* he is a tireless practitioner of "conwiviality" and self-conscious jollity. Mark, who seeks to find credit in being jolly under the most adverse circumstances, tries to bring his bright temperament to the aid of Martin Chuzzlewit, just as Dick, with much less success, attempts to communicate his good spirits to the petulant lout Frederick Trent, who only resents the fact that Dick "can be merry under any circumstances" (7). Dick, as the saying goes, rolls with the punches, and his "composure and self-possession"—qualities repeatedly attributed to Sam in *Pickwick Papers*—his natural resource and resilience, are explained by Dickens as bearing a close similarity to "certain systems of moral philosophy" (34). (Sam, as we remember, was awarded the honorary title of "philosopher" by Mr. Pickwick.) Dickens makes this suggestion in Dick's case on the same page as that on which the theme of antagonistic destiny has been brought suggestively to the fore. We are told that in an animated soliloquy "it may be presumed that . . . Mr. Swiveller addressed himself to his fate or destiny, whom, as we learn by the precedents, it is the custom of heroes to taunt in a very bitter and ironical manner when they find themselves in situations of an unpleasant nature" (34). Dick's attitude is a staunch reversal both of Quilp's "bitter and ironical" taunting of his fate even in death and of Nell's grandfather delivering over his entire will to destiny, to that same gambling at cards which Dick and the Marchioness will make into a fond domestic ceremony. Trent believes that "Fortune will not bear chiding" (29), but Dick knows better, and his comic defiance becomes a saving self-assertion. He is forever bemoaning the "staggerers" with which destiny dogs his life, but his composure and his comedy pull him through, and his final happiness with the Marchioness is itself seen as a destiny. We hear in the book's closing chapter that Dick had "frequent occasion to remark at divers subsequent periods that there had been a young lady saving up for him after all" (73).

When Dick compliments Quilp on his jollity, we are to be warned of the tremendous difference between the dwarf's sadistic sociability and Dick's genial sportiveness. Another scene between these two which generates the same sort of ironic contrast between their widely different imaginations has Dick, intending to hand Quilp his card, accidentally slipping him the wrong "document": " 'By a slight and not unnatural mistake, sir,' said Dick, substituting another in its stead, 'I had handed you the pass-ticket of a select and convivial circle called the Glorious Apollers, of which I have the honour to be the Perpetual Grand' " (13). We are to recognize the mistake, in its widest implications, as being quite unnatural and by no means slight, for Quilp should under no condition gain admittance to this society of poetry lovers. He is excluded by his very nature. Dick's service to the god of poetry invites special analysis in this most "poetic" (in the worst sense) of all Dickens's novels, and while the narrator's prose is grinding into measured and often metrical solemnities, Dick's frivolous verses begin to seem all the more significant. When inquiring about the disappearance of Nell and her grandfather, Dick unconsciously mocks their pastoral longings in a burst of sing-song doggerel: "Has the sly old fox made his fortune then, and gone to live in a tranquil cot in a pleasant spot with a distant view of the changing sea?" (13). Anything so jovial, so light-hearted, Quilp would never bother with. Dick is open and receptive; he believes poetry is to be shared, and so he borrows it to irradiate his conversation. Poetry enters and enlivens the patterns of his thought. But Quilp is closed, inward, unreceptive, and poetry's constructive energy is not for him. His god is Chaos, never Apollo.

I have suggested that Dick's congratulating Quilp on his jolly humor, and his inviting Quilp by accident to visit the Glorious Apollers—that these separate errors are both dramatic ironies. I promised a third. In a moment of intoxicated self-pity, Dick laments his fate as a miserable orphan—like an Oliver or a Nell—and characterizes Quilp as a child-persecuting villain, a latter-day Fagin, a "deluding dwarf" (23). This is hardly casting against type, of course, for it is exactly the part Quilp has chosen for himself in his relation with Little Nell. But Quilp now takes upon himself an even more disturbing role when he defends his good intentions against Dick's charges with this sobering avowal: "I! I'm a second father to you" (23). Mr. Pickwick was for Sam Weller the archetypal second father (we remember that they shared the same first name), but by now this emotional "adoption," as with Fagin's of Oliver Twist, has become a threat, not a benefit. The Pickwickian barriers have been irreparably torn down. It is as if the criminal energies of Daniel Quilp, like those of Fagin or Sikes in the preceding novel, have stolen into and disrupted the main body of Dickens's narrative from the once unencroaching chaos of *Pickwick*'s interpolated tales. And when Quilp's sarcastic claim to the title of "second father" pointedly shatters the illusion of Pickwickian jovial fellowship, we are thrown back again on the important affinities between Sam Weller and Dick Swiveller.

Both Sam and Dick are verbal comedians and Cockney enthusiasts of almost sublime self-possession who extend their imaginations into worlds made of words, but a clue to the difference between them as standard-bearers of the poetic temperament is the primacy of drink as a catalyst for Dick's imagination. Certainly Sam drinks; who does not, and heartily, in *Pickwick Papers*? But Dick drinks *too much*, and the existence of this reservation is a comment on how far we have fallen from the Pickwickian world. There people do drink to excess and fall into delirium, or into delusions of talking chairs and phantom coaches, but this zone of experience is kept safely curtained off in the interpolations, in the stories of either fanciful or feverish imaginations. Both sorts of imagination have come together for *The Old Curiosity Shop* and have broken into the main narrative, for after many alcoholically induced flights of fancy, Dick at last drinks himself into a fever. The fable of the gin and "rosy wine," with which I began this study, has both an emblematic point and a moral. It is a symbol for the transforming power of art and imagination, but it also warns of poetry's closeness to insobriety for Mr. Swiveller. Dick is indeed most poetic, extroverted, and gregarious when in his cups, and it is upon this human tendency that the Glorious Apollers build a community in art. There is a teasingly oblique hint of this at our first meeting with Richard Swiveller, when our attention is drawn to a common (so the relevant dictionaries tell us)[6] slang euphemism of Dickens's day by a redundant high-styled gloss. We hear that Dick "took occasion to apologize for any negligence that might be perceptible in his dress, on the ground that last night he 'had the sun very strong in his eyes;' by which expression he was understood to convey to his hearers in the most delicate manner possible, the information that he had been extremely drunk" (2). The sun itself has stunned our happy acolyte; the god Apollo has been met face to face.

Aside from their differing reliance upon alcohol, however, Sam is also a truer poet than Dick. Mr. Swiveller quotes snippets of poetry as if they were phrases fashioned by himself, whereas Sam, a purer and more disinterested artist, reverses the process, creating comic dialogues out of thin air and then crediting them to others (all the while the voices of his own imagination) by the habitual formula "as the man said when. . ." Dick quotes "scraps of verse as if they were only prose in a hurry" (8) because it is his purpose to divert poetry into the normal, prosaic rhythms of everyday life, as a means of coloring and controlling a reality too bleak if unadorned. If this is a kind of escapism, it still seems a healthier brand than Nell's spiritless spirituality. Dick uses art to extend his response to experience, and it is not at all surprising to catch him at an "extemporary adaptation of a popular ballad to the distressing circumstances of his own case" (50). As a rule, then, Dick's refuge in poetry and imaginative phrase is hurried and artless because it is not really art, but liveliness with a debt to art. Priestley offers something of the same distinction when he assigns Dick Swiveller to that essentially adolescent class of characters who are "sufficiently imaginative to appreciate art, but not imaginative enough to create it,"[7] who "have not sufficient imagination to turn life into art," but who do manage to "turn art into life"[8]—who can through imagination, that is, enliven the pace of their ordinary walk of life.

When exonerating himself in advance from any trouble incurred by the single gentleman's refusal to leave his name—"If any mistake should arise from not having the name, don't say it was my fault, sir"—Dick gaily adds: "Oh blame not the bard—" (35). In a second-hand snatch of poetry he announces himself as a poet, and yet we have seen that art is not really creation for him, it is part of his recreation. Still he is not altogether wrong to call himself a "bard," for his poetic loquacity is, in a sense, a return to the oral or bardic tradition, a ceremonial notion of poetry as part of a shared heritage. This is the concept of poetry as public domain, often associated with the tradition of balladry for which Dick shows such repeated fondness. And we must remember here that the Glorious Apollers are a thriving miniature community, an oral society with their own poetic inheritance. A further point: though Dick's consciousness is derivative, his subconscious mind is revealed as oddly creative. When he falls asleep over his writing desk at the Brasses' from the intolerable monotony of his clerkly chores, the dry and mindless copying, he begins to write in his sleep "divers strange words in an unknown character with his eyes shut" (35)—a remarkable image of the dreamer transcribing his own unconscious fantasies.

Finally, there is a special sense in which Dick is a truly creative agent. Priestley insists that Dick can appreciate poetry but not make it for himself, and this is true until he meets the Marchioness —or rather, until he meets that unformed, unnamed servant girl who must answer to Quilp's inquiry that her name is "Nothing" (51). Dick befriends her and, in fact, by naming her almost brings her into being. For as we learned from the fable of the "rosy wine," to name is to nominate for a reality of one's own choosing. Before their first cribbage game in that dank dungeon below the Brass office, Dick explains that "to make it seem more real and pleasant, I shall call you the Marchioness" (57). This is a romantic daydream in which the "real" and the "pleasant" can be willed at once into conjunction; yet at the same time it bespeaks a mature faith in the possibilities of a better world, a faith nurtured in the love of poetry, where the real and the pleasant, truth and beauty, do regularly coincide. Here, domesticated and made comic, is a true Romantic poet's faith in the sustaining power of imagination. Dick has named (actually entitled) the Marchioness; his jubilant phrase-making has been purposefully directed for the first time, and, in thus conferring new life, his language has become truly "creative." And by his creation he is saved. When his imagination turns feverish it is the Marchioness, this child of his fancy, who nurses him back to health, and we are thereby presented, in a highly indirect but moving way, an image of fancy as salvation.

All this from a name. It is not surprising in Dickens, where names and naming are an important aspect of the author's own style. One need only check off the various names by which Esther Summerson and David Copperfield are known and addressed in their novels, and observe how this variety complicates the quest for identity, to see how Dickens could make thematic capital out of one of his most unforced gifts as a novelist, his ear for names. Many have noted the importance of the name "Dick," one syllable of his author's last name, as a clue to the inherence in this comic character of at least a part of the author's own personality, one phase of his artistic temperament. Further, the family pronunciation of Sam's last name, "Veller," is also contained in Dick's own surname. And there is surely something in "Swiveller" that catches his directionless vitality, that willingness to take the prevailing wind which often makes him seem as though he is merely going in circles.[9] But Dick not only swivels, he seeks; he has a confirmed sense of his identity as a romance hero, and he himself wonders about his first name in connection with that prototypical Richard who became Lord Mayor of London. "Perhaps the bells might strike up 'Turn again, Swiveller, Lord Mayor of London.' Whittington's name was Dick" (50). Here "Swivel again, Swiveller" is indeed a tempting revision, quite faithful to Dick's free-wheeling nature. With the Marchioness, however, he does wish to adapt himself seriously to the Whittingtonian ideal, so important later for Walter Gay in *Dombey and Son*, and it is with the Marchioness at last that he becomes the hero of his own romance. When he has in a manner made good his name, he never forgets that his relationship with the servant girl grew from his first gift of a name to her. No one in Dickens, except perhaps Betsey Trotwood in her eccentric way, has a surer ear for the suggestive reverberations of a name, and when Dick searches his imagination for the perfect name to accompany the title Marchioness, he comes up with the splendidly alliterative "Sophronia Sphynx," which he selects "as being euphonious" (this adjective itself echoed in the syllables of the first name) and also "genteel, and furthermore indicative of mystery" (73). But Dick never deserts his first noble inspiration. This is the last we hear of him in the novel: "And let it be added, to Dick's honour, that, though we have called her Sophronia, he called her the Marchioness from first to last" (73).

Dick is not alone, however, in bestowing a name on the Marchioness. For she in fact renames him after his fever, in a most acute accident. When he finally wakes from his delirium, his little nurse is thrilled into a beautiful misunderstanding of his name which leads him, in turn, to a larger understanding of the episode: "I'm so glad you're better, Mr. Liverer" (64). Dick is moved to a rare moment of reflection: " 'Liverer indeed!' said Dick thoughtfully. 'It's well I *am* a liverer. I strongly suspect I should have died, Marchioness, but for you!' " She has redeemed for him the gift of life he had presented to her, and this past master of words and phrases, brought up short now in gratitude and new sincerity, is forced to attend thoughtfully to someone else's fortuitous pun. Dick's last act before collapsing into fever, after he has been dismissed from the employ of Sampson Brass, is to drop for the first time into silence. This character of ready words and volatile wit, even before his disabling fever, suddenly finds himself bereft of gab, left without even a single appropriate quotation: "Mr. Swiveller answered not one word" (63). He leaves the office in a "profound silence" and is soon very nearly on his deathbed.

The protective walls of interpolation and quarantine have long since been demolished, and the fever to which Dick now succumbs brings into the mainstream of plot and psychology Dickens's study of isolated delirium which was, with its various stylistic "impersonations," the subject of my second chapter on *Pickwick Papers.* Even in the main narrative of Dickens's first book, however, there is an incident that previews the significance feverish states of mind will later assume for his themes of imagination. We remember the hint about midway through *Pickwick* that the "darling child," the inevitable offspring, of the book's sunny splendor is "the madness wild / That sports in fierce fever's train" (*P.P.,* 28). We can scarcely be surprised, therefore, to find Alfred Jingle punished later with such a fever for his illegitimate brightness, his victimizing pretense of convivial high spirits. For the deceits of his style, fancy turns punitive, and this will happen again and again from *Pickwick* on. When Mr. Pickwick first comes upon Jingle in the Fleet, the once extroverted gentleman is found "brooding over the dusty fire" (42), his eyes pathetically "fixed" on the blaze. In this reprisal of imagination, Jingle emerges as the first important fire-gazer in the novels, beginning that line of descent and frittered confidence to be traced in my sixth chapter. His imagination has clearly brought him no comfort, and his fixated attention to the firelight is an image of "misery and dejection." Instead of offering refuge, his mind has turned on him in a revenging fever, as he soon admits with a style that bears witness to this revenge, the language not of burst and freedom, now, but of stammer: "Ungrateful dog—boyish to cry—can't help it—bad fever—weak—ill—hungry. Deserved it all—but suffered much—very."

Fancy's "deserved" retaliation, however, is only one kind of imaginative trial in Dickens, and in his next book it is the hero, Oliver Twist, who suffers from "the dry and wasting heat of fever" (*O.T.,* 12), in an ordeal that becomes a psychic blessing in disguise. For during his delirium, Oliver sees the angelic presence of his dead mother at his bedside, and Mrs. Bedwin gives what she thinks is a psychological explanation: "That was the fever, my dear" (77). As the good nurse Gamp will declare some years later, "There's fevers of the mind ... as well as body" (*M.C.*, 29), and both kinds also attack the villains of this early novel, Fagin and Sikes— creatures far more vicious than Jingle, whose psychosomatic suffering is detailed for us at some length. "Fevers are not peculiar to good people; are they?" asks Mr. Grimwig at one point. "Bad people have fevers sometimes; haven't they, eh?" (*O.T.*, 14), and his sarcasm underscores the variety of feverish traumas we are to meet in Dickens.

On the way to Dick's own in *The Old Curiosity Shop*, for instance, we must pass through the related suffering of old Trent and Nell herself. The old man says at one point, while clasping his head, "There's a burning fever here, and something now and then to which I fear to give a name" (*O.C.S.*, 9). What he fears is that madness which will eventually cause Nell's exile from home and precipitate her own "burning fever" in the industrial wilderness, where a "strange confusion in her mind" will be matched by the frenzy of the external setting. The "noise and tumult" of the mad world in which she there finds herself are such obvious indicators of feverish convulsion that it would be hard to miss the irony when the term "symptom" is applied, not to the frenzied, pathological scene itself, but to its amelioration: "The throng of people hurried by, in two opposite streams, with no symptom of cessation or exhaustion" (44). The whole industrial panorama is made explicit as an intolerable nightmare, "presenting that endless repetition of the same dull, ugly, form, which is the horror of oppressive dreams" (45). As later with *Hard Times*, this "endless repetition" begins to infest the run of the prose itself: "Their way lay through the *same* scenes as yesterday, with no variety or improvement. There was the *same* thick air, difficult to breathe; the *same* blighted ground, the *same* hopeless prospect, the *same* misery and distress" (45, my italics). Narrative style has again become almost psychoanalytic, with the objective passing over into the subjective as external monotonies begin to take their subliminal toll. The effect is more than a matter of fixated repetitions. The regularized rhythm of the second sentence is interrupted, suggestively thickened, by the phrase "difficult to breathe," and the track of the sentence as a whole gauges the internalizing of the industrial landscape as it moves from the specific sensations of "air" and "ground" to the generalized "same hopeless prospect," an amplification of the earlier phrase, "same scenes," yet also a psychological ambiguity which turns us toward the subjective outlook, the inward prospect, of "misery and distress." When the external trauma in the technological wilderness coincides with and extends the crisis of Nell's own illness, we realize that she too, in effect, has undergone "a raging fever accompanied with delirium" (11) like her grandfather's before her.

Just as with everything else about him, Dick Swiveller's fever serves to distinguish his imagination from that of the book's tragic heroine. Often Dick's "modest quenchers" have "awakened a slight degree of fever" (35), and there is that favorite Dickensian pun on "spirit" when the real fever is introduced, as we are told that the "spiritual excitement of the last fortnight, working upon a system affected in no slight degree by the spirituous excitement of some years, proved a little too much for him," and he "was stricken with a raging fever" (63). The first sentence of the next chapter lasts for just under two hundred words, the throbbing participles and gerunds crowding a strained, overloaded syntax almost beyond its hold:

Tossing to and fro upon his hot, uneasy bed; tormented by a fierce thirst which nothing could appease; unable to find, in any change of posture, a moment's peace or ease; and rambling, ever, through deserts of thought where there was no resting-place, no sight or sound suggestive of refreshment or repose, nothing but a dull eternal weariness, with no change but the restless shiftings of his miserable body, and the weary wanderings of his mind, constant still to one ever-present anxiety—to a sense of something left undone, of some fearful obstacle to be surmounted, of some carking care that would not be driven away, and haunted the distempered brain, now in this form, now in that—always shadowy and dim, but recognisable for the same phantom in every shape it took, darkening every vision like an evil conscience, and making slumber horrible—in these slow tortures of his dread disease, the unfortunate Richard lay wasting and consuming inch by inch, until, at last, when he seemed to fight and struggle to rise up, and to be held down by devils, he sank into a deep sleep, and dreamed no more. (64)

The first two participles, the active "tossing" and the passive "tormented," convey the essence of the fever, the fury of restless activity combined with the passivity of relentless assault. The one instance of a doubled pre-nominal adjective is located carefully to elongate the phrase "dull eternal weariness," and the whole grotesquely protracted sentence, with its weakened clutch upon continuity, seems to be "rambling" through its front-heavy expanses without a syntactical "resting-place," producing on its own part "a sense of something left undone."

When Dick awakes, he suspects that he must have "been delirious twice or thrice," and he notices that his flesh is much wasted away. Yet there is no surer token of the fever's severity than the fact that this one-time maestro of curiosity now has "no curiosity to pursue the subject" (64). His spirit is depleted, and his convalescent fancies turn to a kind of involuntary pastoralism, as he "unconsciously fell, in a luxury of repose, to staring at some green stripes upon the bed-furniture, and associating them strangely with patches of fresh turf, while the yellow ground made gravel-walks, and so helped out a long perspective of trim gardens." Dick is "rambling in imagination upon these terraces, and had quite lost himself indeed," when an overheard cough calls his attention for the first time to the Marchioness, the importance of whose ministrations to Dick we have already seen. The robust and voluble gent has been stricken wan and speechless, and only the Marchioness, whose identity is itself the product of Dick's most unselfish fancy, can nurse him back to voice and vigor, to his own identity as a man of extroverted imagination. And so it is only right that she has been the sole witness at Dick's greatest trial, the revenge of his verbal imagination for its years of alcoholic misuse: "But if you could have seen how you tried to jump out o' winder, and if you could have heard how you used to keep on singing and making speeches, you wouldn't have believed it" (64).

We recall that Dick, just before his delirium, had fallen into a "profound silence," and after his fever a speechlessness returns that is even more profound. This acrobat of banter and poetic embellishment has been crippled; he must lose his gift temporarily in order, at last, to appreciate it in connection with the Marchioness—as a shared life in imagination. His first request when he comes out of the fever is that the Marchioness should "have the goodness to inform me where I shall find my voice" (64). His speech is physically impaired, but this is mainly to emphasize that the gravity of his experience has left his expressive powers behind. The imagination has been tested by crisis, humbled and humanized in its greatest trial. The Marchioness waits on Dick with a loving and tender hand, and to all her attentions "Mr. Swiveller submitted in a kind of grateful astonishment beyond the reach of language" (66). Like the Wellers before him, Dick is most likely to be silenced when there is too much to say. But language is simply the way imagination finds voice, and Dickens wants to make the point very clear that Dick has been touched at his deepest springs. Even his imagination is bested, and he cannot stand the strain of a reality which outdoes his wildest dreams; when the cornucopious hamper arrives from his friends, Dick "was fain to lie down and fall asleep again, from sheer inability to entertain such wonders in his mind" (66).

Dick originally named his heroine the Marchioness "to make it seem more real and pleasant," but reality is now pleasant beyond the farthest fetch of his imagination, and he is sobered by this happiness. And if there are any lingering doubts on the reader's part about the fitness of the deprived girl as a soul-match for Richard Swiveller, they are dispelled in this scene by a delightful parallel to Dick's own wine miracle earlier. The Marchioness is telling Dick about her life in the Brass dungeon when she stops to recommend her personal recipe for the transformation of water and orange-peel (even more convenient than gin) into wine; she even advises (as if she would have to remind Mr. Swiveller!) that the imagination is a necessary ingredient for any such concoction:

'So I used to come out at night after they'd gone to bed, and feel about in the dark for . . . pieces of orange-peel to put into cold water and make believe it was wine. Did you ever taste orange-peel and water?'
Mr. Swiveller replied that he had never tasted that ardent liquor; and once more urged his friend to resume the thread of her narrative.
'If you make believe very much, it's quite nice,' said the small servant, 'but if you don't, you know, it seems as if it would bear a little seasoning, certainly.' (64)

Make-believe has been the spice of life for this comic pair, yet when asked by Mr. Garland what might be done for him after his fever, Dick replies: "If you could make the Marchioness yonder, a Marchioness in real, sober earnest . . . I'd thank you to get it done off-hand" (66). "Sober" is now the operative marker, placed next to "real" as a new and finally more satisfying modification. But the imagination in the end holds its ground, and she remains the fanciful Marchioness all her days. Sampson Brass at one point fawningly calls Quilp "quite a Troubadour" (51), but, as usual, especially whenever their verbal energies are implicated, Dick takes up the positive side of Quilp's lascivious excess. Like Sam Weller in his valentining before him, it is actually Mr. Richard Swiveller who is the true love poet and poet-lover in the novel, not only singing the praises of his noble and titled lady, but actually hymning her into existence with her comic name.

In his discussion of *Pickwick Papers*, Chesterton is quite good on the difference between comedy and pathos. His remarks tend also toward a judgment on Dickens's fourth novel: "Humour is expansive; it bursts outward; the fact is attested by the common expression, 'holding one's sides.' But sorrow is not expansive; and it was afterwards the mistake of Dickens that he tried to make it expansive. It is the one great weakness of Dickens as a great writer, that he did try to make that sudden sadness, that abrupt pity, which we call pathos, a thing quite obvious, infectious, public, as if it were journalism or the measles."[10] Before this criticism, Nell's narrative must stand justly and severely accused. But Dickens was great even in one of the greatest failures, and while he gave us Nell only to take her away, he also gave us Dick Swiveller and a humor so "expansive," an imagination so roomy, that it embraces and practically creates another human being. Quilp's humor is of course an exception to Chesterton's rule. Quilp holds his sides to hide his grotesque glee. In laughter, covertness is perversion; it is to joy as masturbation is to love, and Quilp's festering sarcasm is hardly infectious—it is just sick. Dick's laughter, on the other hand, is communicable, and he reaches out. In this novel of curiosities, Dick is the only character who has enough energy actually to be curious. He wonders about the diminutive servant girl, explores her dungeon, and returns with—after many further trials—a wife.

And just as Dick is a humorist who shows Quilp's energy harnessed and harmonized, so we are to think of the Marchioness as an alternative to Nell, whose blanched imagination pits nothing against the world and therefore finds no earthly refuge from it. The Marchioness makes with Dick the home which Nell is never to find, and her career is a happier rendition of Nell's life, just as Quilp's drowning is a terrible reversal of the child's death. The parallels are somewhat cryptic in each case, and are discovered in part by working backward from unobtrusive numerical information. We subtract the days of the journey to find Nell from the number of days she has been dead when found, and we discover that she died almost immediately after Quilp. We are told in passing that Nell is thirteen years old, "nearly fourteen" (7), and if we subtract those "half-dozen years" of education which Dick financed from the nineteen years to which the Marchioness has attained when she becomes Mrs. Richard Swiveller (73), we realize that she too was thirteen years old when Dick met and fell in love with her.[11] Quilp is a hideous mockery of the small, delicate child. Why else is he made a dwarf, who fits snugly into Nell's tiny bed? The Marchioness is also unnaturally small, a second study in the mistreated, the stunted girl child, who is saved by Dick's comic imagination and who in turn saves him. A version of Nell's missed possibilities for living, the Marchioness has found her salvation in Mr. Richard Swiveller, a perennial adolescent who grows into responsibility, with remarkably little loss, by the end of the novel. Together they build that refuge in imagination Dickens is to find ever more fugitive and inaccessible from this point on.

The "He" at the head of this chapter refers to the man of style in Richard Eberhart's poem, a lyric that begins: "Style is the perfection of a point of view, / Nowise absolute, but held in a balance of opposites." Style is brought to this perfection only once in Dickens, when opposites settle to a keen balance in the intelligence of Sam Weller, an intelligence schooled in dualities and able to commute, without insisting on absolutes, between logic and fantasy, gaiety and tragedy, engagement and irony, innocence and acclimation. When Dick Swiveller attempts this poise it taxes him dearly. His is a contingent, an imperfect universe torn between the absolutisms of Quilp and Nell, where balance cannot easily be won. It is Mr. Swiveller, not Mr. Weller, who must learn what has become, by the measures of imagination, the high cost of living; it is Dick, never Sam with his effortless verve, who has "purchased at a great price the gems of elan / In some avid precinct of his personality." After Dick Swiveller the price may sometimes seem too steep to bear, all spirit a simulation, the gems paste. With Sam Weller, his fancy untaxed and prodigal, elan comes easy. With Mr. Swiveller, however, the imagination begins to learn its surcharge.

5 Apollo And The Naughty Company

> What words can paint the Pecksniffs in that trying
> hour? Oh, none: for words have naughty company
> among them, and the Pecksniffs were all goodness.
> —*Martin Chuzzlewit* (4)

This lapsarian notion of language as a fallen and impure medium is a joke for Dickens, an irony fully in line with the pastoral and Edenic satire leveled at the Pecksniff clan in *Martin Chuzzlewit*. Yet in one of Dickens's novels after another, it is the naughtiness of language—its impurities both ethical and esthetic, its moral and metaphorical lapses, confusions, indelicacies, excesses—which is dragged before us in comic review, now delegated to an egregious rhetorician, now to a prissy euphemist, now to a slave of banality and cliché, now to Dickens's own voice as it triggers some verbal absurdity booby-trapped for parody. This satire begins, of course, with the Pickwickians and continues through twelve novels to the sudden end of Dickens's career, where, in *The Mystery of Edwin Drood*, the rhetorical Mr. Thomas Sapsea must lug his frayed, hand-me-down language, those worn and tattered clichés he believes himself to have created, across a narrative geography mined at every turn with Dickens's satiric charges. With Thomas Sapsea, Dickens has in fact essentialized the type in its final appearance. As was more slyly the case for such earlier men of rhetoric as Pecksniff, Chadband, and Micawber, the forms of Sapsea's speech are automatically geared to self-aggrandizement: "I congratulate myself on having the honour of receiving you here for the first time" (*E.D.*,4), he sings reflexively when first meeting John Jasper. With Sapsea, Dickens has also epitomized the punishment which he metes out symbolically to his earlier shoddy talkers, most dramatically to Pecksniff as we are to see. Sapsea has been elevated to mayor on the wings of his rhetoric, and Dickens now speculates on his political future, capping his sarcastic apostrophe with a typical Sapsean cliché—used satirically against itself: "Mayors have been knighted for 'going up' with addresses: explosive machines intrepidly discharging shot and shell into the English Grammar. Mr. Sapsea may 'go up' with an address. Rise, Sir Thomas Sapsea! Of such is the salt of the earth" (12). Samuel Pickwick tended not to mean what he said, and this rhetorical habit blew up in his face with Mrs. Bardell. Afterwards it has regularly been Dickens's method to turn the "explosive machine" of bombast against its wielder, transforming it into the proverbial "petard" on which the linguistic satirist lets the rhetorician hoist himself.

This self-revenging satire is a tactical necessity for most of the novels. There is often no other means of deflation. Blotton tells Pickwick off, and the next year, in *Nicholas Nickleby*, the parliamentary bluster of Gregsbury is impeached by a special deputation, headed by a spokesman who might have been chosen on the basis of his name alone—a pugnacious critic of style when unmet by performance named Mr. Pugstyles (*N.N.*, 16). By no means does this usually happen. Too often, showy or hectoring speech goes unchecked within the novels—unchallenged, that is, by the characters it is designed to dazzle or intimidate. The task is left to the narrator, who must incorporate the attack in the absurdity of the rhetorical showpieces themselves. It may be fair to say that our greatest comic writer is never funnier than in his fantastic impersonations of Pecksniff, Chadband, and Micawber; it may also be fair to hope that Dickens's rhetorical satires will not defy analysis here, for this rich field of humor is itself rigorously dissective.

I will begin with a wonderful interlude in *Dombey and Son* which, after our laughter, also gauges for us the sad falling off since *Pickwick* for the well-intentioned man of words. It is a passage of fine enough comedy to quote whole, drawn finely and stretched to its limit. It gives us Toots, one of the great daydreaming romantics in Dickens, greeting hopelessly his beloved Florence:

'How dy'e do, Miss Dombey?' said Mr. Toots. 'I'm very well, I thank you; how are you?'
Mr. Toots—than whom there were few better fellows in the world, though there may have been one or two brighter spirits—had laboriously invented this long burst of discourse with the view of relieving the feelings both of Florence and himself. But finding that he had run through his

property, as it were, in an injudicious manner, by squandering the whole before taking a chair, or before Florence had uttered a word, or before he had well got in at the door, he deemed it advisable to begin again.

'How dy'e do, Miss Dombey?' said Mr. Toots. 'I'm very well, I thank you; how are you?' (D.S.,18)

The idea of relief through verbal inventiveness is here facetiously overturned, and between the two appearances of Toot's repeated salutation Dickens stuffs his own laboriously high phrases—themselves, by their bulk and mass, an ironic coming true of that single sarcasm "this long burst of discourse."

These are the discrepant techniques of *Pickwick's* linguistic satire, but without the focal presence of that book's masterly technician of such witty juxtaposings. In the absence of Sam Weller, with his free and briskly portable language, there is instead in Toot's case only the impoverished "commodity" theory of language discussed also in connection with Emerson and *Pickwick Papers*,[1] where words are something fixed, immobile, a "property" that can be "squandered." Comedy in this passage from *Dombey and Son* cannot cover for the unfortunate truth that words and phrases no longer obey the good men in Dickens with anything like their former readiness for Sam or Dick Swiveller. In the novel before *Dombey*, Mark Tapley fans what is left of the Weller spark, contending always against the rush, swell, and bellow of Pecksniff's rhetoric. With the opposition of these two characters in *Martin Chuzzlewit* I will begin this selected survey of Dickens's naughty company, contrasting Pecksniff's windy nonsense with the spirit of the "Glorious Apollers" still surviving in Mark. From there to Chadband in *Bleak House* and his oratorical assaults on the speechless Jo, at their best a criminal negligence of communication. And then back to that central contrast of competitive stylists in *David Copperfield*, the title figure's vocational "Apollo" against the professed rhetorician Micawber: a linguistic contest that puts the issue of verbal manipulation into sharpest relief.

Mr. Richard Swiveller has led us, inconspicuously, to a point of no return in Dickens, beyond which the themes of imagination have never been fully mapped out in criticism. For one of the most spottily charted developments in Dickens's novels is the resolute phasing out of volubility from the manner of his heroes. Verbal wit is never for long denied to the narrative voice in the novels, of course, but after Dick Swiveller, with only a brief resurgence for Mark Tapley, and then very much later for Jenny Wren, the characters must increasingly do without. What they retreat to in the face of such deprivation is to be the subject of the next chapter, and what becomes of verbal expression itself will now be watched for in the false rhetoricians who have beaten their own retreats into deceptive labyrinths of words, a numerous company descending not from Sam Weller or even Alfred Jingle, but from Mr. Pickwick himself.

Seth Pecksniff is probably the most frantic of these men of words who talk themselves into themselves, who fashion a personality by forging (in both senses) a persona. Nor are they merely hypocrites, for no one is more completely their dupe than they themselves. Pecksniff is the completest examplar in Dickens of rhetoric's snares for the unwary, the deceptions that make style not art but (in the worst sense) craft. On narrow inspection, he appears to rank among the progeny of the Pickwickian style. Yet it could be argued that, in contrast to Dickens's first hero, Pecksniff is endowed with as much imagination as anyone in the entire canon, gifted with a riot of verbal invention and resourcefulness. No Sam Weller, he is every bit as intense. He is always *on*, always alive with words. Where and how completely his raging, inexhaustible imagination has gone wrong is worth some time to sort out.

After the blustering absurdities of *Chuzzlewit*'s opening (to which I will later return), we encounter in the second chapter the "bluster" of the evening wind grumbling across the landscape and bullying the bellows of the forge, the wind deliberately personified as an "impotent swaggerer" like the famous gentleman, Mr. Seth Pecksniff, whom it soon knocks to the ground. Northrop Frye has discussed the allegory of names in Dickens as a debt, shared by humors comedy, to the morality play.[2] Dickens may be the greatest master of such naming in our literature, and no one has given enough attention to the many-faceted rightness of a name like Pecksniff, which has been taken up by modern dictionaries, in adjectival form, to mean sanctimonious or unctuously hypocritical. With its appropriate falling off from the similar beat of "Pickwick," the name "Pecksniff" rings so immediately true— somehow so petty, so trifling, so sniffy—that its connotations are not pinned down by commentators. Yet with Pecksniff tossed off his feet, the time is right to notice the latency in his name of the colloquial verb "peck" (itself an altered form of "pick"), current in Dickens's day to mean "stumble." That the verb is used especially of a horse is less troubling than it might seem, in view of the well-known passage at the start of the fifth chapter in which

Pecksniff's horse is seen by the worthy man's enemies to bear "a fanciful resemblance to his master." Pecksniff is forever stumbling or being overturned. Given his sham of righteous composure, such spills are indeed "unfortunate falls," and when he arrives for the final exposure scene it is only fitting, on his way up the stairs, that he should have "stumbled twice or thrice" (52). Very soon after this, old Martin "rose up, and struck him down upon the ground," and when Marcus calls this last collapse "a kind of moral prat-fall,"[3] the accusation is really retroactive—as an understanding of all the hypocrite's *pecking* throughout. Even his final departure, after his last "sublime address" in the novel, "was very much impaired by his being immediately afterwards run against and nearly knocked down" (52) by Poll Sweedlepipes.

But this is not all we can discover about the application of Pecksniff's name. Its second syllable is illuminated by his inaugural scene in the novel, just after the wind has "slammed the door against Mr. Pecksniff who was at that moment entering, with such violence, that in the twinkling of an eye he lay on his back at the bottom of the steps" (2). There he remains for awhile without any effort to stand up, until finally he "raised himself on one elbow, and sneezed." And even by his sneeze he is at once recognized: "'That voice!' cried Miss Pecksniff. 'My parent!'" It is as if the sniffing nasality present in his surname has now exploded in a violent, involuntary exhalation, and is at once mistaken for utterance. Something of the same comedy returns in the next novel, *Dombey and Son*, for the satire of Mrs. Chick, whose coughs are described as "monosyllabic" attempts at articulation (*D.S.*, 29). A great admirer of Mr. Dombey's stolid, chilling rhetoric, Mrs. Chick exhibits in her own verbal affectations the danger of oratorical poses as they intrude upon the personal life, upon private communication. When we find her, during a discussion with her husband, in "a state of soliloquy" (29), the odd locution invites us to recall the earlier mention of her voice as "synonymous with her presence of mind" (18). Soliloquy equals mentality: talk is the only "state of mind" the rhetorical imagination has left room for, and the same was implied about Pecksniff. It is not without interest that in this first novel after Pecksniff we get the only laudatory nod at an "orator" in all Dickens's thousands of pages, a creature blessed with no human speech at all: "Diogenes the man did not speak plainer to Alexander the Great than Diogenes the dog spoke to Florence" (18). For some "characters" at least, the language of the heart is not a foreign tongue.

One of the most deflationary critiques of Pecksniff's style, of course, comes—with the sneeze—before we have even heard the huffing bravado of his rhetoric. And just as his voice is no more than a reverse sniff, so Pecksniff is no more than his voice. This criticism is hinted by a sort of choric parallelism as the Pecksniff girls help their father retrieve his footing; the younger cries "He's come to himself!" and her elder sister adds the equivalent phrase: "He speaks again!" (2). Finding his voice he has, by definition, found himself. Not only is his identity verbal, but his virtues also are spoken virtues, his "morality" residing largely in "conversation and correspondence" (2). Here the aphorism "style is the man" has gone beyond the implications of *Pickwick Papers* to its ultimate parody. It has become, in *Martin Chuzzlewit*, a bizarre "anatomy" of morality. Pecksniff is all talk, and all of him talks. "His very throat was moral . . . It seemed to say, on the part of Mr. Pecksniff, 'There is no deception, all is peace, a holy calm pervades me.' So did his hair . . . his person . . . his plain black suit, and state of widower, and dangling double eye-glass," each of which, in a miracle of deceit, "cried aloud, 'Behold the moral Pecksniff' " (2).

When one of the Pecksniff girls brusquely objects to her father's use of his advertising slogan, Pecksniff calls her in reply a "Playful —playful warbler," and Dickens explains, as we have every reason to believe from her curt reply, that she is "not at all vocal, but that Mr. Pecksniff was in the frequent habit of using any word that occurred to him as having a good sound, and rounding out a sentence well, without much care for its meaning" (2). Once again, escapist rhetoric has become a self-incrimination. In dodging his daughter's charge of meaningless rambling by praising her "vocal" nature, Pecksniff has in fact confirmed his own meaningless vocality. It is he who "warbles" rather than speaks, who makes not meaning but melodious gestures. As distinct from content, "a strong trustfulness in sounds and forms was the master-key to Mr. Pecksniff's character" (2). A hypocrite is defined as one who does not mean what he says; Pecksniff carries this degradation of language one step further by not bothering to make what he says mean anything. He finds the perfect audience later at the dedication ceremony for the grammar school young Martin has designed but Pecksniff is taking credit for, simply by *calling* it his; this merely underlines the irony of his declaration to the crowd: "My duty is to build, not speak; to act, not talk; to deal with marble, stone, and brick; not language" (35). His auditors deserve whatever meaningless chatter they get, for they have just listened to the

inscription read "in Latin (not in English; that would never do)."
Not a word is understood, yet it "gave great satisfaction; especially
every time there was a good long substantive in the third declen-
sion, ablative case, with an adjective to match; at which periods
the assembly became very tender, and were much affected." Alien
or otherwise, intelligible or not, rhetoric itself is again the subject,
as the pun on "periods" helps remind us. Pecksniff is soon to tell
the crowd that he, too, is "very much affected," and in Fielding's
sense what is taking place is indeed "affectation." On the large
scale as well as the small, meaning has found itself replaced by
preening "forms," substance by the "sounds" of weighty substan-
tives. The audience that enjoys this Fieldingesque "vanity" is just
the audience to idolize Pecksniff, that parody of a poet with a false
artist's faith in the mere shapes of speech, its outlines and intona-
tions—again its "sounds and forms"—without interest in routine
coherences.

Yet with all this talk about style as style, it still seems to me
that Chesterton gives too little weight to the moral implications
of Pecksniff's rhetoric. In his first book on Dickens, he contrasts
the treatment of Bounderby in *Hard Times* with Pecksniff in one
of his characteristic antitheses: "Dickens exaggerates Bounderby
because he really hates him. He exaggerated Pecksniff because he
really loved him."[4] Five years later Chesterton still cannot "take
Mr. Pecksniff's hypocrisy seriously. He does not seem to me so
much a hypocrite as a rhetorician."[5] Serjeant Buzfuz in *Pickwick
Papers* comes to Chesterton's mind as a prototype,[6] yet he is an
attorney who wheels his rhetoric around in the immediate interest
of others. He lies for his clients, but Pecksniff is his own and only
counsel, and his rhetoric is wholly self-interested. It is not true
that Dickens "exaggerated Pecksniff because he really loved him."
What Dickens loves is the exaggeration itself. For him it is high
comedy and outlandish verbal satire, while for Pecksniff it is a
proficient fog for clouding over even the haziest outline of a moral
issue. As if to stress hypocrisy over rhetorical intoxication, Dickens
often shows us moments when the want of a word seems in the
best interests of Pecksniff's persona, with the hypocrite appearing in
a Brass-like pose of linguistic humility and verbal trepidation: "My
dear Mr. Chuzzlewit . . . for such a man as you have shown yourself to be this day; for a man so injured yet so humane; for a man
so—I am at a loss what precise term to use—yet at the same time
so remarkably—I don't know how to express my meaning . . ."
(10). Even the flourishes of his own natural idiom can be choked

back when there is something to be gained; rhetorical extravagance is only one of his tools. Perhaps an even more glaring stigma of the hypocrite, as distinct from the pure rhetorician, attaches to Pecksniff when he shows himself willing to deny that his conniving words are in fact his own. When making drunken advances to Mrs. Todgers, he pretends that the earnest wishes of his deceased wife are prompting him, and when the widow tries to silence his nonsense with a defensive "Hush!" Pecksniff insists: "It's not me . . . Don't think it's me: it's the voice; it's her voice" (9). No true rhetorician would so humbly disavow his powers.

George Eliot wrote in *Middlemarch* that "all of us . . . get our thoughts entangled in metaphors,"[7] and she meant large evasive fictions like Casaubon's, like Rosamond Vincy's "romance"—escape artistry like the pastoral delusions of Mrs. Skewton or Mrs. Merdle, the amorous fantasies of Mrs. Nickleby or Flora Finching. Pecksniff gets entangled in metaphors in a less comprehensive sense, caught up repeatedly in the threads of his own florid discourse. At one point he cannot find the phrase he wishes to play off against "the promptings of nature," and admits to being "at a loss for a word." What he wants is the "name of those fabulous animals (pagan, I regret to say) who used to sing in the water," and after gratefully entertaining the suggestions "swans" and "oysters" from the members of his audience, the intended "Sirens" at last come to mind, and Pecksniff is able to phrase his unacknowledged self-accusation about "the siren-like delusions of art" (4). The naughty company always consorting with the better elements of language is forever tricking him, and tripping him up. Dickens, in his own voice, travesties this major liability of language, as well as the apologetic verbal temper, when he says about Mary Graham's efforts to free herself from Pecksniff's hold that she was caught in "the embrace of an affectionate boa-constrictor: if anything so wily may be brought into comparison with Pecksniff" (30). Indeed no one knows better than Dickens that it can, for Pecksniff has several times been referred to as a "serpent," and at one point the flailing irrelevance of his own metaphors corners Pecksniff and forces him to deny what, but for his own language, he never would have been "brought into comparison with" in the first place: "But I am not a Serpent, sir, myself, I grieve to say, and no excuse or hope is left me" (31). The self-libelant metaphor of the hypocrite's own rhetoric has once more done the satirist's work.

For a faltering moment there, Pecksniff's own impossible language seems to be taking itself out on him, and indeed it is

Dickens's plan in the novel to administer the ultimate retributions against Pecksniff in deliberate verbal affronts: the revenge of the rhetorical imagination. Often it is an abasement to which Pecksniff is impervious. In their last scene together, old Martin explains how he had attempted long ago to humiliate Pecksniff "syllable by syllable" (52) with a number of vile proposals. Then Pecksniff could not be shamed, but he is finally ruffled by the words "Scoundrel," "Hangdog," and "Ghoul" applied to him by old Martin, whose "fertility in finding names for Mr. Pecksniff was astonishing." The effect of this unmasking seems to be almost magically destructive, the hypocritical spell violently broken, the hoax of rhetoric exposed. Pecksniff's figure has shrunk, and even his "clothes seemed to have grown shabbier, his linen to have turned yellow, his hair to have become lank and frowsy; his very boots looked villainous and dim, as if their gloss had departed with his own" (52). This is what has become of the hypocrite whose whole person, all of his attire in fact, had once rhetorically proclaimed: "Behold the moral Pecksniff!"

There has, of course, been an even more devastating exposure earlier, with a still more symbolically pointed aftermath, rendered in terms of garments other than Pecksniff's own. I refer to Tom Pinch's discovery of his master's villainy. As much as the device of sentimental apostrophe is to be lamented in Dickens's addresses to Tom, its counterpart in the treatment of Pecksniff is most revealing. Pecksniff also uses—and abuses—apostrophe, able to produce on call a parody of virtue's effusions: "'Oh Mammon, Mammon!' cried Mr. Pecksniff, smiting his forehead" (4). Instead of "smiting," he might as well simply point at himself. As a touchstone of sincerity, apostrophe is, like all rhetoric, unreliable. When Martin pleads his case before his grandfather, we find Mr. Pecksniff "assuming the position of the Chorus in a Greek Tragedy" and again taking wings on moralistic apostrophe: "'Beautiful Truth!' exclaimed the Chorus, looking upward. 'How is your name profaned by vicious persons!'" (43). The content of this invocation is, as so often in Dickens's treatment, a stark self-indictment of Pecksniff's own profaning hypocrisy, and the form of the address is ironic too: the apostrophizing impulse which should be reserved for sincere outburst. The irony becomes retributive when Pecksniff is in fact punished by that same form of apostrophe he has so often defiled, a reprisal by language alone. Just as old Martin had attempted to insult Pecksniff "syllable by syllable," so Mary now reveals the truth about him to Tom "word by word and phrase by phrase" (31). The shattering of Tom's illusions is an agony both for him and for the eavesdropping hypocrite. Tom calls out in his grief, without knowing that he is actually speaking to his old master, "Oh Pecksniff, Pecksniff, there is nothing I would not have given to have you deserve my old opinion of you." There is nothing Pecksniff himself would not give to regain that old comfortable idolatry, but he is forced instead to listen as Tom "delivered this apostrophe"—unknown to Tom, a damningly direct address.

For the first time in the novel, since he cannot possibly reveal himself, Pecksniff is allowed no relief of his own in words or phrases, and this frustration seems to turn him inward upon unexpected discomfiture. Tom leaves the church soon, and Pecksniff watches him in the yard leaning now and then against a gravestone, "as if he were a mourner who had lost a friend." So he is. The next paragraph, in effect, portrays the death of Pecksniff in a shattering allegory:

He was in a curious frame of mind, Mr. Pecksniff: being in no hurry to go, but rather inclining to a dilatory trifling with the time, which prompted him to open the vestry cupboard, and look at himself in the parson's little glass that hung within the door. Seeing that his hair was rumpled, he took the liberty of borrowing the canonical brush and arranging it. He also took the liberty of opening another cupboard; but he shut it up again quickly, being rather startled by the sight of a black and a white surplice dangling against the wall, which had very much the appearance of two curates who had committed suicide by hanging themselves. Remembering that he had seen in the first cupboard a port-wine bottle and some biscuits, he peeped into it again, and helped himself with much deliberation: cogitating all the time though, in a deep and weighty manner, as if his thoughts were otherwise employed. (31)

To expatiate on symbolic economy of this order is almost an insult, "a dilatory trifling with the time," yet the risk of paraphrase must be run in order to suggest the hidden implications of the scene. Besides the desecration implied by Pecksniff eating bread and wine in the vestry, it is important to note, after the lacerations just inflicted on his proud sense of identity, that vestments not his own are now projecting Pecksniff's destruction. In the cupboard with the mirror he sees himself; in the other—the parallel is irresistible —he sees himself again in a white and black corpse, a whitewashed and artificial self sustained by hypocritical language, the collapse of which also destroys the black alter-ego, the speechless and unspeakable counter-self. The death of the two selves must be reciprocal, for Pecksniff is literally nothing if not what he seems.

Pecksniff's flights of fancy are wholly verbal, superficial, obsessive, his depths unknowable. This brings us to another hidden significance in his name. When Dickens parodically asks at one point, "What saith Mr. Pecksniff in reply?" (9), he is deploying the same sort of ennobling archaism, like "thy" and "thou" and "doth," that he sincerely (if regrettably) expends in descriptions of Tom Pinch. There is at once a revision: "Or rather let the question be, What leaves he unsaid?" Predictably, the answer is "Nothing." Pecksniff is a man convulsed with talk, his persona a compulsive stream of rhetoric which thickens about him like a private atmosphere, shielding him from observation. His words work upon each other with their own unaccountable friction, grinding to unexpected halts or heaving each other forward with ludicrous new momentum. The office of language for Pecksniff is to create a closed and autonomous world, like poetry's except self-serving and in any final sense unimaginative, a world whose absurd laws Pecksniff will blandly obey. As a self-centered hypocrite, he is the First and Final Cause of his verbal universe, and his very name is a phonetic transcription of "saith Pecksniff," conferring not just designation but existence itself upon the man. For "Seth Pecksniff" is not just a name, it is the most characteristic sentence that can be fashioned for him, and finally the only thing that can truly be said about Pecksniff: he saith.

I have suggested that no one in *Martin Chuzzlewit*, even when Pecksniff's hypocrisy is widely denounced, directly attacks the rhetorical medium itself through which he moves. There is, however, a character who gradually insinuates a set of opposite linguistic values, a man of self-reliant "philosophy" (48) like Sam Weller whose "fertile imagination" (48) shows up by contrast the elaborate but sterile inventiveness of Pecksniff. This man is Mark Tapley, who redeems the private pleasures of style from Pecksniff's abuse the way Sam did from Jingle's. Mr. Bevan's point is well taken when he says of the American nation that "no satirist could breathe this air" (16), and yet here, from the next chapter, is Mark's peculiarly Dickensian (or Wellerian) linguistic turn on the subject of American freedom: "They've such a passion for Liberty, that they can't help taking liberties with her" (17). At home, too, his confidence in satiric language reminds us of Mr. Weller: "It's not in the natur of Pecksniff to shame *us*, unless he agreed with us, or done us a service, and, in case he offered any outdacity of that description, we could express our sentiments in the English language, I hope" (43). As Sam's did for *Pickwick Papers*, Mark's fidelity to honest and vital language helps to focus many of the linguistic festivities of *Martin Chuzzlewit*, a novel of particular moment in the development of Dickens's style. "For the first time," writes Steven Marcus, "Dickens's narrative style becomes consciously mannered ... The sentences of *Martin Chuzzlewit* are long and involved, their syntax strenuous, their punctuation adventurous and peremptory."[8] As he has noticed more recently about *Pickwick*, "style itself is one of its subjects."[9] In addition to a vain and hypocritical rhetorician like Mr. Seth Pecksniff, *Martin Chuzzlewit* also brings before us the deviltry and deception of words in themselves—their self-satisfaction, their waywardness, their thwarting of communication through specialized idiom, obfuscating metaphor, partisan and combative vocabularies of every sort. *Chuzzlewit* might be called Dickens's most fully articulated novel-of-manners-of-speaking; self-conscious verbal analysis, dating back to the parodic styles of *Sketches by Boz* and *Pickwick Papers*, comes forward in such linguistic signals as "in the metaphorical sense of that expression" and "in the figurative language of the day" (4), not to mention an allusion later to Pecksniff's own style when the narrator decides to "adopt that worthy man's phraseology" (8).

The dissection of false style in *Martin Chuzzlewit*, apart from the portrait of Pecksniff, is located most unsparingly in the American chapters, where "vulgarity" of language, either coarseness or crass elevation, has returned to its root identification with the indiscriminacy of the mob. All of Martin's troubles in England stem from a series of arguments with his grandfather in which "words engendered words, as they always do" (6); yet the land to which he has fled represents a monstrous institutionalization of this dangerous tendency for language to beget itself in ever more thoughtless offshoots. Mark Tapley again takes up the Dickensian satire as he blasts the "gammon" rhetoric and "bragging speeches" (23) of this pretentious Eden, where language really has become profane. At a display of the orator Pogram's "genius," an anonymous bystander says to Martin "that he guessed he had now seen something of the eloquential aspect of our country, and was chawed up pritty small" (34). In America, language is not just naughty, it seems almost devouring, a loud, unalleviated assault on the imagination implied in the Transcendentalist motto: "Howls the sublime ... in the whispering chambers of Imagination" (34). Martin has sought refuge from a place where "words engendered words," but he has only been further mired in a world where Pogram and the three literary ladies, out of their rhetorical depths and nearly drowning in an inundation of humbug, "splashed up words in all directions; and floundered about famously" (34). This parodic enlargement upon the commonplace metaphor "flow of words" as a churning torrent of language helps us to see in that earlier description from Putnam Smif's letter of the great national river, "our mighty Mississippi (or Father of Waters)," the perfect emblem for the swollen American rhetoric—where the mythic stream endlessly "rolls its turbid flood" (22). As if in an ultimate pretense of mastery over the principles of what they would call Classical "o-ration," with all the sublime assurance and sway over words which this implies, the Americans have named a Negro slave Cicero (17). But the pretense is no good, for it is they who are slaves to their rhetoric and to its imprisoning limitations.

Besides the American interlude, there is in *Martin Chuzzlewit* another extended satire on the windy bewilderment of rhetoric. This is the novel's opening chapter, as much a treatment of humbug prose as was the start of *Pickwick*, and once again an unrestrained parody that has received mixed reviews. Only Steven Marcus has noted how the immediate "point" of this satiric genealogy, "that the historic past is both misleading and incommunicable," connects with the larger themes of language in the novel, since it "makes that point by demonstrating through a labyrinth of double-entendres, non sequiturs, and puns that language is itself essentially deceitful."[10] But perhaps the salient deceit Marcus does not mention. It is no piece of flamboyant trickery, but instead a quiet fraud that has crept into the actual syntactic plan of the episode. I am speaking of the passive transformations that structure this genealogy, the wily formulas by which the Chuzzlewits are made to subserve the prose intended to extol them. The incidence of impersonal passives in six pages is absurd, as we wade through such lifeless phrasings (to cite only a few) as "should ever be urged," "may be laid down," "is further recorded," "is strengthened if not absolutely confirmed by," "may safely be asserted," and such nested atrocities as "will be observed that no emendation whatever is necessary to be made" or "was supposed to have been communicated." The historical comings and goings of the family are grammatically subsumed by a syntactic logic that directs our attention not to the actual contours of the history, but to the act of recording and confirming and submitting to it as presented. Through this uncompromising use of the passive voice, action is cast out by an indirection which finds nothing out in return, and which keeps us from finding out. The impersonal passive, for all its high-sounding conclusiveness, seems to erase the idea of agency altogether, and thus of responsibility. The language numbs us out of attention and thus disables us for getting at the truth. It is syntax facilitating lie, and a use of language as a tool for hypocritical rhetoricians which is one of the constant themes of *Martin Chuzzlewit.*

This brief survey of linguistic self-reference and stylistic guile in the narrative prose of *Martin Chuzzlewit* took off from our discussion of Mark Tapley's language, and to this champion of earnest and witty expression it naturally returns, for the passive grammar of the first chapter, as a symptom of rhetorical disingenuousness and tactical opacity, finds direct contrast in the vitality and candor of Mark's speech. In fact, Mark thinks of himself as a verb, an *active* verb, offering this definition of his nature: "... a Werb is a word as signifies to be, to do, or to suffer (which is all the grammar, and enough too, as ever I wos taught); and if there's a Werb alive, I'm it. For I'm always a-bein', sometimes a-doin', and continually a-sufferin' " (48). I have already suggested that Mark is the Weller archetype in its last viable manifestation, and there seems to me no clearer indication that Dickens had the Pickwickian ethos in mind—with its parodistic high style—than a direct echo in *Chuzzlewit* of Dickens's first novel. In the second chapter of *Pickwick* there is that encounter where the cabman gives Pickwick the ridiculous misinformation that his horse is forty-two years old, and where Mr. Pickwick enters "every word of this statement in his note-book, with the view of communicating it to the club, as a singular instance of the tenacity of life in horses." Pickwick has not yet met up with his satiric "sidekick," and without Sam Weller he is defenseless in such a case. The prose with which Dickens records what Pickwick records about this singular horse is among other things, as we saw in the first chapter, a parody of Victorian journalese—a style which Sam Weller, once arrived, will be at any moment likely to mock, and which Mark Tapley himself, in almost exactly the same words as Pickwick used, explicitly satirizes as newspaper English in discussing Mr. Pecksniff's horse: "That's a description of animal, sir, as will go on in a bony way peculiar to himself for a long time, and get into the newspapers at last under the title of 'Singular Tenacity of Life in a Quadruped' " (43).

Mr. Pickwick's brand of rhetoric, however silly, was never malign, and the verbal imagination of his "man" was a thing of marvelous vigor and resilience. *Martin Chuzzlewit* witnesses a sad decline when the rhetorical hypocrite Pecksniff plays master to Tom Pinch's man of imagination, and the carrying over of the master and man configuration into the relation of Martin and Mark becomes especially important. Part of the deep psychological bondage of the American people is to live in an unnatural horror of the word "Master." For the author of *Pickwick Papers*, however, the word will always connote first, not slavery, but a liberating reciprocity and devotion between gentleman and his gentleman. Such reciprocity is finally understood by Martin when he says to his own "man": "You are the best master in the world, Mark" (35), a judgment which Mr. Pickwick might well have made about Sam Weller, who taught his master the world the way Mark teaches Martin.

In *Martin Chuzzlewit* the lesson comes partly through fever, in a reworking of Dick Swiveller's trial two novels before. Mark's is only one among no fewer than five fevers in *Chuzzlewit*, and the one that afflicts Chuffey seems to result, unlike Mark's, from a kind of imaginative inadequacy. A barely human fixture of the Chuzzlewit office, Chuffey has been the chief victim of its mechanical routine; as Jonas explains it, "he's been addling his old brains with figures and book-keeping all his life; and twenty years ago or so he went and took a fever." Imagination has here taken one of its retributive turns, with the menial calculations of his daily routine avenging themselves in a feverish, astronomical ledger: "All the time he was out of his head (which was three weeks) he never left off casting up; and he got to so many million at last that I don't believe he's ever been quite right since" (11). When we first meet Chuffey, he is "looking at nothing with eyes that saw nothing, and a face that meant nothing. Take him in that state, and he was an embodiment of nothing. Nothing else" (11). Fever has driven him to the brink of extinction, and no influence has ever quite carried him back. In this novel of assertive and vicious selfhood, Chuffey is the embodiment of anti-self. He pushes selflessness to the point of non-being and is teased into sentience only by his devotion to Anthony Chuzzlewit, who is master to Chuffey's man in a further version of the relationship between Martin and Mark. Wishing to offer a lifeless manikin as a fair analogy for Mr. Chuffey, Pecksniff at one point gets tripped up not in his own metaphors this time but in his search for the very word "metaphorically"; he doesn't quite find it: "I believe that our dear friend Mr. Chuffey is, metaphysically speaking, a— shall I say dummy?" (18). But this malapropism seems once again appropriate, for Chuffey's marginal existence appears to be a comment on the metaphysical limits of selfhood.

In contrast to the fevers that also attack Jonas Chuzzlewit and the mysterious Lewsome, as if for their shared guilt, Mark's trial in Eden is merely a proving, not a punishment. Lewsome's vagrant imaginings during his crisis are worse than any "wanderings of Cain" and are charted again, as in the case of Dick Swiveller's fever, with a grim participial syntax; they serve mainly as an isolated study in diseased fancy that takes up the as yet undramatized threat of "fever and ague" (32) in Mark's and Martin's American subplot: "Oh, haggard mind, groping darkly through the past; incapable of detaching itself from the miserable present; dragging its heavy chain of care through imaginary feasts and revels, and scenes of awful pomp; seeking but a moment's rest among the long-forgotten haunts of childhood, and the resorts of yesterday; and dimly finding fear and horror everywhere" (25). Memory cannot reclaim the "haunts" of the past, yet the loaded word itself seems ironically to press upon the sentence the weight of "fear and horror"—the awesome "pomp" become "awful"—that everywhere haunts his consciousness. Also, the transference of the adjective "haggard" from Lewsome's wasted body to his gaunt "mind" is typical of that psychic emphasis—all the more appropriate when strained—which Dickens always gives to such descriptions.

It is long after Lewsome's fever has run its course that we return to Martin's travail in "Eden." Mark exhausts himself in tending Martin, and the man falls ill himself just as the master recovers, a pattern to be reversed in the exchanged fevers of Charley and Esther in *Bleak House*. "And now it was Martin's turn to work, and sit beside the bed and watch, and listen through the long, long nights, to every sound in the gloomy wilderness; and hear poor Mark Tapley, in his wandering fancy. . ." (33). What he hears is Mark's dislodged imagination grasping at memories and old pleasures in the turmoil of his brain, and the psychology of participial syntax is here uniquely revealing. We remember from the last chapter that Mark associates himself with the grammar of the verb, specifically the present active participles "a-bein'," "a-doin'," and "a-sufferin'." This is the grammar Dickens, too, has deliberately associated with him on his way to America, where his unflagging activity on board ship is given to us in two long sentences boasting fourteen substantial participial phrases, capped by "doing . . . compounding . . . helping" (15). During Martin's delirious illness, Mark forgives him for being "too passive" (33) in their previous adventures, and when Mark's fever strikes later on the same page, we find that his own restless activity is now jumbled and discordant. In the participial account of his "wandering fancy," Mark is "playing at skittles in the Dragon, making love-remonstrances to Mrs. Lupin, getting his sea-legs on board the Screw, travelling with old Tom Pinch on English roads, and burning stumps of trees in Eden, all at once" (33). At such high fever heat, "burning" is last but hardly least among these details.

As in all things, Mark is really Martin's master, and even Mark's fever seems to test Martin in a far more penetrating way than his own bout with nonexistence had done. Realizing that he might lose Mark, he comes to appreciate his spirit and to realize in turn his own selfish disregard for Mark in the past. Mark's fever is thus, in effect, an identity crisis *for Martin,* a shock of self-discovery which brings him to the verge of hallucinatory disturbance, as if feverish himself all over again, when the specter of "Self, Self, Self, dilated on the scene" (33). The threatened annihilation of self in fever brings it at last into perspective for Martin, while in Mark's case fever merely highlights the essential self—for even "in certain forlorn stages" of his disease, when too far gone to speak, "Mark had feebly written 'jolly!' on a slate" (33). Tried by speechlessness like Dick Swiveller, that other fast talker before him, Mark passes with flying colors.

Like his prototypes Sam Weller and Dick Swiveller, Mark Tapley becomes a kind of comic bard, a jovial and hardly ancient mariner back from his Atlantic crossing who entertains the wedding guests at the end of the novel "with short anecdotes of his travels, appropriate to the occasion" (53). And with his own marriage to Mrs. Lupin, Mark has tapped a latent significance in his last name. He gives this name not only to his wife in marriage, but to her popular taproom under the former sign of The Blue Dragon. This tavern is now the Jolly Tapley: "A sign of my own inwention, sir. Wery new, conwivial, and expressive!" (52). In this novel where language tends too often to retreat into moribund and deceptive forms that are the opposite of "expressive" and designed, not to be "conwivial," but to close off all communication, the consciousness of Mark Tapley is uniquely valuable. Words in *Martin Chuzzlewit* are the structural units out of which hypocritical or defensive personas are erected, and this drastic violation of language prophesies an ultimately mute humanity unable to express, even to itself, its "bein'," "doin'," and "sufferin'." Where words are

either fatuous or self-infatuated, where all talk is fraught with
alienating naughtiness, Mark Tapley—in his role as verbal satirist,
as well as in his role as "Werb," a linguistic sign or "mark"—stands
for the vitality that makes language move, and gladden, and yet
hold to the truth.

In *Ben Jonson and the Language of Prose Comedy*, Jonas Barish
alludes at only one place to Dickens: "It is always the 'two dimensional' characters—the Thwackums and Squares, the Miss Bateses
and Alfred Jingles—who pipe away in a strange mock realistic
falsetto, and always the more 'organic' figures, the Elizabeth Ben-
nets and David Copperfields, who speak in a relatively neutral,
flexible, and transparent style."[11] It is the whole point about the
"two dimensional" dramatis personae among Dickens's naughty
company that they are just personae, façades, that they have only
length and breadth and no depth, and that "transparency" in word
or thought would at once expose this. So the false rhetoricians become, in one sense, the most unremitting escape artists in Dickens,
discharging their words as defense mechanisms, spewing forth a
kind of linguistic flak so dense as to make language itself opaque
and impassable. Dickens's debt to the comparable satiric language
of Ben Jonson is, however, surprisingly underplayed in criticism.
In recent comprehensive studies, one on language and one on
satire, we hear from G. L. Brook merely that the name Melchise-
dech Howler in *Dombey and Son* owes something to the Jonsonian
habit of naming,[12] and from Sylvia Manning that there is a "certain
verbal expansion"[13] in common between Volpone and Pecksniff
but that "there is certainly no evidence that he [Dickens] saw himself as the inheritor of Jonsonian tradition, either comic or satiric."[14] As the title of Northrop Frye's important article on "Dickens
and the Comedy of Humors" at once implies, he sees the debt more
clearly, and what Barish calls "mock realism" Frye discusses as
"the rhetoric of the tagged humor" in such characters as "Chadband with his parsonical beggar's whine or Micawber with his
Parliamentary flourishes."[15] These are in fact the two major styles,
in this order, which lie ahead for discussion, as well as those Apollo-
like energies, even when only the narrator's, which offer either
a resistance or an alternative.

Along with Stiggins in *Pickwick Papers*, Frye calls Chadband
"the same type of greasy lout as their ancestor in Ben Jonson, Zeal-
of-the-Land Busy,"[16] and comparisons are therefore invited with
Barish's theory of prose comedy. " 'My friends,' says Mr. Chad-

band, 'Peace be on this house! On the master thereof, on the mistress thereof, on the young maidens, and on the young men! My
friends, why do I wish for peace? What is peace? Is it war? No. Is it
strife? No. Is it lovely, and gentle, and beautiful, and pleasant, and
serene, and joyful? O yes!'" (19). Certainly these sophistic redundancies gather to what Barish calls, in connection with Busy,
the "comic deformation of logic as a means of suggesting hypocrisy."[17] In a marathon sequence like "to wrestle, and to combat
and to struggle, and to conquer" (25), incremental rephrasing can
be strung out even more ludicrously, as if Chadband were reeling
off synonyms from a thesaurus entry. This habit, also shared by
Zeal-of-the-Land Busy, combines with the latter's "egregious fondness for the genitive phrase"[18] in Chadband's oration on
"Terewth," where the Reverend marches out a kind of literal
"double talk," with every noun used twice. The subject is the
"light of truth," and to Chadband it seems "the ray of rays, the
sun of suns, the moon of moons, the star of stars" (25). Not only
does Chadband double his words, he even tries to get extra rhetorical mileage out of his syllables. It is very likely that his
disyllabic "Terewth," his hypocritical effort to make more of less,
provided the inspiration for Philip Roth's satire of Rabbi Warshaw
in *Portnoy's Complaint:* "Mother, Rabbi Warshaw is a fat, pompous, impatient fraud, with an absolutely grotesque superiority
complex, a character out of Dickens is what he is . . . a man who
somewhere along the line got the idea that the basic unit of meaning in the English language is the syllable. So no word he pro-
nounces has less than three of them, not even the word God."[19]
It is also just as likely that Dickens got the idea of Chadband's
pronunciation from Fielding's own oratorical hypocrite, Parson
Trulliber, in whose rhetoric "call" was always stretched out to
"*caale.*"[20]

    In the pulpit Chadband meets with great success, and the gasping
response from the faithful "serves the purpose of *parliamentary
cheering,* and gets Mr. Chadband's steam up" (35; my italics). For
Dickens this could be no arbitrary comparison; the Reverend's
assumed piety is here defrocked, and he stands confessed as an
orator first and last, a self-enthralled verbal demagogue. The be-
witchment of his words does meet some minor resistance, however, and not everyone is enchanted by the mastodon rhetoric. Mr.
Snagsby's meek assessment is that Chadband "has a great deal of
eloquence at his command, undoubtedly, but I am not quite favor-
able to his style myself" (22). Snagsby's mild, tentative language,

which pulls back even from the indisputable with its repeated "not to put too fine a point on it," is the perfect contrast to the Chadband thunder, which bludgeons too much "point" into everything. But the most devastating critic of Chadband is Jo, who lives in mortal dread of his speeches. When Chadband first says "My young friend, stand forth!" Jo is disconcerted, and, "thus apostrophised," he is inspired with evident doubts about Chadband's "intentions" (19). Rightly so, for they are as unworthy as his words, and go no deeper. Out of the glib goodness of his heart, all Chadband sees fit to offer the destitute boy is talk—preachment, pedantry, apostrophe: "Will you come to-morrow, my young friend, and . . . upon the next day, and upon the day after that, and upon the day after that, and upon many pleasant days, to hear discourses?" (19). Jo is "gradually going out of his mind" with all this mutter, and its spurious solicitation is a terrible parody of true moral concern, a parody that makes its way with bold irony into Dickens's own apostrophes to Jo: "Do you hear, Jo? . . . The one grand recipe remains for you—the be-all and the end-all of your strange existence upon earth. Move on!" (19).

The title of this chapter is in fact "Moving On," and amid all of Chadband's claptrap there is a moment of voiceless but eloquent reticence from the quiet-spoken Snagsby that in its own way articulates the tragedy: "Mr. Snagsby says nothing to this effect [about moving on]; says nothing at all, indeed; but coughs his forlornest cough, expressive of no thoroughfare in any direction" (19). This is the trouble with language, with "discourse," in *Bleak House*: it does not open up intercourse between people, it is no medium for human communion, no thoroughfare, but an expressive dead end. Five novels later, when Veneering does a turn as Parliamentary orator in *Our Mutual Friend*, a similar image waits on his pointless words, as he continually "loses his way in the usual No Thoroughfares of speech" (*O.M.F.* II, 3). The impasse of language in *Bleak House* is dramatized as a lethal failure of society. That pillar of the community, the renowned orator Chadband, does not make addresses, he makes grotesque soliloquies, blinding the communal outcast Jo to any possible glimmer of the truth and thus barricading all thoroughfares to salvation. Jo has never been instructed in the silent language of prayer, and he has always confused it with the bogus oratory of the pulpit. He thinks prayer is what Chadband had once seemed to be talking at him while he was actually talking to himself: "Mr. Chadbands he wos a-prayin wunst at Mr. Snagsby's and I heerd him, but he sounded as if he wos a-speakin to hisself, and not to me. He prayed a lot, but *I* couldn't make out nothink on it" (47). Here is Jo, unawares, as perhaps the most astute critic of Dickens's false rhetoricians. He may confuse rhetoric with prayer, but he knows it is not communication. He recognizes it for what it is: a retreat into solipsism and soliloquy, the sublime howling in the whispering chambers of imagination.

It is time to notice that the image of a linguistic cul-de-sac is taken up in the first chapter of *Bleak House,* where, amid the countless blind alleys of Chancery's legal labyrinth, members and advocates are ceaselessly "running their goat-hair and horsehair heads against walls of words." One of the chief architects of these "walls of words" is Conversation Kenge, a famous solicitor who "listened to himself with obvious satisfaction, and sometimes gently beat time to his own music with his head, or rounded a sentence with his hand" (3). Esther Summerson's naiveté is the perfect satiric instrument: "I was very much impressed by him— even then, before I knew that he formed himself on the model of a great lord who was his client" (3). His eloquence is not even his own, a stolen rhetoric that becomes an accurate symbol of the muddle perpetuated in Chancery by the parasitic relation, even linguistically, of lawyer and client. The orator's trick of emphatic repetition is pushed by Kenge to vacuous lengths: "O really, Mr. Jarndyce! Prejudice, prejudice. My dear sir, this is a very great country, a very great country. Its system of equity is a very great system, a very great system. Really, really!" (62). When he repeats these sentiments at the end of the chapter, he is seen "gently moving his right hand as if it were a silver trowel, with which to spread the cement of his words on the structure of the system, and consolidate it for a thousand ages." Here is the "wall of words" metaphor implicitly reenacted, with Kenge as the expert in word masonry who will erect the impassable barrier of language out of his own trumped-up enthusiasm.

Behind the riot of feeling and flourish artificially manufactured by Kenge lurks the lawyer Vholes, his henchman and counter-self, who converses while "shading his mouth with his black glove" (62). Vholes is all stealth and cloaked expression to Kenge's storm of eloquence; they are thus two halves of the same hypocritical character, the persona and that "black" hidden self which we have already seen uncovered in a different way for Pecksniff. Vholes has no rhetorical face of his own, and in scene after scene he merely repeats Kenge's words, "as if his low inward voice were an echo" (65). Even Othello was more alert to Iago's repetitions than Kenge is to Vholes's: "By heaven, he echoes me / As if there were some monster in this thought / Too hideous to be shown" (III, iii). To enfold and protect his motivating "inward voice," Vholes at times finds himself in dire need of Kenge, "the benignant shadow of whose conversational presence he seemed afraid to leave" (65). When stripped of his public shell, that oratorical persona Conversation Kenge provides, Vholes is hideously "inward" and without surface, a devouring void like the "hole" hiding in his name. (The name of the morally empty Skimpole in this same novel, if heard as one of two possible phonetic compounds, betrays the same secret syllable.) When Vholes undresses he seems to flay himself raw, for he "takes off his close black gloves as if he were skinning his hands, lifts off his tight hat as if he were scalping himself" (39). He is the cannabalistic maw behind Kenge's rhetorical front, and the several hints of this reach their climax in the last we hear from Vholes in the novel, as he chases after the "conversational presence" of Kenge without which he is so completely exposed. It is an inarticulate monstrosity of a sound: "one gasp as if he had swallowed the last morsel of his client" (65). His client is the destitute Richard Carstone, and it is from him, the victim of Chancery who has beaten his own head against the "walls of words" until hemorrhage has made him speechless, that we get the most terrible image of inarticulateness in all of Dickens, thrust upon us with bitter simplicity. Richard was found sitting "in the corner of the Court . . . like a stone figure," and in a final effort of defiance "made as if he would have spoken in a fierce voice to the Judge. He was stopped by his mouth being full of blood, and Allan had brought him home" (65).

This is an extension of linguistic satire angrier than anything in *Pickwick Papers*, to be sure, but since all displays of language under study in the present chapter draw on Dickens's diagnosis of false rhetoric in that first novel, it is appropriate to leave *Bleak House* by way of a somewhat clearer descendent of Mr. Pickwick's, though again a more extreme case. When Bucket tells Sir Leicester Dedlock about the disappearance of his wife, the detective "soon detects an unusual slowness in his speech, with now and then a curious trouble in beginning, which occasions him to utter inarticulate sounds" (54). Sir Leicester is completely desolated by the loss of his lady, reduced nearly to the state where "all the living languages, and all the dead, are as one to him" (56), and the reason Dickens wants this linguistic periphrasis for death, this unusual stress on language at Sir Leicester's downfall, is made clear two paragraphs later. Dedlock has lived among rhetoric's naughty company, self-satisfied and pompous, delivering words with only the sound of meaning, and language now takes its revenge in manifest meaninglessness, garbled beyond the possibility of deception: "His voice was rich and mellow; and he had so long been thoroughly persuaded of the weight and import to mankind of any word he said, that his words really had come to sound as if there were something in them. But now he can only whisper; and what he whispers sounds like what it is—mere jumble and jargon" (56). Dedlock has paid the price for his lordly sanction of society's false speaking, which poisons human discourse at every level of the novel. After his ordeal his voice returns, and though the old rhetorical habits are still with him, his humbling experience, like Pickwick's far milder trial before him, has transformed his language from within and brought a chastened earnestness to the once hollow sounds. The following comment on Sir Leicester could well have been written about Pickwick's last speeches: "His formal array of words might have at any other time, as it has often had, something ludicrous in it; but at this time it is serious and affecting" (58).

What remains for discussion in this survey of indulgent, sometimes dangerously negligent loquacity is Mr. Micawber's novel, *David Copperfield*, a book that is also a novelist's (more importantly a stylist's) autobiography. It is a book deeply and variously concerned—one is tempted to say obsessed—with the ways and means of expression, the delights, the responsibilities, the allowable limits of style itself: a preoccupation that renders the prose of *David Copperfield*, as in no other Dickens novel, at times almost reticent. Verbal play on the narrator's part is rarely willful or assertive, and even quite unexceptionable metaphors are hedged, kept tentative by means of recurring apologetic asides like "as I may say" (20, 38), or "if I may call it so" (28, 42) or "if I may so express it" (33, 57). In this search for an authenticity of manner, both personal and stylistic, Dickens as overseeing narrator can go one step beyond his fancied earlier self in David, turning the minutest semantic notation into a searching pun as he has David say, with unwitting irony, that the name "Doady" given him by his childish Dora is "a corruption of David" (41). David Copperfield the Younger is feeling his way toward expressive self-reliance as he is groping toward emotional maturity and self-definition, and the two efforts are seen as complementary. There is a moment when he confesses to Agnes, with his typical cautiousness of phrase: "I get so miserable and worried, and am so unsteady and irresolute in my power of assuring myself, that I know I must want—shall I call it—reliance, of some kind?" Agnes is in no mood to mitigate: "Call it so, if you will" (39). There is an unabashed ethical inversion of this exchange earlier between Steerforth and Rosa Dartle, again eliding the verbal and the moral. Rosa is wondering about "people, who are like each other in their moral constitution—is that the phrase?" and Steerforth answers that "It's as good a phrase as another" (29). Nothing could be more foreign to David's earnestness of mind and style than Steerforth's verbal indifference and its underlying moral laxity. Dickens has indeed used the ethical implications of Steerforth's glibness against him with the first words he speaks in the novel, for on the occasion of David's initial punishment at school, Steerforth's condolence, phrased in a colloquial oxymoron, is meant to register a moral ambiguity—with David's new hero "pleased to express his opinion that it was 'a jolly shame' " (6).

There are other characters in the novel, though, who threaten a far more deleterious effect on David's style itself than Steerforth ever does, and it is ironic that, in retelling his favorite childhood stories to his friend, David develops a "simple earnest manner of narrating" (7) that is the artistic reverse of that pervasive lack of "earnestness" in Steerforth's charmingly facile manner. Following his story-telling with Steerforth in the line of his artistic growth, David later admits to concocting "astonishing fictions" about London in which he "fitted my old books to my altered life, and made stories for myself, out of the streets, and out of the men and women" (11). Here we recognize an autobiographical account, one of the fullest Dickens ever gives us, of the imagination's refuge, the first sheltered stirrings of creative fancy. And when we hear that such daydreaming is transferred to a more verbal escape artistry in David's first "fragments of English versification" (26), we realize that even by such poetic juvenilia we are being called upon to compare the other "author" figures in the novel. With Mr. Dick and his abortive Memorial, there is even an autobiographer such as David will become. There is Dr. Strong and his dictionary, into which Mr. Dick finally directs his authorial energies. When David was a child, the Doctor's "looking out for Greek roots" was "supposed to be a botanical furor" (16), but David has succumbed to the poetical "furor" and become the artist of words who can manufacture just this sort of double pun. The Old Soldier's praise of the dictionary is hardly without relevance for David's craft:

"What a useful work a Dictionary is! What a necessary work! The meanings of words! Without Doctor Johnson, or somebody of that sort, we might at this present moment be calling an Italian-iron a bedstead" (45). In addition to the lexicographers, there is Traddles as an assistant author of an encyclopedia, the exact opposite of David on the score of imagination: "I am not a bad compiler, Copperfield . . . but I have no invention at all; not a particle. I suppose there never was a young man with less originality than I have" (27). And there is Miss Mills and her prose-poetic journal, an insincere tribute to her "wonderful flow of words" (38). David learns to distrust her "romantic style" as mere show, suspecting that under pretense of extravagant sympathy she actually took a "dreadful luxury" in his and Dora's plight. David is always embarrassed when he finds himself carrying on, like Julia Mills, in "a rhapsodical style" (36), and yet he seems naturally to fall into this artificial mode when communicating with her. For David as an apprentice stylist, this "dreadful luxury" of her prose is itself her greatest danger.

Yet there is a still more powerful enemy, as we find from the close of this letter sent by David to Miss Mills: "I informed her that my reason was tottering on its throne, and only she, Miss Mills, could prevent its being deposed. I signed myself, hers distractedly; and I couldn't help feeling, while I read this composition over, before sending it by a porter, that it was something in the style of Mr. Micawber" (38). Here we come to the most important of David's author-counterparts in the novel, and with "the style of Mr. Micawber" we must now come to terms. In *Hard Times* Bounderby is accused by the narrator of having "a moral infection of claptrap in him" (*H.T.* I, 7), by which his humbug boasting contaminates those around him into likewise reciting his praises. More generally, it is a useful phrase for rhetorical style that is "infectious" in the worst sense. Miss Mills languishes in the shabby poetry of romantic anguish, bathes herself in bathetic rhapsodies, and she seems able to pollute David's style in a similar fashion. Yet in writing to her, his prose reverts to the epistolary preenings of Micawber, the grandiose clap-trappings of his style. It is in this sense that Micawber is the great rival author in *David Copperfield*, a commanding stylist against whose prose David must define his own expressive tendencies.

In this light, it hardly seems accidental that when David is just beginning to mix reality with his "mist of fancy" and create his own "imaginative world," when he is thus coming into creative self-awareness for the first time, we learn in the same scene that Mr. Micawber has already fully assumed his "author's vanity" (11). We watch Micawber as he listens proudly to Captain Hopkins read "in a loud sonorous voice" the former's own petition to the House of Commons, a document ablaze with rhetorical fireworks like "The people's representative in Parliament assembled," "Your petitioners therefore humbly approach your honourable house," "His gracious Majesty's unfortunate subjects." Captain Hopkins gave "a certain luscious roll" to such phrases "as if the words were something real in his mouth, and delicious to taste," and in this he is a man after Micawber's heart, mistaking words for palpable delicacies in themselves nourishing, and the mouth, as an organ of communication, for an organ of pleasurable self-gratification. It is after the reading of Micawber's document that David closes his chapter with the memory of his former self, "an innocent romantic boy, making his imaginative world out of such strange experiences and sordid things," a world that now passes before him in review once again, "to the echo of Captain Hopkins's voice!"—that is, to the perhaps "sordid" yet unforgettable sonorities of the Micawber rhetoric.

The case against Mr. Micawber is certainly ambiguous. The indomitable ostentation of his style is a true inebriation with words. Compared to the verbal exultation of Micawber, Pecksniff and Chadband are little more than hypocrites, who use language without delighting in it. They tell their lies with rhetoric largely for the lie's sake, Micawber for the sake of rhetoric—for the sheer joy of so much *telling*. Words to this man are as good as gold, verbal resources tantamount to financial resources. Micawber seems sincerely to believe that an I.O.U. from his pen has a kind of poetic autonomy, and when he "was at any particularly desperate crisis, he used a sort of legal phraseology: which he seemed to think equivalent to winding up his affairs" (28). The letter to which this remark is prefaced displays not only such "phraseology" as "legal possession of the premises," "the undersigned," "appertaining," "the before-mentioned," but also a smattering of Micawber's favorite poetic phrases. Here the two types of diction try to consort: "If any drop of gloom were wanting in the overflowing cup, which is now 'commended' (in the language of an immortal Writer) to the lips of the undersigned" (28). The letter also contains one of those super-substantives of parliamentary rhetoric in which Micawber delights, the juicy "supererogation." Micawber lavishes words upon anything that comes to mind, and he is the greatest single master of circumlocution in Dickens. When reminiscing about his days of bachelorhood, he speaks of "the period when I was myself in a state of celibacy, and Mrs. Micawber had not yet been solicited to plight her faith at the Hymeneal altar" (28). Hoping that his family may someday be better located, he speaks of a "more ambitious domiciliary accommodation" (39), and on the same page refers to getting paid as "the drawing of stipendiary emoluments." In the first chapter I discussed Alice Meynell's treatment of contemporary linguistic parody in Dickens's style. In connection with Micawber specifically, Meynell says that a "portly phrase" such as " 'gratifying emotions of no common description' hits the whole language with one sure arrow."[21] By describing a letter of Micawber's as a "roundabout communication" (49), David himself offers us another useful term for the unrelieved "portly" circumlocution of the Micawber rhetoric, a linguistic high road which makes a wide arc of words on its way toward meaning and sometimes fails to reach home.

At the last moment in any given speech, Micawber is likely to essay one of his famous rhetorical "short cuts," and a single amazing sample should do: " 'The twins no longer derive their sustenance from Nature's founts—in short, said Mr. Micawber, in one of his bursts of confidence, 'they are weaned' " (17). "In short" is a descent that can be taken either as a condescension or an apology, and when Micawber does not bother to abbreviate, he may well pause to ask permission. Here he is to David's aunt on the subject of Mr. Dick: "The friendliness of this gentleman . . . if you will allow me, ma'am, to cull a figure of speech from the vocabulary of our coarser national sports—floors me" (49). This self-conscious phrasing, which turns up repeatedly in his talk, is a parody of David's own verbal wariness and humility. As a further control, there is also the abject pretense of humility in Heep's speech: "I am really unequal with my umble powers to express. . ." (35). Heep is the incarnation of hypocrisy, and his faked humility clears David's reticence of excess or self-indulgence, just as it sets Micawber into relief (and here what Chesterton said of Pecksniff does apply) as much less a hypocrite than a self-hypnotized rhetorician.

It is surely in his climactic denunciation of Heep that Micawber has his finest hour, and he knows it. Delivering his accusations in the favored epistolary form, Micawber "cherished an artistic admiration of their style of composition," paying homage to his own language "with a roll of his head, when he thought he had hit a sentence very hard indeed" (52). His one act of just moral outrage thus becomes merely a platform for his rhetoric, and David notes that he reads a certain passage in his letter "as if it were from an Act of Parliament; and appeared majestically refreshed by the sound of the words." We know what Dickens thinks of this kind of rhetoric, and we even know that David too detests "the music of the parliamentary bagpipes" (48) from his earlier days as a stenographer. "I wallow in words" (43), he had then lamented; it has now become Micawber's boast. Here, for example, is a lump of his predictable "legal phraseology" from the denunciation scene, in which everything is not only recorded or filed but actually stated in triplicate (italics mine): "HEEP has, on several occasions, to the best of my *knowledge, information, and belief,* systematically forged, to various *entries, books, and documents,* the signature of Mr. W.; and has distinctly done so in one instance, capable of proof by me. *To wit, in the manner following, that is to say . . ."* (52).

David, speaking for Dickens, follows these waste phrases with the most detailed piece of stylistic criticism to be found in any of the novels, a long paragraph belittling such "formal piling up of words" while recognizing that it is "not at all peculiar to" Mr. Micawber, but unfortunately the "general rule." Again, legalistic triplets serve David as example: "In the taking of legal oaths, for instance, deponents seem to enjoy themselves mightily when they come to several good words in succession, for the expression of one good idea; as, that they utterly detest, abominate, and abjure, or so forth." David feels that "too large a retinue of words" is in fact a British national dilemma. "We talk about the tyranny of words, but we like to tyrannise over them too; we are fond of having a large superfluous establishment of words to wait upon us on great occasions; we think it looks important and sounds well" (52). No one needs reminding at this point that such an attack on the "superfluous establishment of words" is nothing new for Dickens. Nor is it a surprise that the most idiotic instances of "several good words in succession, for the expression of one good idea" convene in great numbers for that satiric matrix at the opening of *Martin Chuzzlewit,* where we are pummeled with such luminous redundancies as "inflammatory and combustible," "highly respectable and in every way creditable and unimpeachable," "noble and illustrious," "high and lofty," "utterly settled and clenched," "invariably peculiar to and only make themselves apparent in."

Any of these might "make themselves apparent in" Micawber's

speech, and David's exposé of verbal phoniness was indeed spurred by his distaste for the Micawber style. Yet such cool satire as this hardly does justice to the real glee and gusto, however misplaced, with which Micawber dispenses his language. Perhaps a modern analogy will help. W. C. Fields, who loved and seemed almost to live his Dickens, was the perfect choice for Micawber in the Metro-Goldwyn-Mayer film of *David Copperfield*. After his first marriage, according to one biographer, Fields spent a great deal of time re-reading his favorite authors; they were Dickens, Swift, and Mark Twain.[22] He was such an incarnation of the Dickensian spirit that Kenneth Tynan goes back to Dickens for his appreciative analogies when he says that "Fields breakfasting with his screen family be-haves with all the wariness of Micawber unexpectedly trapped in Fagin's thieves' kitchen,"[23] and certainly Fields was following in Micawber's footsteps in his repeated efforts "to outwit the agents of calamity with sheer pomp."[24] Again and again Fields's humor reminds us of Dickens's mockery of magniloquence. Periphrasis runs amuck in Fields's gravelly patter: "quite the antithesis" re-places "on the contrary," a barber shop is called a "tonsorial parlor," Mae West is complimented on her "symmetrical digits," and the high and low get ludicrously mixed in a phrase like "mit in the melange." In characterizing his humor, Delmore Schwartz writes that Fields is "overwhelmingly articulate, not to say verbose (redundant is one of his favorite words),"[25] and he calls him "as oratorical as a barker."[26] He might as well be talking about Micaw-ber. So too when he indirectly connects Fields's personal career with the patterns of Jonsonian comedy, observing that "in Fields's life there was really little that was humorous—except in the old sense of the word."[27] Without mentioning Dickens, Schwartz says some suggestive things for any comparison of Micawber and Fields. Noting that Fields's father was a Cockney Englishman, Schwartz surmises that "there may well have been some connection between Fields's Cockney antecedents, his attitude toward the English, his use of the comedy of names, and his rich feeling for the comic possibilities of pompous, pretentious, or hypocritical language."[28] In a literary line, then, it would seem that Sam Weller must also be one of his "Cockney antecedents."

Fields was the greatest linguistic satirist in American film comedy, and the ideal comedian to have impersonated Micawber. It is no coincidence that the year before the filming of *David Cop-perfield* in 1934, Fields was cast in the Paramount production of *Alice in Wonderland* as Humpty Dumpty, the character who says that he can make a word mean anything he wishes it to mean. This lordly dominion over language was Micawber's province, and Fields's after him. In *Martin Chuzzlewit*, Pecksniff's unmasking before Tom Pinch finds metaphorical elaboration as yet another pratfall, since from "the lofty height on which poor Tom had placed his idol it was tumbled down headlong," a fact the narrator follows with these appropriated (and appropriate) lines: "Not all the king's horses, nor all the king's men, / Could have set Mr. Pecksniff up again" (*M.C.*, 31). And as if to complete the circle, Fields, who has already played Humpty Dumpty and a Dickensian rhetorician, writes his own screenplay for "You Can't Cheat an Honest Man" and has himself denigrated near the end of the film as a "Pecksniff."

If part of Micawber's destiny is to find a home in the comedy of W. C. Fields, another part of his fate is realized in his lifetime, as he becomes a prominent rhetorician and public figure in Australia. J. B. Priestley has seen the fitness of this: "Is there anything nearer Micawber in the world than the early Colonial and American Press, existing sumptuously on magnificent phrases, rhetoric, and capital letters?"[29] More recently, Randolph Quirk has written of Micawber in terms that are interesting for our purposes: "It is a regular symptom of Micawber's retreat from reality that he should find a sufficient reality in words."[30] Micawber's life in language is indeed a retreat, and he has emigrated as far as Australia in order to make possible a continuing career as an artist of words. He is in the long run more of an honest "escape artist" than a peer of language's naughty company. He does not try to alter or falsify reality; he is not a hypocrite, and his own private world is more than merely "sufficient." David may hate his rhetoric, but Micawber would never be able to imagine why. He takes refuge, but he also takes joy in it. It is exultation, then, that sets Micawber apart and finally exalts him when, for his powers of speech in Australia at the end of the novel, he is elected to the public post of Magistrate.

A word about last words. After his unfeeling encounters with Jo early in *Bleak House*, we see nothing of Chadband in the second half of the novel until he is recalled for a final exposure of his hypocrisy. He comes with his wife and Grandfather Smallweed to blackmail Leicester Dedlock with their knowledge of Lady Dedlock's past, and in a last outburst of his oily rhetoric Chadband "delivers himself" of his disingenuous language almost as if the false words made up the only "self" he has left to offer: "Air we in possession of a sinful secret, and doe we require corn, and wine, and oil—or what is much the same thing, money—for the keeping thereof? Probably so, my friends" (*B.H.*, 54). Pecksniff, too, had tried to pay his way with defrauding rhetoric, and the last we hear of him in *Martin Chuzzlewit* he has begun to set down his words on paper as a "drunken, squalid, begging-letter-writing man" (*M.C.*, 54). Micawber has the only propitious exit of the three; he has taken to pen and ink in Australia, but, unlike the squalid Pecksniff, he has become a "diligent and esteemed correspondent" (*D.C.*, 63) of the *Port Middlebay Times*.

Letter-writing is an obvious symbol for language as interchange and communication. Yet whether the written words of such "stylists" are churned up as self-pleading or mere self-display, whether they bubble from the pen of a Pecksniff or a Micawber, still this transcribed verbosity, like the vocal torrents of these men—and despite crucial differences between them—is finally, as Dickens shows, negligent and wrong. No longer communication at all, it is style given over to the noise and honk of rhetoric. Linguistic egomania is often a matter of "conciet," and even the freshest metaphors from this naughty company seem self-promotional. Their unappeasable language constantly runs afoul of its own overexertions and ends in a style bulbous and blunted. It is Pickwickianism incensed, exacerbated. The first person whose voice we hear in the novels of Dickens has a presence that too often appeared to be little more than verbal; the very obesity of Pickwick seemed to embody the rhetorical dimensions of his selfhood. Yet he emerged several hundred pages later as a more than oratorical being, a moral agent whose essential goodness and humility waited only to be cured of too much talk. No such essence can be thought to lurk beneath the verbal surface of a Pecksniff, a Chadband, a Micawber, for there alone is their life. Carry on though he did, loud and long, Pickwick was never "all talk." At the end of his novel, therefore, he could submit to a divesting of rhetorical excess in a manner that would leave his irresponsible successors not only naked but vacant. When spoken and written language has devolved into such unworthy hands, the custody of authentic imagination must, needless to say, go elsewhere. Exactly where, and in what forms, we are about to see.

To take stock at this point is to discover a much shrunken inventory of imaginative possibility. Rhetorical excess in Mr. Pickwick, verbal wit and fanciful intuition in Sam Weller, words whipped up to deceit in Jingle, and dream turned to nightmare in the interpolated tales—these materials from *Pickwick* converge once more, and for the last time confidently, in *The Old Curiosity Shop*, where Sampson Brass is the false wielder of elaborately empty language, Dick Swiveller has what is left of Sam's stylistic ingenuity, Quilp is Sam's or Jingle's satiric energy gone over into sadism, and the revenge of imagination is suffered by Dick Swiveller, the pivotal hero, in an ordeal by fever. These themes have a powerful momentum in Dickens, but by now they are primarily running on only two tracks. Satiric language on the part of the characters, however sadistic, was too vibrant to last, and, as we know from this chapter, verbal energy seems to have merged almost entirely with a linguistic bypass engineered out of rhetorical deceit. Pickwick and, worse yet, Sampson Brass have had more followers than either Jingle or Quilp—even than Sam, along whose independent and spontaneous trail few manage to make their way. In fact, the course of Sam's vocal energy has yielded to the path of a fancy nearly deprived of style, verbal wit all but disappearing into the privacies of unspeaking dream and their frequent reprisals in fever. I call this rerouting of imagination "escape artistry." It is more than just wit relaxed or canceled. It has its own regimen, its own vigilance, and these are the subject of the next chapter.

6 Escape Artists

'If they would only leave us a little more of the
poetry of existence in these terrible days!'
—*Dombey and Son* (27)

William H. Gass writes in *Fiction and the Figures of Life* that
"When Dickens' creatures speak, subjectivity flows as from a
tap into the world: personal, poetic, unique; their talk is testimony,
and a pure quality of soul,"[1] and his high estimate of Dickensian
dialogue is in more than one way partial. For such a judgment to
stand, it must be allowed to ignore those hypocrites and poseurs
who have so vociferously read their "testimony" into evidence in
the foregoing chapter. Gass's happy claim can be substantiated at
large in the later novels only as a dwindled ideal, for the characters
who spurt "poetry" in Dickens tend more and more after *Pickwick
Papers* to do so as a way of substituting for or obscuring a "quality
of soul" blackened or altogether absent. They are less "figures of
life" than they are the mere figures of speech they brandish. Which
is why the irony is more than a little puzzling when, after one of
his fat speeches of "abominable nonsense" (*B.H.*, 19), we are told
that Chadband "retires into private life" for a time; but it seems he
has nowhere to go, and what inner life he could possibly lead
beneath the roll and swell of his language is beyond any reader's
fathoming.

Through a style felt and flexible, however, we see a character like
Sam Weller wedding essence and presence, the inward man and his
verbal projection. Imagination bridges the gap. But not for long;
Jingle begins to pervert and falsify the tap-flow of his verbal self,
and by the middle of Dickens's career even the energy needed to
sustain such a linguistic false front is so attenuated that villains

146

and heroes alike begin to labor under the curse of a language ever more dreary and inert. Though fancy can no longer meet the public world on (and with) its own verbal terms, still it must be trusted to, sometimes to armor characters against this world. When the privileges of spoken style have been largely revoked, emergency measures are necessary, and, by cunning and struggle, fancy goes underground. Since characters can no longer speak their minds, as it were, no longer communicate their dreams, the imagination becomes secretive and mute. Yet against the beguiling tug of despair, fatigued, bruised by routine, still it holds on. When the coalition of style and imagination is forcibly dissolved, other directions for the fancy must be searched out, fresh courses for the spirit to adventure upon, new channels for an imagination hoping to stay fluid and abundant, to keep free. Increasingly, romanticism offers and leads the way.

Dickens's novels show us that the irrational impulse alone can ransom us away from a world that makes neither rational nor poetic sense, a reality of neither rhyme nor reason. They show fancy to be our only deliverance, yet they know too that "the poetry of existence" can be a destructive sham, not honest relief but a mere subterfuge. These are the two sorts of escape we are to look for here, fair and foul, genuine and empty. After Dick Swiveller, the guardianship of imagination is rarely assigned to vocal characters, and this privation of verbal style begins a new privacy of imagination evident in such different people as Dickens's true and false "pastoralists" and his habitual fire-gazers, in such opposite escapist mentalities from the same novel as Sairey Gamp and Tom Pinch of *Martin Chuzzlewit*, in a reserved and guarded artist like David Copperfield, and in the later "antiheroes" of imagination like Arthur Clennam and Philip Pirrip. These are the often verbally deprived lives that will guide the course of this chapter. When fancy no longer has words in which to clothe itself, other provisions must be made, and the theme of imagination takes an unexpected but momentous turn—a turn inward.

Two brief instances can condense my point about the curtailment and exhaustion of personal style in the later novels. The examples are in themselves linguistic condensations, one of sense, one of sound, a pun and a pattern of alliteration—deployed not out of creative gaiety by the characters, but for sheer psychic relief. Ebeneezer Scrooge, a villian to be transformed, it might be said, by a revenge of his own repressed imagination in instructive hallucinations, like Gabriel Grub in *Pickwick Papers*, must dredge up his verbal fancy as a defense against the initial sight of Marley's ghost. Hoping to explain away his apparition as the result of indigestion, Scrooge remarks to the ghost, "There's more of gravy than of grave about you, whatever you are!" (*C.C.*, 1) The narrator, whose comic voice Scrooge seems at that moment to have borrowed, is compelled to an explanation: "Scrooge was not much in the habit of cracking jokes, nor did he feel, in his heart, by any means waggish then. The truth is, that he tried to be smart, as a means of distracting his own attention, and keeping down his terror; for the spectre's voice disturbed the very marrow in his bones." Sam Weller might have responded in this way, but then Sam was "waggish" at the drop of a hat, a reveller in such bald puns. Scrooge's imagination is instead erratic and tactical, a refuge in only the most perilous straits. Sam's penchant for sarcastic alliteration also surfaces in just as unlikely a place when Tom Gradgrind appeases himself in *Hard Times* with its soothing symmetry: " 'No Loo; I wouldn't hurt *you*. I made an exception of you at first. I don't know what this—jolly old—Jaundiced Jail,' Tom had paused to find a sufficiently complimentary and expressive name for the parental roof, and seemed to relieve his mind for a moment by the strong alliteration of this one, 'would be without you' " (I, 8). Though couched in the narrator's own comic overwriting, such a desperate "poetic" alleviation is anything but style, just as Scrooge's "play" with words is the farthest thing from game. Spontaneous invention in language—whether, as in the present cases, facetious or mellifluous or both—has become one of the casualties of imagination, crippled by its own disuse. Once a quickening function of the free-sprung mind, brisk, ventilated by delight, it is now narrowly functional. It deflects and fends off. Were it not for Jenny Wren in Dickens's last masterpiece, who wins back for pun and alliteration, among other verbal entertainments, some kind of spirited autonomy, the decline of fancy would have seemed even more complete and irreversible.

Before establishing a perspective on the individual motifs of pastoralism and fire-gazing, I would like to pair two more examples of that fallen world whose spiritual frustrations the later novels must chronicle. Incidents from the only books in the canon with frankly descriptive titles, *Bleak House* and again *Hard Times*, sum up the problem. The place called Bleak House is ironically the best place in its novel, where community is made, sheltered, and where disruptive energies are easily routed into the Growlery, that room where Jarndyce goes to isolate his despondencies and which thus becomes another self-enforced domestic quarantine. In contrast to such programmatic dampening of negative energy are the manic rages of Boythorn on one side and the impatient, fretful urges of Richard Carstone on the other, neither wired into the circuit of active imagination. The entire novel seems to be about an energy crisis where, due to various drains and overloads, the fancy can be only weakly, intermittently powered. Even a genuine romantic impulse like pastoral nostalgia, though wholly imagined out of the thinning air of the novel by men who have never seen the country, spends itself in the process and comes to nothing.

Take the case of Mr. Snagsby, "in his way, rather a meditative and poetical man; loving to walk in Staple Inn in the summer time, and to observe how countrified the sparrows and leaves are" (B.H.,10). That passive modifier "countrified" marks the transformation of a summery urban nook into a romantic locus. Another linguistic hint is dropped in the subsequent description where Snagsby, after misquoting a romantic simile, reminds us that the proper name "Turnstile" was once a common "countrified" noun; his own imagination is not verbal, however, and the satiric abbreviation "Vices" is Dickens's joke, not his:

He solaces his imagination, too, by thinking of the many Chancellors and Vices and Masters of the Rolls, who are deceased; and he gets such a flavour of the country out of telling the two 'prentices how he *has* heard say that a brook 'as clear as crystial' once ran right down the middle of Holborn, when Turnstile really was a turnstile, leading slap away into the meadows—gets such a flavour of the country out of this, that he never wants to go there.

"Turnstyle" is seen by Snagsby as the geographic equivalent of a dead metaphor, but his pastoral nostalgia is hardly rejuvenating, and offers no real motivation. There is something blocked, congested, indeed "snagged" about this imagination; it has no thrust. Dickens has reconstituted the dilemma in another theater of the novel's action as Phil Squod, on a winter morning, awakens from "dreaming of the country," and Mr. George, having learned that Phil has never "clapped . . . eyes upon the country—marshes and dreams excepted," asks, "Do you want to see it?" "No," Phil answers surprisingly, "I don't know as I do, particular . . . I doubt if I ain't a-getting too old to take to novelties" (26). Dreams may be a "solace" for the imagination, but the thirst for waking novelty, a prime nourisher of the fancy, cannot dare to be so easily slaked.

As with Snagsby, the dream is clearly one of escape, yet it is weakened by imaginative timidity and fails to convert to urgency even the lives of the characters who share it. Neither Snagsby nor Squod sees the pastoral world he dreams of, and by the time the reader does, ironies have buried all trace of human fancy, displaced entirely the romantic impulse. We heard early that Leicester Dedlock's gallant deference to his wife was "the one little touch of romantic fancy in him" (II), and this we may recall at the opening of the full-scale description of their country place at Chesney Wold: "The weather is so very bad, down in Lincolnshire, that the liveliest imagination can scarcely apprehend its ever being fine again. Not that there is any super-abundant life of imagination on the spot, for Sir Leicester is not here (and, truly, even if he were, would not do much for it in that particular)" (7). The prose has knotted back over itself as if to fix our attention on the point, and the three long paragraphs of conjecture that follow, about the possible "motions of fancy among the lower animals at Chesney Wold," build to a showpiece of bravura writing in which the narrator's style is made bold and inquisitive with that fancy denied to any other human consciousness on the scene.

The horses in Sir Leicester's stables "seem to be always consulting—*they* may contemplate some mental pictures of fine weather on occasion, and may be better artists at them than the grooms." Dogs, rabbits, turkeys all dream of summer, and even the "discontented goose" gabbles out a "waddling preference" for better days to come. That last quoted adjective is a transferred epithet, no longer attached to the locomotion of the goose but to its preferential consideration, a "human" or rational quality which exists only (or does it?) in the preferences of the narrator's fancy. But the most ingenious verbal trick in the entire passage comes in that second paragraph about the dozing mastiff who (notice the personal pronoun to which we are led) was "very much wanting something to worry, besides himself and his chain." Dickens turns the simple parallel compound into a complex form of that sylleptic word play (one verb governing two objects in different senses) in which he so often delights—merely by unchaining a semantic duplicity in the verb "worry," the pun that turns on the double meaning of to tear or bite and to induce anxiety, and thus on the idea of animals as imaginative creatures around which the whole passage turns.

The pun is a type of ambiguity which here typifies not only the theme of displaced imagination but also the wit and elasticity of the narrative style itself, the one remaining refuge for human fancy. This is style as the standard of imaginative value which is to be undermined in the next novel, *Hard Times*, where Dickens's remorseless satire will have foreclosed even this final outlet of fancy. The ironies of *Bleak House* are only a step behind, and the Chesney Wold episode becomes a devastating pastoral which asks what would become of the pastoral mode if the sheep were more romantic than the shepherds. It is no wonder that the aberrant artistic or poetic imagination, when it does rear up in the human brain, tends to seek escape from a world in which horses are "better artists" than their stableboys.

This kind of imaginative poverty in *Bleak House* is again placed under the microscope in the chapter on "The Smallweed Family," where Dickens probes to the psychological roots of their ugly, ganglious "family tree" in the arid upbringing of the children, a clear sketch for the "Never Wonder" mentality of *Hard Times*. In the voice of official neutrality, the coolly impersonal style that will become the norm for the next novel, we are informed that the Smallweeds' "narrow world of fact" has "strengthened itself in its practical character, has discarded all amusements, discountenanced all story-books, fairy tales, fictions, and fables, and banished all levities whatsoever" (21). The young Judy has outdone the pastoral parody of her family name and has taken to "the art and mystery of artificial flower-making," while her brother Bart "could as soon play at leap-frog, or at cricket, as change into a cricket or a frog himself." By criss-crossing the terms, chiastic ingenuity has surprised us first with the less apparent of the two incarnations in the pun on "cricket," but again this act of verbal wit, as with all "play" in the scene, is exclusively the narrator's. In the Smallweed mind there is no place for game and daydream, no tenable ground this side of metamorphosis for simply pretending to be a "leap-frog," no room for make-believe, let alone impossible magic. Yet to build and maintain such an imaginative space is often the way of redemption in Dickens's novels, for the narrative voice at least if not for the characters. Style alone is frequently consigned to the tenancy of this space, as in the impersonal satiric flights of *Bleak House*, but by the next novel the times are harder yet for imagination, and the line between the satire of deluding fancy and participation in it, between parody and narrative capitulation, is in *Hard Times* insidiously thin.

The Dickens novel with the most generic title, *Hard Times* paints the most explicit, the most harrowing picture of the Victorian assault against imagination, and thus it is a good focal point for this survey of escapist fancy in the novels. The inimical Gradgrind world does indeed represent everything from which the imagination must make its retreat and take its refuge. Otherwise it is proscribed and exterminated. And more unflinchingly than in any other book, the prose of *Hard Times* displays this chilling alternative, where the most pervasive threat to being is that monotony will aggravate it into derangement: a danger latent in the fixated patterns of the style itself. The usual narrative gaiety of Dickens is deliberately minimized for *Hard Times*, where there is considerably less play of mind over the vagaries and private elations of language than in any other of his novels, less unassimilated love of words themselves. The relentless style of the novel is a success precisely (and this is just the word) because it scores against the satiric adversary on its own ground: logical argument, tabular reasoning, itemization, mensurable considerations only. Nowhere else in Dickens, for so long at a time, is the writing so assiduously paced, the antithetical structure so automatic and tenacious. One can quote almost at random: "Stephen bent over his loom, quiet, watchful, and steady. A special contrast . . . to the crashing, smashing, tearing piece of mechanism at which he laboured" (I,11). The contrast of opposed syntactic triads, the quiet and steady adjectives against the grating kinetic participles, has a tightness unfamiliar in Dickens's usual prose, including those affronts to compression in the famous opening chapters to his later novels. There, as in *Bleak House* for example, we meet a profusion barely contained by parallelism and repetition, whereas in *Hard Times* we are faced with a world narrowed to the bounds of a punctual and peremptory antithesis. Yet there are ironies beyond this in the passage I selected, for that "special contrast" asserted between hero and machine is partly subverted by the similar three-pronged grammar of their balanced descriptions, and is in fact contradicted by that extra-syntactic parallel throughout the novel which insists that men in this society are slowly being turned into machines.

The rigor of a similar deterministic prose, a stylistic impersonation of the Gradgrind system's own strict sequential logic, is later used to point up the danger more explicitly, as Dickens warns the oppressors of the poor that "in the day of your triumph, when romance is utterly driven out of their souls, and they and a bare existence stand face to face, Reality will take a wolfish turn, and make an end of you" (II,6). Here is an explicit danger signal about the revenge of imagination that follows upon its improper cultivation—for society at large, this time, rather than for the private consciousness. If "romance" is expelled completely, "Reality" itself will turn wolfish: the psychic danger becomes for the industrial society a revolutionary threat. There is a perfect dramatic example of this process when Tom "the whelp" is captured finally and admits his crime to the astonished Mr. Gradgrind; Tom has been treated as a cipher all along, an item in a general statistical theory, and now the statistical "reality" has taken its own whelpish turn: "So many people are employed in situations of trust; so many people, out of so many, will be dishonest. I have heard you talk, a hundred times, of its being a law. How can *I* help laws? You have comforted others with such things, father. Comfort yourself!" (III,7). This pattern of the revenging turn in the case of Tom Gradgrind is even prepared for earlier in the novel, when Tom explains that he has been treated for so long as a mule or donkey that "I should like to kick like one" (I,8).

The style in which *Hard Times* is conducted also makes a "wolfish turn" upon itself, a turn into parody and mechanistic simulation. Nothing more light-hearted will do, no brisk alternatives by which, as in so many of Dickens's novels, the healthier tenor of the prose itself becomes a kind of counter-argument: the medium as message.[2] Readers who look for this expected foothold in Dickens's style tend to be deceived by *Hard Times*. Two different critics have in fact discovered a kind of narrative affirmation in a well-known simile from the novel,[3] and they are both, I think, mistaken. "The lights in the great factories, which looked, when they were illuminated, like Fairy palaces—or the travellers by express-train said so—were all extinguished" (I, 10). What Dickens is after at this point is crucial for *Hard Times*, as well as for the larger development of escapist refuge among his characters. No one would disagree that the reference to "Fairy palaces" is in some sense ironic, that these factories are merely temples to fact, not palaces at all but places of toil and the expense of spirit, products of a system which denies the existence both of fairies and of their architecture as absurd castles in the air. The problem comes when we try to decide whether the narrator is proud of having introduced this lively, albeit false, trope.

Here we meet a further irony, enrolled this time at the expense of style and imagination themselves. Though the fancy about "Fairy palaces" seems to the commentators another tribute to the gusto and variety of the narrative voice, it is instead a trenchant parody of the whole romantic sensibility as it becomes an aestheticizing indifference to human pain. Once more, style is revenging itself on those who value it too cheaply, a facile romanticism turned on its perpetrators. Dickens is not proud of self-display here; rather, the world he is drawing for us is so inhuman that even the narrator himself cannot afford the natural and effortless manipulations of his fancy. Too much is at stake for such unearned "poetry of existence" to be anything but a callous fiction. By no means a complacent testament to imagination, the simile here is rather an exposure of fancy as at times a dangerous, an unfeeling indulgence. From a public world that knows only the death of fancy—either by edict and extinction or suicidally, through its own prevarications—there must be some honest means of escape. The chief release for the Gradgrind children is the activity of fire-gazing soon to be considered in this chapter, one of the primary romantic employments of Dickens's characters before and after *Hard Times*.

I want first to account in some way, however, for the gradual influx of romantic preoccupations into a career that began with the epitome of an eighteenth-century picaresque novel. *Pickwick Papers* is, in this sense, a kind of last word. It might be thought of for English fiction as the final pre-modern masterpiece, followed thirty years later by *Our Mutual Friend*, perhaps even now the quintessential modern novel. Book by book, richly, decisively, romanticism effected the transition. Sam Weller, with his debts to the verve and exuberance of the preceding century, is no romantic character; Jenny Wren, who will speak for herself in the next chapter, may be, despite her countering cynicism and flaws of spirit, the most brilliant such character in our prose. Yet Sam and Jenny have perhaps more in common, and more deeply, than any other characters in Dickens. That they must inevitably frame my reading of the novels is one of the commanding facts about the theme I am tracing, and yet the question remains how Dickens moved, and how criticism should after him, from Sam's brio toward a partly derivative energy in Jenny that is by turns vitriolic and visionary. Without Mr. Weller, we would have no solid sense of the Dickensian ideal of personality. Without Miss Wren, years and much turmoil later, we would never have known what Dickens thought could be salvaged and consolidated out of the psychic wreckage of the new industrial society, that depersonalization against which the romantic must always pit itself. Resisting the tides of urbanized anonymity, Jenny erects a persona that holds, and behind it she harbors her dream; style guards the vision with the fending energies of wit. Like no character before her, Jenny contests the Pickwickian disinheritance and assumes her share of Sam's verbal legacy. If she makes it defensive, at least she makes it work, and she brings it, too, into some rhythm with those romantic impulses her vocal satire never wholly conceals or demeans.

So the standard of wit, under whose banner Sam so jauntily moves, has derived from the previous century as a visible posture of style, an imaginative stance and gait. It is fancy's public manner. Dreams are a different case, and they may become, demoralizingly enough, the sole escape from the imaginative blockage of the industrial city, the hostile new earth. It is to just this imaginative exit that the Romantic poets, when necessary, pledged their best energies. Their dreams wavered between pastoralism and metaphysics, between retreat and transcendence, and from the former recourse to the latter is one path through the novels of Dickens toward *Our Mutual Friend*. Along this uneven way, the myth of pastoral haven, with all its protective artistry of escape, tends either to be privately enshrined or falsely broadcast, and Miss Wren's "golden bower," symbol of her quartered, glorified fancy, is one of the few achieved instances of romantic assurance and recouped vitality in the later novels.

As we have seen, beginning even with *Pickwick Papers*, neither style nor imagination can be easily trusted in the novels of Dickens, and just as narrative fancy can at one time seem a healthy liberty of mind, at another a desensitized, almost brutal delusion, so the pastoral impulse, sometimes true and improving, can easily be perverted. Indeed it is a motif more often than not savagely ironic in Dickens, where his satire scores repeatedly against such loudly vaunted but fraudulent pastoral sympathies as Mrs. Skewton's "Arcadian" longings in *Dombey and Son* to live "entirely surrounded by cows" (*D.S.*,21), the bogus and parasitic romanticism of Harold Skimpole in *Bleak House,* who takes an aesthete's delight in the downfall of Richard Carstone, characterized by Skimpole as the "present shepherd, our pastoral Richard" (*B.H.*,37), or that final ostentation of sensibility in *Little Dorrit* when Mrs. Merdle sings mechanically of a lapsed Arcadia: "If we were in a more primitive state, if we lived under roofs of leaves, and kept cows and sheep and creatures, instead of banker's accounts (which would be delicious; my dear, I am pastoral to a degree, by nature), well and good. But we don't live under leaves, and keep cows and creatures" (*L.D.I.*,33). That prepositional phrase "by nature" attached to the adjective "pastoral" becomes a kind of punning deceit; beyond its idiomatic function, it is at once a redundancy and—like the atheist claiming "I am religious, by God"—a blasphemous lie.

In *Dombey and Son* the child hero Paul, when he is not staring into fires, indulges his fancy in other ways. He has, for instance, a dream of pastoral flight more active than Snagsby's or Phil Squod's, a myth of liberation with which he too "solaces his imagination." In a single notion he transforms the lust for capital which characterizes his father's position in the industrial society into a wholesome romantic determination: "I mean . . . to put my money all together in one bank, never try to get any more, go away into the country with my darling Florence, have a beautiful garden, fields, and woods, and live there with her all my life!" (14). But all his life is not long, and when he was very young his first nurse, Polly Toodle, had explained the idea of death in pastoral terms, saying that his mother was "buried in the ground where the trees grow." Death is at one with transfiguration and rebirth:

'The cold ground?' said the child, shuddering again.
'No! The warm ground,' returned Polly, seizing her advantage, 'where the ugly little seeds turn into beautiful flowers, and into grass, and corn, and I don't know what all besides.' (3)

The only occasions "seized" by Paul's second nurse, Mrs. Pipchin, are for him disadvantages, and her relation to the pastoral ideal sets the tone, for her "embowerment" is "uncommonly prolific" with such grotesque vegetation as "writhing" cactuses "like hairy serpents" and "several creeping vegetables possessed of sticky and adhesive leaves" (8).

At least with Mrs. Pipchin we meet no pretense of the congenial, the natural, and there is more danger to the standards of imagination in the synthetic chatter of that other aged crone, Mrs. Skewton, the mad escapist romantic to whom we owe the epigraph about "existence" and its "poetry." When she proudly claims to "want Nature everywhere" (21), the satire Dickens has just used to expose her comment about "wanting heart" again applies—for the pastoral effusion, too, "was frightfully true in one sense, if not in that in which she had used the phrase." The moral vacancy at the center of such hollow romanticism is most dramatically shown up in Mrs. Skewton's cruel victimization of her daughter Edith, whom she has married off first to a man whose name is a mockery of the pastoral, one Mr. Granger (we remember what Mark Twain is to do with the names Shepherdson and Grangerford in *Huckleberry Finn*), and finally to a man whose name has hybrid suggestions of Doom and Tomb. Edith has become an accomplished but uninspired artist, with no delusions about herself and no escapist antidotes for the barrenness of her existence. She is a satire of herself as artist, and there is no more telling obliquity in the novel than Edith's matter-of-fact announcement when asked to make a sketch: " 'My pencils are all pointless,' she said, stopping and turning them over" (27).

Certainly it is Skimpole of *Bleak House,* in the same novel with a passivist of fancy like Mr. Snagsby, who is the most treacherous of all the false escape artists in Dickens, the showy poetizers, and he has told his lies so often that even the otherwise clear-sighted John Jarndyce believes that "he is all sentiment, and—and susceptibility, and—and sensibility—and—and imagination" (*B.H.,*43). Skimpole's poetic indulgences do not enhance reality; they exploit it by putting an aesthetic distance between the mind and the world. In order to escape responsibility, Skimpole turns people and all natural objects of sympathy into mere *objets d'art,* and we cannot help imagining him, the next year, among those "travellers by express-train" in *Hard Times* who see "Fairy palaces" where there is only filth and misery. When Skimpole says about the suffering American slaves, "they people the landscape for me, they give it a poetry for me" (18), he has substituted the picturesque for the ethical imagination, and morality has become a landscape with figures. Afraid of contracting Jo's illness later, Skimpole suggests that the boy should get himself imprisoned for some energetic crime, since at least there would be a sort of "poetry" (31) in that fate.

Such use of the term "poetry" disgraces imagination, and there is certainly no character in *Bleak House* to redeem its reputation. The mad Miss Flite, with a name that predicts Jenny Wren's but sets its emphasis on flight exclusively, on escape, rather than on the natural artistry of the songbird, indulges a pastoralism eroded by her fruitless dream of a Chancery Judgment. Her "bower" thus becomes merely a respite and a waiting-place, and there is a sense of this suspension in her hesitant, clipped syntax: "This is the garden of Lincoln's Inn. I call it my garden. It is quite a bower in the summer-time. Where the birds sing melodiously" (*B.H.,*5). The immediate antecedent of "where" seems to be the time of year, and this locative adverb (where we might expect "when") coalesces time and place in an interval, a breathing space, of melodious peace from the proceedings of Chancery. "I spend the greater part of the long vacation here. In contemplation." The last phrase isolates that aspect of her nature which reminds us of the "contemplative and poetic" Snagsby in the same novel, content with his own urban bower. Yet Miss Flite's contemplation looks beyond to a satisfactory decision in the Court when "the vacation is fulfilled; and the sixth seal, mentioned in the Revelations, again prevails." Miss Flite looks to the otherworldly for a reparation on earth, whereas Jenny's appetite for the divine, fed by private "Revelations" of her own, will somehow capacitate her for this world; transcendence with her is not a way out but a way back.

Between the "bowers" of Miss Flite and Miss Wren there appears in *Little Dorrit* one of the most heartily endorsed and explicit pastorals in all of Dickens. Just as, in *Bleak House*, a feel for the "countrified" spirit on the part of Miss Flite or Snagsby or Phil Squod is grotesquely polarized by the skimped, insincere romanticism of Harold Skimpole, so in *Little Dorrit* the pastoral fabrication of Mrs. Merdle, with her "cows and sheep and creatures," meets refutation in the honest fancy of Mrs. Plornish. Hers is no sentimental idyll but a domestic comedy in one paragraph, describing a "little fiction in which Mrs. Plornish unspeakably rejoiced." Her parlor displays a painted wall mural representing an exterior view of "a counterfeit cottage " that becomes "a perfect pastoral to Mrs. Plornish, the Golden Age revived" (*L.D.* II,13). The "little fiction" is here no destructive "counterfeit," no lie, but a delightful game— and that "most wonderful deception" which is art itself.

After the ruthless boasts and blather of Skimpole, it is a wonder that the life of fancy, especially the pastoral imagination, is ever given another chance. Yet Mrs. Plornish, and after her Wemmick in *Great Expectations*, manage to build a pastoral idea into their ingenious domestic arrangements. Wemmick is the most direct rebuttal to Skimpole, for the simple refusal to talk publicly about his fancy seems to have made it operable. To borrow and rethink an aphorism: silence gives consent. This was implied even in Mrs. Plornish's case by the pun tucked away in that vernacular hyperbole quoted above, for when she "rejoiced" in her fictional haven, it was in two senses "unspeakably." But Wemmick's retreat at Walworth Castle becomes the most complete dramatization of escape artistry in all the novels. At Jagger's office in London, Wemmick is little more than some useful piece of office furniture like Chuffey before him in *Martin Chuzzlewit*, a serviceable item in the inventory of "portable property," with a "mechanical appearance of smiling" that "was merely a mechanical appearance" (*G.E.*,21). But when he makes his way home to Walworth and can demonstrate to Pip his ingenious drawbridge, he is able to smile "with a relish, and not merely mechanically" (25). Gladness itself has found a home, and neither the strict dichotomy of Wemmick's existence nor the strict antithetical prose with which he announces his escapist strategy, a starkly contrastive style that might have come straight from the severities of *Hard Times*—neither is meant here to be cautionary: "When I go into the office, I leave the Castle behind me, and when I come into the Castle, I leave the office behind me" (25). This is no longer a rigor coerced, but a balance won.

Wemmick is among those "practical" men of business in Dickens whose "private life" (25), as he calls it, must be kept secret to be kept alive at all. At the same time, he brings to a climax another important Dickensian motif in one of its few nonsatiric appearances, for Wemmick's moated world of literally garrisoned imagination at Walworth Castle is also a pastoral enclave. Wemmick's fancy has sheared off from the daily round of his existence into a defensive privacy, an emotional schizophrenia that necessitates his rigid sequestering of imagination. Only when he is safely within the confines of the Castle, far from Jaggers's office, is Wemmick's fancy allowed to take root, and it flowers there amidst a thriving natural stronghold: "—At the back, there's a pig, and there are fowls and rabbits; then I knock together my own little frame, you see, and grow cucumbers; and you'll judge at supper what sort of salad I can raise" (25). The Castle is "in point of provisions" a place of bounty and fruition, staunchly defended against siege by drawbridge and cannon. And in the center of this walled garden, fulfilling its pastoral promise to the letter, there is even a "bower," and an "ornamental lake, on whose margin the bower was raised."

Wemmick is the sole architect of the miracle, the Prospero of this magic place: "I am my own engineer, and my own carpenter, and my own plumber, and my own gardener, and my own Jack of all Trades ... Well, it's a good thing, you know. It brushes the Newgate cobwebs away, and pleases the aged." As this last admission shows, the Castle is not just art for art's sake; by means of it Wemmick has provided a blooming and delightful home for his aged parent, who recognizes it for the "pretty pleasure-ground" it is. The Castle also houses a "museum" that displays "among small specimens of china and glass, various neat trifles made by the proprietor of the museum, and some tobacco-stoppers carved by the Aged." The champion in London of "portable property" and its accumulation, Wemmick now, as a maker and connoisseur, stands for an opposite view of "things," which are no longer portable at all but stabilizing—the fixed fortifications of his fancy. When the sojourn is over at the end of this remarkable chapter, when the necessary return to the world has begun, Wemmick turns gradually "dryer and harder" as "the Castle and the drawbridge and the arbour and the lake and the fountain and the Aged" disappear all at once into the guarded recesses of his profoundly divided consciousness. A dozen novels after *Pickwick Papers*, the idea of a quarantined imagination has found brilliant restatement, and Wemmick, whose artistry has carved out an ideal if transitory escape from a world well lost, becomes the most thoroughgoing refugee of imagination in Dickens.

His fancy closeted, laconic, Wemmick is as far from Weller in the graph of imaginative life as a character can get. Yet the way he has chosen has become steadily more incumbent on Dickens's people since Sam's time. When nearly all talk is balked, or suborned to the vulgar lip service of romanticism, these characters must seek elsewhere than in style for their "solace"; in looking at fires, as in pastoral dreaming, they often find it. A diversionary tactic of the mind under duress, fire-gazing becomes one of Dickens's most important symbols for the everyday liaisons with imagination. It made its first appearance—a remarkable debut—with the furnace-tender's fire in *The Old Curiosity Shop*, and there Dickens was perhaps harkening back even to the Romantic *locus classicus* in Coleridge's "Frost at Midnight," where a mere piece of soot, or "film," lingering after a hearth fire is felt to perform, like the midnight frost, its own "secret ministry":

> ... the thin blue flame
> Lies on my low-burnt fire, and quivers not;
> Only the film, which fluttered on the grate,
> Still flutters there, the sole unquiet thing.
> Methinks its motion in this hush of nature
> Gives it dim sympathies with me who live,
> Making it a companionable form,
> Whose puny flaps and freaks the idling Spirit
> By its own moods interprets . . .(ll. 13–21)

Certainly the foundryman who gives Little Nell a warm place to lie down amid the volcanic industrial landscape of *The Old Curiosity Shop* "interprets" the fire he stokes as a "companionable form": "It has been alive as long as I have . . . We talk and think together all night long" (O.C.S.,44). As the fire is personified, it emerges as a sort of *genius loci* in the center of this industrial hell. Amid the hammering engines whose power it supplies, the foundryman's fire becomes, so to speak, a *deus inter machinas,* a protean and enduring force, the prime mover and special providence of the furnace-tender's affections and fancies. Here is his astonishing confession of faith: " 'It's like a book to me,' he said—'the only book I ever learned to read; and many an old story it tells me. It's music, for I should know its voice among a thousand, and there are other voices in the roar. It has pictures too. You don't know how many strange faces and different scenes I trace in the red-hot coals. It's my memory, that fire, and shows me all my life' " (44). After the death of his mother in his infancy, the worker's father brought him to this unusual hearth, where "the fire nursed me—the same fire. It has never gone out." The furnace fire is the worker's private myth of continuity, and, as the nurse of his life and fancy, it becomes a productive image for Dickens of the ministering imagination.

Having taken shape in *The Old Curiosity Shop,* the idea of fire-gazing immediately takes a turn it cannot afford. For by the time of *Barnaby Rudge,* the next novel, it has become an index to insanity. The idiot hero Barnaby exhibits the fate of escapist fantasies that have become too potent and overbearing, as he reports on one of his favorite games: "I like to lie before the fire, watching the prospects in the burning coals—the rivers, hills, and dells, in the deep, red sunset, and the wild faces" (B.R.,17). After a seeming climax, the series of imagined scenes snaps back with the clinching instance of dementia, those "wild faces" that obtrude as if by involuntary afterthought. It is up to Paul Dombey, two novels later, to pull back from this pathological fancy into something less fevered, more wholesome. Yet for him the autonomy of imagination, as evidenced partly in his fire-gazing, seems to have retreated, by forced march, into a kind of spiritual autism.

Paul's constrained world in *Dombey and Son* is very much like that to follow in *Hard Times,* where Mr. Gradgrind says to his daughter Louisa at one point: "It has always been my object so to educate you, as that you might, while still in your early youth, be (if I may so express myself) almost any age" (H.T.I,15). Paul Dombey enjoys the benefits of a similar educational system. He is given over to the care of the gruesomely "embowered" Mrs. Pipchin, "who had devoted all the energies of her mind, with the greatest success, to the study and treatment of infancy" (D.S.,8)— as if it were an infectious disease needing cure. He is also farmed out to Dr. Blimber, who, "in some partial confusion of his ideas, regarded the young gentlemen as if they were all Doctors, and were born grown up" (12). When Blimber offers "to make a man" of Paul, Paul replies: "I had rather be a child" (11). Exactly what kind of child is a grave puzzle to Mrs. Blimber, who soon "opined, with something like a shiver, that he was an unaccountable child" (11). That weighted adjective is a direct anticipation of *Hard Times* and its satiric terminology for human arithmetic. It is the irreducible mystery of every human soul, when properly understood, that it is by nature "unaccountable," in no way susceptible to logical or tabular account—wholly impervious, in other words, to anything like the "Analysis of the character of P. Dombey" (14) later performed by Dr. Blimber.

At Doctor Blimber's Academy, Paul Dombey falls victim to what Wordsworth might have called the "pygmy theory" of child development, in which children are denied the uniqueness of their vision and considered to be merely, in Mr. Dombey's own words, "little people" (8). When the "old-fashioned" Paul first meets Blimber, the boy admits to being six years old (12), and Dickens may well be alluding here to the Romantic poet he apparently knew best, to Wordsworth's "Intimations Ode" and its "six-years' Darling of a pygmy size" surrendering to a forced maturity. The allusion would be most appropriate, since it is Paul Dombey's struggle, against the unnatural strictures of the Blimber system, to retain as much of "the visionary gleam" of childhood as he can, and to persist in his "obstinate questionings / Of sense and outward things" while surrounded by an "arabesque work of his musing fancy" (12). An important part of this musing imagination has found vent in fire-gazing, and the key scene coincides with that famous crisis in Paul's education where he asks his father for a definition of money. Paul is sitting with his father before the fire, and like Wordsworth's "best Philosopher" he is "peering into the red perspective with the fixed and rapt attention of a sage . . . entertaining Heaven knows what wild fancies, half-formed thoughts, and wandering speculations" (8). Suddenly he blurts out: "Papa! what's money?" Disconcerted only for a moment, Mr. Dombey quickly regains his composure and begins to explain the holy principle of money as if it were the child's catechism, while Paul goes on "cogitating and looking for explanation in the fire." The same blaze that had been Paul's "advisor and prompter" in questioning his father now provides the child's weird, unearthly entertainment, with Paul "looking in between the bars of the grate, as if

some ghostly puppet-show were performing there." And we leave
the scene with Paul's face "addressed towards the flickering blaze,
until the nurse appeared to summon him to bed."

The chance of a pun in "addressed" opens surmise about Paul's
secret converse with the confined fires of his own imagination.
Just as the furnace fire in *The Old Curiosity Shop* substituted for
"books" in the imagination of the foundryman, and just as "the
hollow down by the flare" in *Our Mutual Friend* will later do
service for Lizzie Hexam's "library," so Paul Dombey not only
"addresses" his thoughts to the fire, but reads in the flames themselves his odd fictions, "studying Mrs. Pipchin, and the cat, and the
fire, night after night, as if they were a book of necromancy, in three
volumes" (8). Part of this "study" seems to bring him in closer
touch with his own premature instincts and with mortality itself,
for it is in one of those "old old moods of his," before the fire in
this same chapter, that he is induced by the flames to wonder, as
he admits to Mrs. Pipchin, "how old you must be." The hint of
"necromancy" in his curious soundings is also linked with the
earlier mention of Paul as a changeling, "like one of those terrible
little Beings in the Fairy tales, who, at a hundred and fifty or two
hundred years of age, fantastically represent the children for whom
they have been substituted" (8). D. H. Lawrence, who carried the
romantic novel into the Freudian era and who borrowed in the
process so many techniques and speculations from Dickensian
psychology, reproduces the "changeling-as-fire-gazer" image with
Anna Brangwen in *The Rainbow*. As the child Anna Lensky, she
seems "bewitched . . . like a changeling"[4] and appears like the old-
fashioned Paul Dombey before a hearth fire: "The fair head with
its wild, fierce hair was dropping towards the fire-warmth, which
reflected on the bright cheeks and clear skin of the child, who
seemed to be musing, almost like a grown-up person."[5] As in the
case of Paul Dombey, there is also a strange reciprocity with the
fire, an internalizing of its energies, for Anna's "face was illuminated till it seemed like wax lit up from the inside."

When Dickens, and Lawrence after him, blend the figure of the
sensitive romantic child, alive to a world of "musing fancy" from
which adults are excluded, with the fairy-tale motif of the changeling, the result is a peculiar anticipation of modern science fiction
and its recurring figure of the demonic child, in touch with alien
and unearthly energies, often possessed by an extraterrestrial intelligence. There is, of course, the transition ambiguously provided
by James in *The Turn of the Screw*. Yet the conception reaches its

apotheosis, after a cruder rendering in the fifties films *Village of the Damned* and its sequel, *Children of the Damned*, with Arthur C. Clarke's script for Kubrick's *2001: A Space Odyssey*. There the child is a kind of "changeling" for the entire race, rising triumphant at the end. His birth is the Second Coming, and a judgment on all mankind. It is no longer the isolated, supernatural child who is doomed, but everyone else. The race itself, embodied in Keir Dullea's nearly automatized Everyman, grows more and more "old-fashioned" before our eyes, and the Star Child, through the genetics of apocalypse, is born for our sins: a new order out of the old.

On the cover of the Signet edition of *Dombey and Son* (1964), Paul, presumably dead or dying, is laid out horizontally at the bottom, silhouetted in a spectral white—the ambiguous white of Coleridge and Melville. Mr. Dombey's profile rises from the left of the illustration, tinged with what looks like reddish firelight; it is the only light in the picture, fading off into the inky purple background, and it seems to emanate from a small reddish flame located at a point just below the base of Paul's brain—as if, like Lawrence's child, he were "lit up from the inside." It is an intriguing and suggestive cover, and it reminds us of the important connection, in this novel and in others, between the internal fire that sustains life and the external fires that characters must at times seek out to foster and fuel their imaginations. The symbol is completed when, long after Paul's fatal waning of energy, the hearth becomes an emblem of "Retribution" for Mr. Dombey in the chapter so named. Just before the reconciliation with Florence, we find Paul's desolate father surveying his image in a mirror, and what he finds there is a "spectral, haggard, wasted likeness of himself" that "brooded and brooded over the empty fire-place" (59).

In *David Copperfield*, one of Steerforth's few brooding moments is before the blazing hearth at the Peggotty's boat house, where David comes upon him by surprise. When Steerforth stirs the fire and David objects that his own chance for studying the pictures has been spoiled, Steerforth's answer underscores their private, subjective character: "You would not have seen them" (22). We soon learn that firelight, so often the "nurse" of benevolent fancies, so often a bright world where improving fictions are played out and dreams find habitation, has been a mockery and a confusion for Steerforth—where nursery tales carry dim warnings of disaster: "I believe I have been confounding myself with the bad boy who 'didn't care,' and became food for lions—a grander kind of going to the dogs, I suppose." And identity itself has not only been confounded, it has become frightening: "What old women call the horrors, have been creeping over me from head to foot. I have been afraid of myself."

Such refuge in fire-watching will, much later in the novel, revenge itself even upon David. After spending a "pleasantly fanciful" evening with Traddles, David returns to Gray's Inn and "gradually fell from consideration of his [Traddle's] happiness to tracing prospects in the live coals, and to thinking, as they broke and changed, of the vicissitudes and separations that had marked my life" (59). Though David had not seen a "coal fire" since he left England three years before, "many a wood fire had I watched, as it crumbled into hoary ashes, and mingled with the feathery heap upon the hearth, which not inaptly figured to me, in my despondency, my own dead hopes." Suddenly the present fire seems almost magical, as David finds his eyes "resting on a countenance that might have arisen out of the fire, in its association with my early remembrances" (59). The face belongs to Dr. Chillip, who apparently fears the effects of authorship on his old patient and who, three times in the course of their conversation, inquires about David's mental health. David has already twice "waived that question" when the Doctor, forced into some other topic of conversation, begins recounting his wife's theory that the Murdstones "undergo a continual punishment; for they are turned inward, to feed upon their own hearts, and their own hearts are very bad feeding." But immediately: "Now, sir, about that brain of yours, if you'll excuse my returning to it. Don't you expose it to a good deal of excitement, sir?" The transition seems abrupt, distracted, yet there is an important parallel between David's case and the Murdstones'. They feed on their own hearts, he feeds on his own brain. Their unhealthy inwardness seems to suggest to Dr. Chillip David's own imaginative introversion and the dangers of his creative fervor. Just as the Murdstones' evil is self-retributive, so Dr. Chillip is worried that David too is undergoing a revenge of imagination. And how does David react to the suggestion this third time? "I found it not difficult, in the excitement of Mr. Chillip's own brain, under his potations of negus, to divert his attention from this topic to his own affairs."

If Dr. Chillip is inordinately preoccupied with lunacy and derangement, like the obsessive storytellers in Dickens's first novel, for instance—and he has just the last name for it—then David, in his turn, is guarded and defensive like Pickwick himself, preserving what remains of his emotional equilibrium, even his sanity, by ignoring whatever would upset it. David Copperfield is a creative artist who has lived a life of productive fancy. He has drawn heavily on his imagination, yet it has somehow failed to replenish him. Though he has worked long and earnestly with imaginative language, words themselves have not worked the wonders for him that they did for extroverts like Sam Weller and Dick Swiveller, and when, late in the novel, Dr. Chillip happens to appear before him, David is confused and despondent. We are helped to see David's case as Dr. Chillip does—a revenge of imagination—by the way in which their encounter is framed: for Chillip "might have" (the subjunctive of fancy) sprung up with those troublesome questions on his chilling lips out of that same fire where, before it betrayed him, David had been exercising his brighter fancies.

Two novels later, the initial fire-gazing scene in *Hard Times* comes appropriately in the "Never Wonder" chapter, with Louisa and Tom Gradgrind at their father's hearth, a place where the "fanciful imagination" is indeed a "treason." Louisa seems transfixed by the flames, and she speaks "slowly, and in a curious tone, as if she were reading what she asked in the fire, and it were not quite plainly written there" (I,8). When Tom looks into the fire to see what engrosses his sister, he finds nothing; to him it looks "as stupid and blank as everything else looks." An important exchange follows. "What can you see in it?" Tom asks. "Not a circus?" And Louisa replies, "I don't see anything in it, Tom, particularly. But since I have been looking at it, I have been wondering about you and me grown up." The fire brings on wonder. Tom is looking for some substantial relief from the mulish drudgery of his life, and of this the circus is Dickens's chief representation in the novel; hence Tom's question. But as Louisa's response shows, the fire-gazing reaches deeper into the psychic life, inducing the very wonder upon which circus-going and all imaginative enterprise are founded.

The metaphor of fire appears often in *Hard Times*, where Louisa's "starved imagination" is described as "a fire with nothing to burn" (I,3), and where we hear later that her repressed energies "smouldered within her like an unwholesome fire" (III,1). That last description then opens out into a vision of reality turning back on itself in destructive reprisal, the imagination's revenge when denied a refuge in fancy: "All closely imprisoned forces rend and destroy. The air that would be healthful to the earth, the water that would enrich it, the heat that would ripen it, tear it when caged up. So in her bosom now; the strongest qualities she possessed, long turned upon themselves, became a heap of obduracy, that rose against a friend." For Dickens this psychic retaliation is a kind of natural law, and part of Louisa's tragedy is that only she seems to sense this. When discussing with her father her proposed loveless marriage to Bounderby, she looks hopelessly into the distance, and Gradgrind asks if she is "consulting the chimneys of the Coketown works" (I,15). " 'There seems to be nothing there but languid and monotonous smoke. Yet when the night comes, Fire bursts out, father!' she answered, turning quickly." Here is Gradgrind's only response: "I do not see the application of the remark." Louisa's hours of fire-gazing drew her to a sense of wonder and provided Dickens with an icon for her constrained but vital energies, both fanciful and sexual. But these energies have stagnated, and she can now find symbolic expression for them only in the smouldering, incendiary nature of the Coketown furnaces waiting for their violent discharge.

By the close of the novel, however, Time does seem to have healed many wounds, and in the valedictory section we find Louisa "watching the fire as in the days of yore, though with a gentler and a humbler face" (III,9). Now prophecy is possible, and the question "How much of the future might arise before *her* vision?" is answered in a long series of noun fragments and participles in an overall present tense of anticipated futurity, which foresees in the fire, among other things, Louisa "grown learned in childish lore" and dedicating herself, on behalf of Sissy's children, to "those imaginative graces and delights, without which the heart of infancy will wither up." Much like the way the coda of *Pickwick* widened to the scope of the author's whole creative imagination bidding farewell to the characters of his own brain, here the chronicler's expected resumé of the future and of the fate of his characters is internalized as Louisa's private and habitual fire-gazing raised finally to a visionary power.

When we turn to the fire-gazers in Dickens's last completed novel, *Our Mutual Friend,* we return to a brother and sister pair like the Gradgrinds whose emotional bond is not only symbolized but sustained by their time together at the family hearth. When Charley Hexam sees nothing at all in the fire, Lizzie explains that "It wants my eyes, Charley." She then makes an effort to translate for him what she can glimpse of past, present, and future in the dance of the coal blaze, and the insensitive Charley at least seems to understand the fire's importance for his sister: "You said you couldn't read a book, Lizzie. Your library of books is the hollow down by the flare, I think" (I,3). With this idea Dickens has returned through ten major novels, especially through Paul Dombey's almost voodooistic use of the fire as a book of black magic, back to the foundryman in *The Old Curiosity Shop,* for whom the furnace fire was "like a book to me . . . the only book I ever learned to read." Yet it is typical of Charley that he later wants to deny Lizzie the continuing reality of her fiery visions, as part of his habitual effort to escape the moral and emotional burden of his past. " 'You are such a dreamer,' said the boy, with his former petulance. 'It was all very well when we sat before the fire—when we looked into the hollow down by the flare—but we are looking into the real world now' " (II,1).

In the center of the dust-heaped squalor and greed of *Our Mutual Friend,* a world of ever-worsening potentialities, a world defaced everywhere by bodily and spiritual mutilations, the hollow down by the flare is able to "real-ize" something far better, yet Charley will have none of it. In a later interview between Lizzie and Bella Wilfer by another fire that "might have been the old brazier," with a glow that "might have been the old hollow down by the flare" (III,9), Lizzie again hints at the fire's healing power. A silence falls between the two girls, with Lizzie glancing down "at the glow in the fire where her first fancies had been nursed, and her first escape made from the grim life out of which she had plucked her brother," and these lines again closely echo the furnace-tender's belief that "the fire nursed me—that same fire." Lizzie now makes of her fire-gazing an unselfish gift to Bella, an act of imaginative mercy, when she reads an encouraging future for the despondent girl in the glow of the coals.

That phrase "escape . . . from the grim life" is a clear statement of the escapist refuge in imagination which tends to be detested by characters who cannot avail themselves of it, and when Charley repeats to Bradley Headstone the idea of the fire as Lizzie's "books," speaking even of her "wise fancies . . . when she sat looking at it," Headstone is triggered into a brief self-condemning outburst: "I don't like that" (II,1). Here is an enemy of fancy even less lenient than Charley, a man who we have already heard has a certain "stiffness" in his manner "recalling some mechanics in their holiday clothes" (II,1). This barely more than casual analogy at once takes off on its own in a complex monotony of repetition reminiscent of the mechanical drone in some of the satiric prose of *Hard Times:* "He had acquired *mechanically* a great store of teacher's knowledge. He could no mental arithmetic *mechanically,* sing at sight *mechanically,* blow various wind instruments *mechanically,* even play at the great church organ *mechanically.* From his early childhood up, his mind had been a place of *mechanical stowage"* (II,1, my italics). The dead metaphor "store . . . of knowledge" is prodded back to life in order to expose Bradley's own deadness of soul, along with such ironic diction as "stowage" above and, later in the same paragraph, the idea of Bradley "taking stock" of his "mental warehouse."

Though there is almost nothing human left, though romance has been almost entirely driven out, still, as in *Hard Times,* fires wait to flare up, and through all of Bradley's mechanically "constrained manner" there was "enough of what was animal, and of what was fiery (though smouldering) still visible in him." (II,1). Jenny Wren in her own way predicts the explosion when comparing him, not without demonic overtones, to "a lot of gunpowder among lighted lucifer matches" (II,11). The pattern of the "wolfish turn" from *Hard Times* is by now expected, and, after the assault on Eugene which only serves to bring him and Lizzie together, Bradley's subsequent murder of Riderhood becomes at the same time his own suicide. Just before the murder, however, Bradley has become one of the most obsessive fire-gazers in Dickens. Repeatedly he stares into the blaze with what is called "intent abstraction," the oxymoron neatly responding to the deep disturbance of reality in the scene. Prose is also used suggestively in the stiffly isolated two-word main clause of the following sentence, a startling vision of fire-gazing in its ultimate ironic decline: "Rigid before the fire, as if it were a charmed flame that was turning him old, *he sat,* with the dark lines deepening in his face, its stare becoming more and more haggard, its surface turning whiter and whiter as if it were being overspread with ashes, and the very texture and colour of his hair degenerating" (IV,15; my italics). The firelight which has elsewhere, in this novel and before, evoked the instinctive energy of life itself—as in Rogue Riderhood's "spark of life" (III,3)—called forth the vitalizing imagination, summoned up memory and carried the gazer back to the wholeness and warmth of childhood here has the opposite effect, "a charmed flame" draining the very life from Bradley in a necromantic horror far worse than anything suffered by Paul Dombey.

Machines menace the imagination in Dickens, but at the heart of the machines, at the source of their mimic life but very real power, is an energy, a fire, that only the imagination can fully harness. This idea was the source for Dickens's private archetype of the shaping fancy in *The Old Curiosity Shop,* and out of that first image of the furnace fire came one of his most potent and versatile symbols for the energies of imagination. With Bradley Headstone, as foreseen in *Hard Times,* the man has at last become merely the complete machine, well oiled and monotonous. The schoolmaster in *Our Mutual Friend* is the culmination and the final dreadful critique for the themes of destructive education and the mechanical operation of the spirit. And as so often happens when these subjects converge, firelight illuminates the darker ironies. Bradley hated Lizzie's fire-gazing, but his own smouldering fires have finally erupted in criminal violence, and when he himself looks intently at a blaze for the first time, it begins to destroy him—in a way which suggests with brilliant irony that he has become not only a machine but, just before the last "spark of life" is drowned out of him, a dying fire as well, his face "turning whiter and whiter as if it were being overspread with ashes."

Here is Angus Wilson's Mrs. Eliot on a February day in her middle age: "Gazing into the jutting, craggy landscape of the fire that flickered and glowed each instant, she was carried back to the thousand times she had peopled with her thoughts these burning caves and mountains snow-topped with wood ash—Alice-like, drying her hair, or like Maggie Tulliver, her book fallen to the floor."[6] In addition to Lewis Carroll and George Eliot, Wilson might well have invoked here the Victorian author with whom he is most closely identified. For in Dickens, as we have seen, it is this same imaginative act of fire-gazing which often lays claim to such landscapes of wonder. It is willed retreat, a sojourn, the winning of a temporary refuge from times that are very hard indeed. Gazing at fires in Dickens is a variety of domestic romanticism, a hearthside entrance to a world of brighter conjecture which, by the nature of its medium, also becomes a symbol for the flux, the impermanence of such vision, the never more than temporary shelter its images bring. Then, too, the greatest virtue of this activity, its quiet privacy, is in the end its major limitation. The intimate monitoring of one's own fancies in fire-gazing becomes a closed-circuit imagination that is, though not wholly passive, receptive only, rather than truly creative. When Paul Dombey "addresses" the fire, for instance, it is an "expression" of his imagination in a narrowed sense, and he is, in the last analysis, endowed more meagerly with the Dickensian energy than are those real men of expression like the Wellers, or Dick Swiveller, or even Quilp.

In the wake of liberating talk, the aftermath of style's ascendancy, personality has an increasingly hard time of it. Perhaps the tyrannous supremacy of Pecksniff's false verbal life in *Martin Chuzzlewit* first made unmistakable the crumbling of style's rightful harmony and empire, the Pickwickian dethronement. Before moving to the later consolations for this partly lost, partly abdicated reign in characters like David Copperfield, Arthur Clennam, and Pip, there are two unique creatures of fancy, Mrs. Gamp and Tom Pinch, who flank Pecksniff in his novel and who deserve close attention for the eccentric alternatives, equivocal, highly unstable, which they pose to his rhetorical absolute.

Sairey Gamp is one of the most stubbornly escapist personalities in Dickens, and her unrelieved, spasmodic language is not expressive so much as defensive. In her first encounter with that other compulsive talker in *Martin Chuzzlewit*, the notorious Seth Pecksniff, her pointless declaration—"I am not a Rooshan or a Prooshan, and consequently cannot suffer spies to be set over me" (19)—seems to Mrs. Gamp an impregnable refuge, and we find her "entrenching herself behind her strong point as if it were not assailable by human ingenuity." Besides this use of language as fortification, Mrs. Gamp's earthy babble does have something in common with the street wit of the Wellers. With similar linguistic luck, her slipshod language takes shape as a pun when she speaks of Mr. Mould, the mortician, having "undertook the highest families in the land" (19), and Sairey is allowed a Wellerian creative accident with words later when she tells Chuffey to get some life into himself (i.e., some color into his cheeks): "Rouge yourself, and look up! Come!" (46).

We also notice something more characteristic in that sloppy "g" which so often strays into her words, a partner to that syntactic malpractice for which the lady is even more infamous among linguists—her use of "which" as a sort of vague, all-purpose coordinator, seen here in the company of the dauntless "g": "which fiddlestrings is weakness to expredge my nerves this night."[7] This abuse is a grammatical liberty which sets Sairey free from the normal rules and responsibilities of subordination; she uses the relative pronoun as a conjunction, often just as empty filler, as if to imply syntactical rigor without the necessary expenditure of effort. It is a verbal laxness that joins with that soft, lazy "g" in informing us with surprising completeness about Mrs. Gamp's temperament, for it would seem that she relieves the harshness of language itself with the palatal "g" in a small effort to make her life easier, more palatable. This softening is not synonymous with euphemism, for Mrs. Gamp insists on all the sting, all the savor of life which her gin and her vinegar can bring her, and her only "motives of delicacy" have to do with hiding the gin in the teapot (49). In the world of *Martin Chuzzlewit*, Sairey Gamp stands for everything that euphemism would fumigate from consciousness, all the grit and squalor of daily living. It is only fitting that Mrs. Gamp should have an irreparable falling out, for whatever reasons, with anyone named Prig, and it is ironically fitting that Dickens should spin out perhaps the most flagrant circumlocution, the most improbably priggish euphemism in all of his writing, about Mrs. Gamp's services during "labor": "It chanced on this particular occasion, that Mrs. Gamp had been up all the previous night, in attendance upon a ceremony to which the usage of gossips has given the name which expresses, in two syllables, the curse pronounced on Adam" (19).

To labor by the sweat of her brow is of course Sairey's curse too, and the purpose of her being, throughout the constant emergency of keeping herself alive, is to ameliorate this curse as much as possible, to find peace from her labors by every devious means available. When she pours out her almost impenetrable language, often laced with illicit biblical allusions and dilapidated gentility, her purpose is to forestall response and thus to dodge responsibility. Using language as a defense against numbness and the loss of will, Sairey becomes a latter-day Alfred Jingle, and her "entrenchment" in words meets its greatest trial with her imaginary idolatress Mrs. Harris. What we recognize here—and it is unusual for the kind of character I am now discussing, except for those dishonest figures who simply lie their way into postures of artistic sensibility—is language itself articulating the escapist fiction. When Mrs. Gamp talks a character into existence who then talks in her imagined turn about nothing but Mrs. Gamp, words have closed out reality in a last embattled stand. The word itself, the name "Harris," brings succor "as if it were a talisman against all earthly sorrows" (49), and Sairey is profoundly disturbed when this nominalist magic is attacked by Mrs. Prig in a brilliantly set and performed scene of "exorcism" that anticipates Edward Albee by over a century (49). At what a deep subconscious level the self-realizing name Harris—the word which is the thing itself—has brought comfort is revealed when, after Mrs. Prig has denied the existence of Mrs. Harris and thus undermined the very bulwark of Sairey's imagination, Mrs. Gamp "was heard to murmur 'Mrs. Harris' in her sleep" (49), a kind of reverse prayer of supplication from the goddess to her devoted creation.

For Tom Pinch in the same novel there is no such debacle of imagination. Denied the rewards of manhood, both sexual and emotional, Mr. Pinch is given the sureties of fancy in return for celibacy. When Mark Tapley, however, tells Tom, "Your conversation's always equal to print" (5), he says so with a "broad grin," for Mr. Pinch has none of the lively verbal wit of his predecessors in the line of imaginative men. In fact, Tom Pinch is not a comic character at all, but merely a "funny" man. It is Dick Swiveller, in Dickens's fourth novel, who is the last comic hero in the works of our foremost comic writer. The books are not less funny after *The Old Curiosity Shop*, but the heroes are, and so the theme of imagination must submit to surprising revisions. Tom Pinch, the all too obvious representative of idealizing fancy in *Martin Chuzzlewit*, is as different from Mrs. Gamp as his friend Mark Tapley, in the role of spokesman for the verbal life, is from Mr. Pecksniff. Dickens addresses Tom in quaint, antiquated, biblical apostrophes, a patron's beneficence which Mrs. Gamp hardly requires. Dickens talks *to* Tom as if to make up for how much less he has to say *about* him, and how much less Tom has to say for himself. As "imaginist," Tom is entirely a child of grace, his fancies granted and guaranteed for him by his creator, in the image of whose imagination they are made. Tom sees and believes to be true what Dickens has fancied for him, and, unspoiled by deluding self-interest, seeing becomes the warrant of being. Tom's journey to Salisbury and his ecstatic perceptions along the way make this clear. Dickens begins to mediate the animistic scene for us with such tried and serviceable qualifiers as "like" and "might" and "as if," but we are made aware that for Tom Pinch there is no mediation—things *are* as they seem, each fanciful hypothesis finding instant confirmation in Tom's mind. The passage, scarcely one of Dickens's most inspired, needs quotation; the italics are mine:

The sheep-bells rang as clearly in the vigorous air, *as if* they felt its wholesome influence *like* living creatures; the trees, in lieu of leaves or blossoms, shed upon the ground a frosty rime that sparkled as it fell, and *might have been* the dust of diamonds. *So it was to Tom.* From cottage chimneys, smoke went streaming up high, high, *as if* the earth had lost its grossness, being so fair, and must not be oppressed by heavy vapour. The crust of ice on the else rippling brook was so transparent and so thin in texture, that the lively water *might* of its own free will have stopped—*in Tom's glad mind it had*—to look upon the lovely morning. And lest the sun should break this charm too eagerly, there moved between him and the ground, a mist *like* that which waits upon the moon on summer nights—*the very same to Tom*—and wooed him to dissolve it gently. (5)

This imaginative revision of the world, however stilted, has broken free of any fallacious distortion; it is neither falsifying nor self-centered, and stands in exact contrast to the later vision of Pecksniff in Nature, a parody of the pathetic fallacy by which the "summer weather in his bosom was reflected in the Breast of Nature" (30).

Dickens must have realized that he had discovered a functional shorthand in Tom's journey to Salisbury for the depiction of wish-fulfilling fancies, and he uses the formula again for Walter Gay in his next novel, another watery young man blessed with a "strong infusion" of the "spice of romance and love of the marvellous," amused and consoled by "indistinct and visionary fancies" (*D.S.*, 9), who listens to Florence's strange adventures with old Mrs. Brown "as if . . . they were rambling along among the broad leaves and tall trees of some desert island in the tropics—as he very likely fancied, for the time, they were" (6). Again the materialized "might have," the "as if" briefly realized, that was Tom's romantic grace in the preceding novel; the conception is again uninspired, the point inescapable.

There is in *Martin Chuzzlewit*, however, an encapsulated study in the malign potential of imagination almost unparalleled in Dickens. I speak of the famous "View from Todgers's" which gives the title to Dorothy Van Ghent's important article,[8] and which few critics after her have missed the opportunity to discuss. To my knowledge, though, no one has connected the Todgers's vision with its pleasant obverse, the other side of the coin of fancy in the experience of Tom Pinch. After a description of the Todgers's roof in a sentence beginning "Whoever climbed to this observatory" (9), there is a move to a generic second person: ". . . there were things to gaze at from the top of Todgers's, well worth your seeing." The shifting point of view (or viewer) is part of a carefully varied focus designed to isolate the act of perception itself as a disembodied, an impersonal experience, and the first thing one gazes on is, as promised, worth attention: "For first and foremost, if the day were bright, you observed upon the housetops, stretching far away, a long dark path: the shadow of the Monument: and turning round, the tall original was close beside you, with every hair erect upon his golden head, as if the doings of the city frightened him." Designed by Sir Christopher Wren to commemorate the Great Fire of London; the Monument is a large Doric column surmounted by a flaming brass urn.[9] But something is wrong, for it appears like a frightened human form with its hair (the sculpted flames of the urn) standing on end. Personification is here a premonition, and before the inanimate world even begins to frighten the onlooker, it is itself scared "by the doings of the town."

The observer soon sees why, for now things really start happening. This is meant literally: things do not simply exist, they *happen*, they swarm and start to life, and before long they have startled and harried the observer, and worse. By the end of this passage,

the tumult swelled into a roar; the hosts of objects seemed to thicken and expand a hundredfold; and after gazing round him, quite scared, he turned into Todgers's again, much more rapidly than he came out; and ten to one he told M. Todgers afterwards that if he hadn't done so, he would certainly have come into the street by the shortest cut; that is to say, head-foremost.

The colloquial descent of the last lines, especially the chatty "ten to one," serves to alleviate slightly what Van Ghent calls a seizure of "suicidal nausea at the momentary vision of a world in which significance has been replaced by naked and aggressive existence."[10] The softening of the passage at the end matches the deceptive safety of the opening, as explained by Van Ghent: "Much of the description is turned upon the conservative 'seemed to be' and 'as if,' and the pathetic fallacy provides a familiar bourgeois security, but the technique changes in the middle, betrayed by a discomfort which the 'as if's' are no longer able to conceal."[11]

Tom's vision during his journey to Salisbury, also recorded with these tentative locutions of fancy, was very much like the temporary security of the rooftop prospect—but without betrayal or discomfort. "Tom's glad mind" dismissed the necessity of mediation, and saw beauty face to face as truth, whereas mediation deserts the Todgers's spectator above as "might-have-beens" swell into terrorizing realities. The nakedness and aggression of this sort of imagination is far more like that of the idiot Barnaby Rudge in the preceding novel than like Tom's. In fact, the "gambols of a piece of cloth upon the dyer's pole," as seen from Todgers's, directly echo Barnaby's vision of clothes on a line as they "roll and gambol" like the strange figures who "live in sleep" (*B.R.*, 10). Barnaby is acquainted not only with the residents of pleasant dreams, but with the inmates of nightmare, and this becomes explicit as a waking threat when we hear of something very much like the Todgers's vision, Barnaby's "strange imaginings" that produce a "terror of certain senseless things—familiar objects he endowed with life" (25). There is a further unusual anticipation of the view from Todgers's in *Barnaby Rudge*; it is John Willet's advice to his son for amusing himself in London, which begins with typically muddled grammar: ". . . and the diversion I recommend is to go to the top of the Monument, and sitting there. There's no temptation there, sir—no drink—no young women—no bad characters of any sort—nothing but imagination" (13). This stupid man, who misunderstands the nature of fancy so far as to have said of Barnaby, after his speech about the clothes on the line, that he "wants imagination" (10), here has no suspicion of the imagination's possible uneasiness. Yet it seems as if Dickens let this idea of the isolated imagination sit in his own mind until the Todgers's passage resulted, where, as a prelude to human confoundings, the Monument itself is nervously animated by the frightfulness of its own vertiginous prospect.

The two halves of imaginative experience, the refreshing and the frightful, come together in the mind of Barnaby Rudge, where derangement makes the balance unsteady. In *Martin Chuzzlewit* the two sorts of fancy are held in isolation, and Tom's glad imaginings are untouched by the Todgers's vision. This is, in a sense, Tom's quarantine of imagination, and I think it goes a long way toward explaining the unexpected intrusion of the Todgers's experience into this particular novel. It is there because Tom is there, to complete the scheme, and its being precipitate and obtrusive is a large part of the point Dickens is making. He has isolated for us a trauma of the imagination, the dark underside of fancy all the more terrible because it comes unannounced, and because it can come to anyone—with the exception of Tom Pinch, of course.

Dickens goes to great lengths to prove this immunity. Much later in the novel there is a detailed passage about Tom's morning excursions to the docks, where, included among the "turmoil" of a densely populated world of things, were "church steeples, warehouses, house-roofs, arches, bridges, men and women, children, casks, cranes, boxes, horses, coaches, idlers, and hard-labourers . . . all jumbled up together, any summer morning, far beyond Tom's power of separation" (40). This is a confusion for Tom that does not confound, with Dickens exercising an unnatural restraint on his own customary ethics of description. The lapsed "power of separation" in this indiscriminate listing of people and things would ordinarily be an accusation against the dehumanizing fancy; yet Tom is exonerated. In another burst of animistic detail,

Dickens now records that the "incessant roar from every packet's funnel . . . quite expressed and carried out the uppermost emotion of the scene," making them appear "to be perspiring and bothering themselves, exactly as their passengers did." As in the nervous bristling of the Monument, here the inanimate sea-going machines are themselves reduced to "a state of mind bordering on distraction." This neurotic imagination is now completely displaced, ascribed only to the inanimate world this time, without reverberations for the spectator. To Tom the frenzied "disorder" of the place is only "amusing," for indeed it is presumed to be his own fanciful animation of the scene, without anxiety or aggression. In the first description of Tom, we hear that he is "extremely shortsighted" (2). Dickens probably made a strategic decision simply to ignore Tom's visual limitation when he made him the receiving consciousness for some of the most minutely detailed landscapes and cityscapes in his writing. But even if Dickens expects us to remember that Tom could hardly have seen such wonders with any clarity, we are still very much in the grip of his theme, for "Tom's glad mind" sees not as ordinary men do, but as the romantic dreamer does—not what is, but what should be.

Tom, we later learn, has "read himself half blind" (31) as a student of Mr. Pecksniff's, but his near-sightedness could also be explained by his avid reading of imaginative literature, especially Shakespeare, whose complete works he keeps by his bedside. One night, before reading one of the plays to Martin, the two men have been discussing the vicissitudes of Martin's love life, and Tom alludes to the now proverbial lines from *A Midsummer Night's Dream* (I,i) by suggesting that ". . . what never ran smooth yet, can hardly be expected to change its character for us" (6). There is a later and more significant allusion to the same Shakespearean play, this time by Dickens himself in one of his own apostrophized asides to Tom—an allusion which Mr. Pinch is meant to catch and, I think, to complete. Tom is moving on foot across a bitter cold landscape, and Dickens enjoins him in this own iambic pentameter (one of Shakespeare's least happy influences upon the novelist) as follows: "Look round and round upon this bare bleak plain, and see even here, upon a winter's day, how beautiful the shadows are! Alas! it is the nature of their kind to be so. The loveliest things in life, Tom, are but shadows; and they come and go, and change and fade away, as rapidly as these!" (12) The best are but shadows; "and the worst are no worse, if imagination amend them" (V,i). Since he has recently alluded to the same play, Tom should be in a fine position to "amend" Dickens's statement with the crucial idea of "imagination."

Throughout *Martin Chuzzlewit*, in uneasy company with the Todgers's vision, Tom has stood for the rewards of imagination, and has been rewarded. He has been Dickens's provision (*pro vision*) against the fatality of fancy. Contained and framed by the mind alone, secure against the violations of society, what Tom Pinch is allowed to envision in the world at large is what the fire-gazers can usually see only in the hearth: a finer rendition of the real. Insofar as Tom's amending refuge has become a fortification against life, however, an uncreative "solace," to the extent that it cuts him off from the anxieties and intimacies of maturity, then Mr. Pinch is not so much an artist as a mere tactician of escape. He is certainly to be forgiven his forced retreat, for the Dickens world is not an easy world, and he is even partly to be envied, for with Tom Pinch the imagination is for the last time in Dickens an inviolable asylum.

In a world where the imagination is in such inhuman decline, where the "poetry of existence" is so coarsely bruited about, more and more characters begin to air their fancies at self-enforced distances from a society scarred everywhere by an un-visionary dreariness. These men and women refuse to concede to the prosaic, to the adamant blankness of living only day to day, without contour and by rule. Yet it is no surprise in such a world that an announced denial of fancy, an escape into wordless privacy, seems one of the few effective gambits left. This retreat is often merely a stepping back into disclaimer, a public disowning of privately held powers. There are, of course, certain characters who say they have no imagination and who are simply telling the truth. When Gaffer Hexam in *Our Mutual Friend* says "I ain't one of the supposing sort" (*O.M.F.* I,3), he means it, as we have already learned from the conclusion of the novel's first chapter, where Gaffer has a corpse in tow: "A neophyte might have fancied that the ripples passing over it were dreadfully like faint changes of expression on a sightless face; but Gaffer was no neophyte and had no fancies" (I,1). Given his situation, few of us are so rigorous as to wish imagination upon him. Gaffer's world is such a black and horrible place that he must expel fancies in order to fend off neurosis. This is the quarantine of imagination at its most desperate and final. More often we meet characters who disclaim fancy while holding to it in secret—characters like Mr. Morfin in *Dombey and Son*, who claims to be merely a clockwork man but who consoles himself in private with his cello, those "practical people," Mr. and Mrs. Meagles, who indulge among their many domestic fantasies a delightful pastoral idea about birds "being practical people too" (L.D. I,16), Miss Pross, that woman "of business" with, as she insists and we know better,[12] "no imagination at all" (T.T.C. II,6), or finally Mr. Grewgious, who pretends to have "not a morsel of fancy" but who, on the contrary, illustrates "the unexplored romantic nooks in the unlikeliest men" (E.D.,11).

To explore such "nooks" of the private imagination in Dickens throughout their long and troubled history—the efforts by which they are won and defended, the homes for the spirit they sometimes make—is the task this chapter has set itself. Pastoralists both good and spurious, the devoted fire-gazers in novel after novel, escapist men and women of every fanciful persuasion, have all demanded representation here, including the late and variously wasted "heroes" of imagination yet to be treated, like David Copperfield, Esther Summerson, Arthur Clennam, Pip, and John Harmon. Any study that hopes broadly to explain how, under what pressures, and after what setbacks Sam Weller comes to be resurrected in Jenny Wren obviously needs such a transitional survey. The interiority we cannot for a minute believe in with Chadband must, nevertheless, be shaped and held to by any character in search of wholeness, despite that entropy of imagination which everywhere seems to characterize the psychic life in the later novels. The art of escape among Dickens's characters is often to withdraw, deeply and finally, into that very "private life" I began this chapter by calling into question for the unfathomable Chadband: an artful retreat into some kind of artistic adequacy.

This is precisely what Twemlow cannot accomplish in Our Mutual Friend, and he emerges as one of the most economically brilliant and sympathetic satires in Dickens on the retreatist mentality. With a Shakespearean convergence of "love" and "imagination" in the term "fancy," we hear that Twemlow "once had his fancy, like the rest of us, and she didn't answer" (I,10). "Brooding over the fire ... Twemlow is melancholy," we are told, and no reviving "fancies" are conjured up at this domestic hearth—only a pervasive sense of "waste." The biographical information about Twemlow's "fancy" deepens in retrospect that initial description of him as a man with "cheeks drawn in as if he had made a great effort to retire into himself some years ago, and had got so far and had never got any farther" (I,2). The imagination has retreated from its defeat and has withered in "retirement," with the "private life" once again failing a man cut off from sustaining fictions.

To deter monotony, to war against the intransigent, the degrading flatness of things, characters like Tom Pinch in *Martin Chuzzlewit*, on the other hand, have sought out in a detour from reality their own "romantic nooks." Pecksniff in that novel is what is wrong with style; Mark Tapley, what is still left of the "Apollo" ideal; Mrs. Gamp, a Jingle turned harried, jangled, with a neurotic language no longer style but merely a transient anodyne against madness or stupor; Tom Pinch, a man escaped to silence, fled into myopic fictions. *Martin Chuzzlewit*, though a manifest turning point, leaves almost nowhere to turn. Whatever the remaining figures of imagination will be empowered to do with their lives, however little, it will have to be something new.

They must, for one thing, look to time for its restorative potential. Tom Pinch has outstripped the normal course and downgrade of time by getting ahead of it at the start; he is middle-aged in body and spirit while still technically a young man: an escape from time that is of course self-defeating. So too with the "old-fashioned" Paul Dombey in the next book, who manages to die while still a child. But in the novel following *Dombey and Son*, the hero who stands for the novelist himself must take time as it comes, suffer its insults and losses, garner its benefits in the end. When David Copperfield was a child playing with Little Emily, the "days sported by us, as if Time had not grown up himself yet, but were a child too, and always at play" (*D.C.*,3). Then, blissfully, David "had no future," but when this feeling returns after Dora's death, it is the desolating revenge of time: "I came to think that the Future was walled up before me, that the energy and action of my life were at an end" (54). That depletion of energy which is one of the prime enemies of imagination has left him physically and spiritually debilitated, and in the "Tempest" chapter near the end of the book he becomes feverish and loses all "clear arrangement of time and distance" (55).

Mr. Dick, the novel's other autobiographer, has also been thrown long before "into a fever" by cruelty and unkindness, but he has managed, as Aunt Betsey explains, to transmute his pain into art, not into the Memorial which he will never complete, but into a small poetic token of his ordeal in the repeated symbolism of King Charles the First, who quite literally lost his head: "That's his allegorical way of expressing it. He connects his illness with great disturbance and agitation, naturally, and that's the figure, or

the simile, or whatever it's called, which he chooses to use" (14).
David's "allegorical way of expressing" his overstrained nerves is
to project his disturbance into a different sort of external "simile,"
the raging "Tempest" during which "Something within me, faintly
answering to the storm without, tossed up the depths of my memory, and made a tumult in them" (55). Time itself seems disrupted,
and David's desperate search for Ham during the storm becomes
a search for time's spokesman in the novel, its hero and martyr.
Shakespeare's Hamlet, for whom Ham is no doubt partly named
(along with Noah's son, saved upon the water as the present Ham
will not be), found himself in a time murderously out of joint,
but at the climax of his drama he could say serenely, "If it be now,
'tis not to come; if it be not to come, it will be now; if it be not
now, yet it will come" (V,ii). Just before the sacrifice that will at
last purge the guilt of Ham's own family, he says likewise to David:
"... if my time is come, 'tis come. If't an't, I'll bide it" (55). Unlike
the uncle in Shakespeare, Mr. Peggotty here is also a hero, and in
his last scene in the novel he tells of a special providence which
seems to justify Ham's death: " 'Theer's been kiender a blessing
fell upon us,' said Mr. Peggoty, reverentially inclining his head,
'and we've done nowt but prosper. That is, in the long run. If
not yesterday, why then to-day. If not to-day, why then to-
morrow" (63).

For David Copperfield, writer and thoughtful critic of language
though he is, words have not served the emotional life as they were
able to do for Sam or Dick or Mark, and the autobiographical hero
of this middle novel becomes another key transitional figure in
that reluctant devaluation of verbal fancy which undermines the
life of words in Dickens's later novels. David's case is a paradigm,
for while Micawber dwells heedlessly with words, David must
turn, in the absence of such verbal resort, to that internalized
romantic experience which comes to characterize the later heroes.
Seeking breadth and scope for his fancies once more after his
feverish trial during the storm, David travels to the Alps, where
he retrieves his native instinct for "sublimity and wonder" and
hears the "soothing songs" of Nature almost as if they were "not
earthly music" (58). This part of the novel, where "great Nature
spoke to me; and soothed me to lay down my weary head upon
the grass," is no success. Dickens is not at home in the Wordsworthian outdoors, and yet the strain in the writing is somehow
vital, for we can feel Dickens scouting out once again some new
novelistic projection for the romantic aspirations of his characters.

David's redemptive episode after fever is a wholesale reworking of the temporal renovation afoot in the preceding novel. After Paul Dombey loses his battle with time, it turns healing for, among others, those cohorts in romantic pipedream, Captain Cuttle and Sol Gills, men whose determination to skirt the prosaic has made their lives more feeling, more festive. Again we are exploring an unlikely "romantic nook" of personality where characters entertain fancies and are entertained by them. By the novel's last chapter, in the true fashion of a romance, these men have been rewarded, with Sol Gills, his "chronometer in his pocket," emerging as time's beneficiary. His investments have begun to pay off in "the fullness of the time and the design," and his partner Captain Cuttle brightens his imagination with "a fiction of a business . . . which is better than any reality." The core of false mercantile values in the novel is stabbed through with a single revisionist fancy, another skirmish won for imagination. Yet optimistic fictions about time have laid hold of their best symbol earlier in the novel, during the Captain's ministry over Florence when she lay ill at the Midshipman. "At this stage of her recovery, Captain Cuttle, with an imperfect association of a watch with a physician's treatment of a patient, took his own down from the mantelshelf, and holding it out on his hook, and taking Florence's hand in his, looked steadily from one to the other, as expecting the dial to do something" (48). Here the Dickensian genius assumes its finest stride, and in one brilliant move symbolizes an entire romantic faith in the curative nature of time itself.

David Copperfield, and after him Arthur Clennam in *Little Dorrit*, must work through their traumas of will and spirit and sexual identity toward such an understanding of time. With Arthur, for whom memory is no balm but merely a chill restoration of his blighted past, the question is largely whether his imagination can hold on long enough. What David Copperfield said of himself late in the novel, about the future seeming walled up before him, is true for Arthur at the beginning of his story: "Will, purpose, hope? . . . All those lights were extinguished before I could sound the words" (I,2). Clennam is one of Dickens's most important studies of the extirpation of fancy from infancy, the casting out of all "graceful or gentle" influence from "childhood, if I may so misuse the word as to apply it to such a beginning of life" (I,2). When he returns to his old garret room in the third chapter, and looks out upon his prospect there, Dickens gives us no description but the remembered one, that nightmarish vision of hell in which the "blasted and blackened forest of chimneys" seemed "but a nightly reflection of the fiery environment that was presented to his childish fancy in all directions, let it look where it would" (I,3). Yet for all the early brutalization of Arthur's mind, the vistas of brimstone and damnation painted for him by his mother's ferocious religion—for all the violence done to his charred, parched fancy he is, nevertheless, one of Dickens's heroes of imagination, a man still susceptible to "the bright glories of fancy" (I,3), still a member of the dreamer tribe searching for a healing and final refuge. At the close of this same chapter, ironically called "Home," Arthur looked out again upon the burnt chimneys and "began to dream," for "it had been the uniform tendency of this man's life—so much was wanting in it to think about, so much that might have been better directed and happier to speculate upon—to make him a dreamer, after all."

Clennam's "uniform tendency" (the clinical diction symptomatic of that rigidity he must work free of) has been to resist the dulling uniformity of his spiritually reduced circumstances, but "after all," what will it come to? Time has certainly not been kind to that character who reflects and distorts Arthur's own leanings toward escapist fancies, one of the great satirical portraits in Dickens of failed but craving romanticism and another instance of the diagrammatic logic in his novels by which characters repeatedly encounter their own parodies. She is the vegetative Flora Finching, both of whose names are travesties of the natural and whose furious effusions also align her with the disasters of volubility who have followed in the wake of Dick Swiveller and Mark Tapley. She has no rhetoric, but her paratactic blabber, in its flailing sincerity, is the Jingle energy gone witless, Mrs. Gamp gone sentimental. She is fancy disenchanted, the razing of romance. Here Flora offers a nuptial pie to Arthur and Amy: "If Fancy's fair dreams," she began, "have ever pictured that when Arthur— cannot overcome it pray excuse me—was restored to freedom even a pie as far from flaky as the present and so deficient in kidney as to be in that respect like a minced nutmeg might not prove unacceptable if offered by the hand of true regard such visions have for ever fled and all is cancelled but being aware that tender relations are in contemplation beg to state I heartily wish well to both and find no fault with either not the least" (II,34). The allusions to "Fancy's fair dreams" and "visions . . . fled" are pallid with the vocabulary of romantic decline. They are inefficacious fictions, and they contrast with the fancies of Mr. and Mrs. Meagles, those "practical people" who disclaim romance in the process of making room for it, and who may also recall the opposite "practical character" of the Smallweed mentality in *Bleak House*. The idea of the Meagleses being most "practical" at their most fanciful is a nice irony, but taken straight it has its earnest message, for in this novel, as in *Bleak House*, the romantic imagination may be, in "practice," the only salvation. Flora's debilitation by it is a warning only against excess and disproportion.

Fancy wants a certain drive, a push and rapidity. Whether in words or in wishful fictions, it must quicken, enliven. Sam Weller had it; Jingle, by trying to cash in on it, began to sell it short; Dick Swiveller and Mark Tapley had to make ends meet with this reduced and questionable legacy; Mrs. Gamp drew too heavily on its depleted funds; and by the time of Flora Finching the reserves of imagination are hopelessly unbalanced, the fancy, spoken and otherwise, indeed bankrupt. Only the psychic investments of Jenny Wren's verbal and visionary energy three novels later can return the imagination to a kind of emotional solvency. Flora exemplifies the self-deluding "dreamer" that Arthur must labor not to become, while at the same time, as in the speech just heard, she gives witness to an honesty of heart that her jabbering cannot dislodge. Arthur has tried to effect his own negation throughout the novel by thinking of himself as "Nobody," his errors and failings as "Nobody's Fault" (see titles, for instance, to chapters 16, 17, 18, and 26, Part I); eschewing the euphemism which ordinarily characterizes her speech, however, Flora "cannot overcome" the sincere need to call him by his own name. Her genuineness marks his own return to a sense of proper self, just as the ensuing ironies, when she rambles on in the same speech after stumbling over nothing more imposing than a comma, signal the wasting sense of time from which Arthur has manged to break clear: "... it may be withering to know that ere the hand of Time had made me much less slim than formerly and dreadfully red on the slightest exertion particularly after eating I know when it takes the form of a rash, it might have been and was not." Hardly "withering" to her person, time has worn thin her spirit, and the "might have been" is all she has left to cling to.

As a "dreamer" Arthur Clennam fares better "after all," but he must suffer for it. Like so many romantic figures in Dickens, his career must reach its climax in nightmare; like so many men who seek relief in imagination, he must be tested by its revenge in fever. There is in *Little Dorrit* an unusual forewarning of Clennam's eventual disease. During an unexpected overnight stay in the prison early in the novel, Arthur's mind is troubled by "involuntary starts of fancy," the last of which is an elliptical premonition: "As to Fire in the prison, if one were to break out while he lay there?" (I,8). One does not this time, but fifty-seven chapters later Arthur lies in the prison as an inmate, stricken with a fire in the brain. What began as a "burning restlessness" for escape has "settled down in the despondency of a low, slow fever (II,29). From the beginning of his incarceration, his fancy had been under severe strain, and he could not manage to find escape in reading, for he "had not been able to release even the imaginary people of the book from the Marshalsea" (II,28). But now the "morbid state of his nerves," irritated by fever, has called up vivid, unwilled hallucinations. He feels himself "going astray" and hears "fragments of tunes and songs, in the warm wind, which he knew had no existence . . . and voices seemed to address him, and he answered, and started" (II,29). He has been denied "the power of reckoning time, so that a minute might have been an hour and an hour a minute," yet in the midst of this delirium "some abiding impression of a garden stole over him—a garden of flowers" like the pastoral perspective that greeted Dick Swiveller on his recovery. And just as Dick was saved by the Marchioness, Arthur is now saved by Little Dorrit. Dick thought he must have been dreaming, and so thinks Arthur, yet the repeated verb of imagination brings his vision true before his eyes in a way that recalls in a nobler key the visionary experience of Tom Pinch: "One of the night-tunes was playing in the wind, when the door of his room *seemed* to open to a light touch, and, after a moment's pause, a quiet figure *seemed* to stand there, with a black mantle on it. It *seemed* to draw the mantle off and drop it on the ground, and then it *seemed* to be his Little Dorrit in her old, worn dress. It *seemed* to tremble, and to clasp its hands, and to smile, and to burst into tears" (II,29; my italics). Indeed it *is* "Little Dorrit, a living presence," who "called him by his name," as Flora does more hesitantly. *Seeming* is no longer hallucinatory; the fever has passed, "Nobody" has returned to life and identity, and the imagination has turned beneficent once again. For Tom Pinch—to reverse the cynic's maxim—believing is seeing. It is an unearned grace and a dream. For Arthur Clennam, pain has paid the way. The "dreamer" is awake to hope at last, and an apparent blessing has deservedly been born out by reality.

The motif of fever has been almost as widespread in *Little Dorrit* as it will be for Dickens's next novel, *A Tale of Two Cities*. Like the national "leprosy of unreality" in the *Tale*, the Merdle financial craze in *Dorrit* sweeps England like an "epidemic" or "moral infection," and "so rife and potent was the fever in Bleeding Heart Yard, that Mr. Panks's rent-days caused no interval in the patients" (II,13). After Arthur Clennam's fever, Dickens makes the following observation: "The changes of a fevered room are slow and fluctuating; but the changes of the fevered world are rapid and irrevocable" (II,33). We are then reminded of the ministering and almost divine presence that unites the public and private, the social and the psychological hemispheres of the book: "It was Little Dorrit's lot to wait upon both kinds of change." And to make out of change something lasting. She has indeed been the constant nurse and surrogate mother for the retarded Maggy, whose tragedy Amy has explained to Arthur: "When Maggy was ten years old . . . she had a bad fever, sir, and she has never grown any older since" (I,9). The perennial child is the opposite of Clennam, who had no "childhood" at all. And just as Amy watches over Maggy, she will later watch over Arthur after his fever, reading to him as he could not do for himself—and releasing not only imaginary creatures from the walls of the prison, but, as we are about to see, freeing Arthur's own imagination as well.

Here is the opening of the novel's last chapter: "On a healthy autumn day, the Marshalsea prisoner, weak but otherwise restored, sat listening to a voice that read to him." The adverbial phrase "On a healthy autumn day" is then repeated at the head of a long and liquidly styled ode to autumn, a private and apparently unmotivated lyric exultation in Dickens's most pellucid "secret prose,"[13] announcing to itself the mellow beauties of the temperate weather. The prison, of course, "had not a touch of any of these beauties on it . . . Yet Clennam, listening to the voice as it read to him, heard in it all that great Nature was doing, heard in it all the soothing songs she sings to man" (II,34). Dickens's experiment for *David Copperfield* seems to have borne belated fruit, and, without recourse to Switzerland and its "sublimity," the romantic consolation of Nature comes to Arthur in one of the fullest dramas of imaginative rehabilitation anywhere in the novels. A fever has held Maggie within the retarded confines of childhood; a fever now helps Arthur to childhood's awaited refuge. The "playful fancies" denied to Arthur as a child are now vouchsafed to him after his trial by fire, conjured by the voice of Little Dorrit. "At no Mother's knee but hers [Nature's], had he ever dwelt in his youth

on hopeful promises, on playful fancies, on the harvests of tenderness and humility that lie hidden in the early-fostered seeds of
imagination; on the oaks of retreat from blighting winds, that have
the germs of their strong roots in nursery acorns." Nature has been
sole nurse of Clennam's imagination, but Little Dorrit is now able
to provide a vital link to this "tenderness and humility," for "in
the tones of the voice that read to him, there were memories of an
old feeling of such things, and echoes of every merciful and loving
whisper that had ever stolen to him in his life" (II,34). Time has
once again become curative, memory at last a blessing, and the
pastoral imagery in this scene, which advances and completes the
"abiding impression of a garden" that "stole over" Clennam immediately after his fever, also offers a saving revision of that
"blasted and blackened forest of chimneys" in his childhood vision
of hell. Amy's affection now builds for Clennam an internalized
and perfect pastoral, a haven in the mind girded round by "oaks
of retreat" that have sprung from the life-giving "seeds of imagination." Here, for Arthur Clennam and Little Dorrit, is that final
refuge of fancy in Dickens: human love on earth.

The recourse to what Dickens calls in *Little Dorrit* "playful
fancies" stands the hero of *Great Expectations*, long before his
own fever, in rather ambiguous stead. They are not denied to him
so much as perverted by him. In Arthur they were never cultivated; in Pip they did not have to be, for from the start of the
novel he was a child of intense and yearning fancy. Yet the scenes
offered to his imagination were hardly "playful," and we see him,
for instance, committing a sympathetic fallacy on behalf of the
two convicts when "the pale afternoon outside almost seemed in
my pitying young fancy to have turned pale on their account, poor
wretches" (*G.E.*,5). It is the young boy's almost morbidly sensitive
imagination which, through Dickens's style, lends such masterly
life and shading to the early chapters of first-person narrative in
Great Expectations, and it is only when the boy's imagination
turns to self-"pitying" fantasies that he is endangered, that dreams
start converting themselves into lies under the influence of Satis
House and its romantic deceptions. It is in the ninth chapter that
Pip is goaded by his sister and Pumblechook into telling a series of
glorious fibs about his first visit to Miss Havisham's, and his guilt
on this occasion is clearly limited: "Toward Joe, and Joe only, I
considered myself a young monster." And so, importantly, it is
only with Joe that Pip feels the need to confess and repudiate his
lies.

It is one of Miss Havisham's "sick fancies" that Pip should exercise his own fancy in front of her, when she informs him that she "wants to see some play" (8). Under such duress Pip's imagination is at once frustrated, quite incapable of "playing to order," and instead he must eventually fall back on a game of cards he knows by rote. Yet under compulsion later to tell Mrs. Joe and Pumblechook the literal truth about Miss Havisham, Pip evades the "order" this time by forging under pressure a series of stunning "fancies" that strike us as anything but "sick." What Angus Wilson says about this episode places it at the climax of the developing theme of imagination in Dickens, and his remarks are worth quoting at length:

Pip, the imaginative, dreaming boy must be torn from that sick room of Miss Havisham's (the very realm of fairy story, of morbidity, of solitary rejection of the world's busy cares and responsibilities). Exactly those stories, grotesque, poetic and childish that have marked Paul Dombey's refutation of the calculating materialist world, that presumably have made David a novelist of fame, must now be relinquished. When Pip tells his stories of the black velvet coach and the dogs and the veal cutlets, drawing upon the same fancy that had made him at the opening of the book visualize his parents and his brothers and sisters from the shape of their tombstones . . . he is told once and for all, however lovingly, by Joe, his good half, that 'lies is lies' and 'that ain't the way of getting out of being common, old chap.' It was, of course, exactly by his wonderful poetic talent for such absurd flight that Dickens himself stepped out not only from the company 'of common boys and men' but of all but a handful of his compatriots of every century.[14]

It seems that Wilson oversimplifies the matter slightly. Here is Pip's actual owning-up to Joe: "And then I told Joe that I felt very miserable . . . and that I knew I was common, and that I wished I was not common, and that the lies had come of it somehow, though I didn't know how" (9). Dickens signals the complexity of the issue when he has Pip add: "This was a case of metaphysics, at least as difficult for Joe to deal with, as for me." For this reason, "Joe took the case altogether out of the region of metaphysics, and by that means vanquished it." He takes it instead into the realm of pure morality, a realm defined by what Joe calls the "one thing you may be sure of . . . namely, that lies is lies" (9). This is a tautological axiom in morality, and, morally speaking, Joe is right to warn against falsehood. So far from heeding this advice, though, Pip begins to tell lies to himself, lies which distort his sense of time and render daydreams into false and unnatural nostalgia. Here is the self-deluding retreat of Pip's grammatically and morally "imperfect" tense: "I fell asleep recalling what I 'used to do' when

I was at Miss Havisham's; as though I had been there weeks or months, instead of hours; and as though it were quite an old subject of remembrance, instead of a new one that had arisen only that day" (9).

These lies *are* lies, yet there is still a troublesome "metaphysical" residue in the preceding scene that simply cannot be reduced to moral certainty. For there are in the region of imagination lies which amuse and delight. To these Joe himself is susceptible, and he adds at the end of his sermon to Pip: "—which reminds me to hope that there were a flag, perhaps?" Pip must disappoint him, for he made the flag up with everything else. Still, no amount of morality can dim Pip's triumph of defensive fancy, with which he stopped the ignorant nastiness of Mrs. Joe and Mr. Pumblechook dead in its tracks. This is the child's thwarted but still thriving imagination in its finest hour, routing his enemies and finding in fancy itself a shelter from cruel mistreatment. His immediate defensive motivation is thus not touched upon at all in his statement that "I wished I was not common, and . . . the lies had come of it somehow." But they do come of his wish to be uncommon in the sense that they are its fulfillment, his sensitive imagination setting Pip apart from all things coarse and ordinary. This Wilson is right to suggest, but we must recognize that it is not "lies" like these, such free-swinging fancies, which "must be relinquished." The trouble is, except for this last defiant moment of childish imagination, that they already have been.

Fantasy's covenant has been broken, and Pip has begun to abdicate the proper exercise of a disinterested fancy to the false romance of Miss Havisham. Very soon daydream has been enslaved entirely by expectation, and the once sensitive boy has no access to the beauty of nature or, as they were called in Arthur Clennam's case, to "the bright glories of fancy" except through the one great lie of Satis House. It is, in its own way, a sort of pastoral rape, the violation of all authentic romance. "Whenever I watched the vessels standing out to sea with their white sails spread, I somehow thought of Miss Havisham and Estella" (15). The even stride of the prose itself then responds to what has happened in an almost sublimal manner, for "whenever the light struck aslant, afar off, upon a cloud or sail or green hill-side or waterline, it was just the same.—Miss Havisham and Estella and the strange house and the strange life appeared to have something to do with everything that was picturesque." The steady fluid rhythm of this strongly paralleled description, with the fourfold cresting of nouns in series, sets up a kind of dangerous undertow, the very quadratic cadence of the prose indicating by its repetition the way in which Pip's fraudulent dream world has tainted his vision of the natural landscape. The false "prospect," as Dickens puns in the next sentence, has spoiled the true one.

The "acorns" of Pip's fancy, those "early-fostered seeds of imagination"—which we see in Pip's case as we never do in Arthur's—are sadly stunted by Pip's escapist expectations. Arthur had never known real love of any kind, while Pip has snobbishly disowned it, and where Clennam suffers a fever that brings Amy to his side at last, Pip must suffer a fever in order to recall Joe to his. The psychic energy crisis in Dickens, signaled most dramatically in *Bleak House* when it made inevitable the imaginative blackouts of several characters, has hardly been rectified by the later novels, where even a Byronic isolation is now slack and listless for characters like Arthur Clennam, Sydney Carton in *A Tale of Two Cities*, John Harmon or Eugene Wrayburn in *Our Mutual Friend*, men whose escape artistry becomes a flight from self. Childe Harold is called in Book III of Byron's famous narrative a man "self-exiled" (1.136)—or, as the point is made earlier, a "wandering outlaw of his own dark mind" (1.20). Even Pip, without conscious design, has submitted himself to such a destructive renunciation, become bereft of his native identity in an attempted escape from the rigors of being, of responsibility—is in fact exiled from himself, by himself. As with similar characters in Dickens, Pip must suffer a fever that threatens the absolute extinction of self and that hallucinates this end in a specialized symbolic imagery.

The ordeal comes in the fifty-seventh chapter, where we hear in the first sentence that Pip "was left wholly to myself." The result is a trauma which in fact shatters the wholeness of personality and brings on the dissolution of self in a series of febrile visions that "confounded impossible existences with my own identity"— the symbolic revenge of the self-exiled imagination. Style dramatizes Pip's delirium, the inverted subordination straining attention and coherence in an impersonation of oppressed mentality:

That I had a fever and was avoided, that I often lost my reason, that the time seemed interminable, that I confounded impossible existences with my own identity; that I was a brick in the house wall, and yet entreating to be released from the giddy place where the builders had set me; that I was a steel beam of a vast engine, clashing and whirling over a gulf, and yet that I implored in my own person to have the engine stopped, and my part in it hammered off; that I passed through these phases of disease, I know of my own remembrance, and did in some sort know at the time. (57)

In the images of the brick and the steel beam yearning to be dislodged, we meet one of the strangest and most persuasive config-
urations of fever in Dickens: the nightmare of severance. It seems
to be an image of suicidal escape, and having used it once before
in *Bleak House,* Dickens is to use it once again in *Our Mutual
Friend.*

Here is Esther Summerson's timorous recollection of the most
terrible throes of her fever: "Dare I hint at that worst time when,
strung together somewhere in great black space, there was a flaming necklace, or ring, or starry circle of some kind, of which *I* was
one of the beads! And when my only prayer was to be taken off
from the rest and when it was such inexplicable agony and misery
to be a part of the dreadful thing?" (*B.H.,*35). Such a vision is almost
"inexplicable" in its elusive psychology. Esther's having been
blinded by fever may account for that "great black space" against
which her tortured brain burns like a flaming atom of unillum-
inating brilliance. What alone is clear from this lurch into surreal-
ism is the passionate wish for divorce, for removal. It may be that
Dickens's symbolism for Mr. Dick's fever in the preceding novel
was the germ of this recurring motif of severance, for with the
decapitation of Charles the First we have an unmitigated "simile"
for the dismemberment of the mind itself during its own feverish
revenge. It may also be that Dickens owes something to Charlotte
Brontë's famous heroine, who, five years before Esther Summerson
first appeared, suffered a similar "feverish" ordeal in the twenty-
ninth chapter of *Jane Eyre.* Not only is Jane "self-exiled" at this
point from the consequences of her own desire for Rochester, but
the prose of her crisis also enacts her trauma as if in a muted
Dickensian "impersonation."

Brontë seems deliberately to invert the locating prepositional
phrase at the start of Jane's second sentence below in order to bind
her ideas more tightly together, in an interlocked syntactic counterpart of meaning: "I knew I was in a small room; and in a narrow
bed. To that bed I seemed to have grown; I lay on it motionless as
a stone; and to have torn me from it would have been almost to
kill me."[15] During the interval of her fever, Jane recalls "no actions
performed," and the predicative format of the passage as a whole
has accordingly been kept for the most part either passive or intransitive. The very idea of transitive action (with Jane the passive
object), as put before us in those equated infinitive phrases above,
threatens to disrupt far more than a mere syntactic pattern; such
action, if "performed," would prove almost lethal. Brontë has an-

ticipated Dickens in what we might have assumed to be his own idiosyncratic sign for the release from fever. It is again an image of severance, that freeing which is also fatal, and it is symbolized as always by the rending or wrenching free of insensate objects—a stone in Jane Eyre's case, for Esther a starry bead, a beam or brick for Pip, and for John Harmon in *Our Mutual Friend*, a tree.

To return for a moment to *Bleak House*, we notice that Esther has undergone a feverish dislocation of identity other than her suicidal hallucination about being dislodged from the starry ring, in a displacement used precisely to locate the significance of the episode. Jo carries the fever to Bleak House, society's victim now plaguing society with a sickness bred of its own neglect, and Esther becomes society's martyr when she contracts the dread illness through her beloved servant Charley. Though the connections between Charley's illness and Esther's are the more direct, Dickens makes clear the thematic connection between Jo and Esther by a close parallel in their respective fevers. Jo watches what is done to save him "with the languid unconcern I had already noticed, wearily looking on at what was done as if it were for somebody else" (31). Four chapters later, Esther describes herself "lying, with so strange a calmness, watching what was done for me, as if it were done for someone else whom I was quietly sorry for" (35). But when she recovers, this displaced sympathy turns to self-help, to reclaimed identity, and the reflexive grammar mirrors this transformation as Esther "became useful to myself, and interested, and attached to life again" (35). This is the homecoming from "self-exile," that usual recuperation from fever for the emasculated "Byronic" figures of the later novels as well.

John Harmon, another "Nobody" like Clennam, a "Man from Somewhere" untold, might well have written those last words of Esther's about his own return to the world of the living in *Our Mutual Friend*. There is a point in the novel, a long and improbable monologue, where Harmon calls up for his own review, in a first-person narrative like Pip's or Esther's, the mysterious events surrounding his return to England (O.M.F. II,13). His own voice, as it moves from information "literal and exact" to "sick and deranged impressions" begins to impersonate his drugged struggle for life in images of the typical Dickensian fever. As usual, time is warped, and the "spaces" between his impressions "are not pervaded by any idea of time," with "days, weeks, months, years" being all the same to him. Harmon attacks one of his kidnappers, and in the struggle there seems to be a "flashing of flames of fire

between us." As if this were not enough to establish the analogue
of fever and delirium, the mystery itself turns on a typical displacement of identity, what the psychologists of the Dopplegänger
would call an autoscopic phenomenon: "I saw a figure like myself
lying dressed in my clothes on a bed." From this confounding of
other existences with his own identity, Harmon, like Pip and
Esther, also moves into a complex and oddly refracted nightmare
of severance: "The figure like myself was assailed, and my valise
was in its hand. I was trodden upon and fallen over. I heard a
noise of blows, and thought it was a wood-cutter cutting down a
tree. I could not have said that my name was John Harmon—I
could not have thought it—I didn't know it—but when I heard the
blows, I thought of the woodcutter and his axe, and had some dead
idea that I was lying in a forest" (O.M.F. II,13). Like Esther and Pip
before him, Harmon suffers an hallucinatory crisis of identity in
which he is finally chopped rather than hammered off, and after
the "dead idea" of himself as a felled tree, the motif of fever returns when the attempt to drown Harmon is accompanied by the
image of "a great noise and a sparkling and a crackling as of fires."
This feverish nightmare has somehow responded to the pattern of
suicidal escape-wish by materializing an actual murderous assault,
but what is needed for Harmon, as it was for Esther, is not severance but rebirth. They each achieve it in their own qualified ways,
as does Philip Pirrip.

I must return now to Pip's fever in *Great Expectations*, where
the ideas of endangered selfhood and imaginative revenge are most
fully and movingly worked through. With Jenny Wren and her
new hope waiting in the wings, Pip brings to an unmistakable climax the negative drama in Dickens of the forfeited imagination—
and to a conclusion this chapter's scan of escapist fancy in the
novels, its temptations, its perils. The neurotic working of subordination in that passage about Pip's crumbling and confounded
identity quoted earlier is a strained variation, literally an inversion,
of the syntax which describes his "first most vivid and broad impression of the identity of things" in the opening chapter. There
the cognitive verb precedes and defines a series of parallel *that*-
clauses moving coherently across the widening sweep of Pip's
growing awareness, a chain of equative clauses which identifies
Pip's first impressions of his world and of himself, and which
seems to contain his first understanding of the use of words for
reference: "At such a time I found out for certain, that this bleak
place overgrown with nettles was the churchyard . . . and that the

dark flat wilderness beyond . . . was the marshes; and that the low leaden line beyond was the river." And so on, until his first act of self-record, almost his imaginative christening: ". . . and that the small bundle of shivers growing afraid of it all and beginning to cry, was Pip." For all his fear, like that of a bawling infant first greeting the world, the copula here marks a confident act of discovery, of identification and naming. But syntax itself has gone mad by the time of Pip's fever, his agony of split and nearly obliterated personality, and there is only uncertain, hallucinatory terror in the predications ". . . was a brick . . . was a steel beam of a vast engine." That passage continues as follows in its reversed and overwrought subordination: "That I sometimes struggled with real people, in the belief that they were murderers, and that I would all at once comprehend that they meant to do me good, and would then sink exhausted in their arms, and suffer them to lay me down, I also knew at that time" (57). Pip has deserted the proper alleviations of fancy for a false and meretricious romance. He has never known what was good for him, and this nightmarish transformation of ministration into murder is his imagination's retributive parable. The overtaxed syntax has eased into normal order by the next sentence, and the clinging stress on cognition marks Pip's struggle for awareness and clarity: "But, above all, I knew that there was a constant tendency in all these people—who, when I was very ill, would present all kinds of extraordinary transformations of the human face, and would be much dilated in size —above all, I say, I knew that there was an extraordinary tendency in all these people, sooner or later, to settle down into the likeness of Joe." The conflation of "constant tendency" and "extraordinary transformation" into "extraordinary tendency" combines with the repetition of "in all these people" for a phrasing which shifts, repeats, elides, in order to suggest the visual transformations of Pip's ordeal as they finally relax and settle down, after the long paragraph, into the appearance of Joe. After moral blindness, this is seeing redeemed.

The next paragraph opens again on mimetic repetition, for "while all its other features changed, this one consistent feature did not change." The five remaining sentences of the paragraph all close down at the end on the word Joe:

Whoever came about me, still settled down into Joe. I opened my eyes in the night, and I saw in the great chair at the bedside, Joe. I opened my eyes in the day, and sitting on the window-seat, smoking his pipe in the shaded open window, still I saw Joe. I asked for cooling drink, and the dear hand that gave it to me was Joe's. I sank back on my pillow after drinking, and the face that looked so hopefully and tenderly upon me was the face of Joe.

Five times repeated, this is the constant focus toward which the words themselves and the impressions they set down have wavered, narrowed, and telescoped. Over and over the scene resolves, syntactically as well as optically, into the image of Joe, the one certain identity reclaimed from the mania of Pip's fever. At a single stroke the entire "monomaniacal" style[16] has been delivered into a more serene impersonation, and after all the terrible monotonies of automatism and fever—"that endless repetition of the same dull, ugly, form, which is the horror of oppressive dreams" (O.C.S.,45)—repetition is now no longer a dread hallucination but a litany of recognition. Pip has been forced by Magwitch's anonymous stipulation always to keep the name Pip, a provision taking us back to the original day on the marshes and the first meeting of the child and the convict. Pip complied with the letter of the request, but he lost that sense of himself as humble and unselfish with which the name was meant to be associated. Now, after his terrible test on the edge of nonexistence, the long struggle for identity nearly lost, now three pages after the crisis has passed, Pip returns at last to his original self at the novel's quiet climax, in a beautiful serial grammar proceeding to new health and old assurance: "I was slow to gain strength, but I did slowly and surely become less weak, and Joe stayed with me, and I fancied I was little Pip again" (57). Again the copula of assured identification, but subordinated now to the verb "fancied" in a newly predicated imagination. Having learned to see Joe again with some clarity, Pip can take a new look at himself as a man reborn. False visions are expunged, the vain dream burnt away by nightmare, but for a mind formerly gifted with poetic devices and invention like Pip's, and for an author so inclined, this is bitterly little. Pip, short for Pippin as well as for Philip Pirrip, is one of those "early-fostered seeds of imagination" (L.D., II, 34) that has come to no true fruition.

There may be no austerity in Dickens like the fate of Philip Pirrip, the plangency of a nostalgia that can never wholly rejuvenate the youthful fancy, but merely recover after great struggle the ethical perspective of uncorrupted childhood. Only at one remove can there be full imaginative rebirth, and after eleven years away from England, during which time he had not seen Joe and Biddy with his "bodily eyes" but only with his "fancy" (57), Pip returns to find his displaced salvation in their son, his namesake. The novel of identity which began with the bundle of shivers that "was Pip" and which rounded its major crisis with "I was little Pip again" has engaged once more the copulative verb and the adverb of recurrence to bring this very "fancy" true before Pip's "bodily eyes," for there at Joe's hearth, "fenced into the corner with Joe's leg, and sitting on my own little stool looking at the fire, was—I again!" (57). After the psychotic doublings of his personality[17] to which Pip has been subjected with characters like Orlick at the forge fire or, later, the kiln fire, and especially with Bentley Drummle staring into the hearth blaze alongside Pip in the forty-third chapter, now there is the happy projection of his second self as a relaxed and comfortable fire-gazer, haunted neither by that incipient guilt associated with the convict which once rose before Pip in the "avenging coals" (2) of Mrs. Joe's hearth fire, nor by those later delusions of grandeur which "would seem to show me Estella's face in the fire" (14) at the forge. The second "little Pip" is a new life whose as yet unspoiled "prospect" opens on the chance for fancies great, expectant, but enlarging this time, not imprisoning. Yet the poignant minor key still holds, and when Pip implausibly suggests that "you must give Pip to me, one of these days, or lend him, at all events," the answer must be emphatically "No, no" (57). We are given, lent, one life; nothing in "the fullness of time" can rescind this law. Regardless of fever's penance, we cannot have back the imaginative innocence we devastate and cast away.

It is tempting to speculate about the extent to which Dickens's own interest in feverish states of mind is meant to inform the ironic climax of Evelyn Waugh's *A Handful of Dust*, where the hero, Tony Last, after suffering a tropical fever in South America which renders him "fitfully oblivious to the passage of time"[18] and bedevils his mind with "a constant company of phantoms,"[19] is nursed back to health by one Mr. Todd—only to find that he will be forced by this illiterate man, at gunpoint and for all foreseeable time forward, to read aloud from the collected works of Charles Dickens. The heroes of Dickens's own novels are usually better rewarded for the pains of their sickbeds. The tribulation of fever becomes the ultimate trial of imagination in Dickens, an ordeal of constructive suffering. There is a moment in *Pickwick Papers* when Mr. Grummer slips into a malapropism in speaking of "our sufferin Lord the King" (*P.P.*,24). There the adjective is merely a slip. But looking back over Dickens's career it seems to take on the resonance of a rather comprehensive pun. Even in that first novel, and especially because of Alfred Jingle's own fever there, the Fleet episode provided a genuine test for the quarantine of imagination, and from that book forward, in those scenes of fever that cast off forever any sense of complacent fancy—in the creative trials of Dick Swiveller, Mark Tapley, and David Copperfield, of Esther, Arthur, Pip, and, as we are next to see, of Eugene Wrayburn— Dickens seems to be saying, once and for all, that suffering *is* sovereign. It is often how we must pay our way for the "poetry of existence."

After *Pickwick Papers* and the exits right and left of Sam Weller and his own corrupt double, Alfred Jingle, in our subsequent meetings with the many escape artists in Dickens's novels, as in our encounters with Romantic poets, we have been asked to confront, and also to formulate as we go, a peculiarly modern definition of imagination, not as the reason-leavening wit of Dickens's eighteenth-century masters Fielding, Smollett, or Sterne, with its evident swift fervor and penetration, but as a certain irreducible impulse of trusted disquiet, loyally private by nature, even antisocial: a secret freeing, nervous, yearning, vivid but often incommunicable. Ideally such imagination becomes a thing rounded, enveloping. Call it romantic wish-fulfillment, a fiction made habitable. Failing this, it may still manage a thrust and a direction. Call it longing. If this new stance of imagination, on whichever footing, be a subtle form of self-cajolery, still it has earned the right, by its gains, its good works, to be known as a faculty sane and cleansing. Fictions can indeed be made serviceable, yet they can also be foiled by diversion or aimlessness, fall to neglect, shrivel into mere lie, become mired in self-aggrandizement. All these are Pip's delinquencies, the ultimately mortal sins against his imagination. The most beautiful, perfect, and satisfying novels Dickens gave us are, for me, the last two he finished, and their central statements about the creative imagination from which they themselves have sprung, with such unflagged genius and integrity, are each, though oppositely, quite final. Pip's story has been about the suicide of the imaginary life. Jenny Wren's, unforeseen, will tell of its continuous potential for rebirth.

7 The Golden Bower of "Our Mutual Friend"

'You are talking about Me, good people,' thought Miss
Jenny, sitting in her golden bower, warming her feet.
'I can't hear what you say, but *I* know your tricks and
your manners!'—*Our Mutual Friend* (III,2)

The last feverish trauma in Dickens, the last trial of imagination, comes near the end of the last book Dickens finished. It
comes to Mr. Eugene Wrayburn in *Our Mutual Friend*, and his
nurse during this distracted time, while his fancy wanders "with
the misery of a disturbed mind, and the monotony of a machine"
(*O.M.F.* IV, 10), is Miss Jenny, summoned by Wrayburn because
of her own lenitive and healing fancies, and placed at his bedside
by his friends so that "the rich shower of hair" (her "golden
bower") might perhaps "attract his notice" when he regained consciousness. The meeting of Miss Jenny and Eugene Wrayburn
there at his sickbed is one of the most wonderful moments in
fiction, the climax of perhaps Dickens's greatest novel and of his
career-long interest in the mending power of imagination.

Miss Jenny is of course Fanny Cleaver, alias Jenny Wren, the
crippled seamstress in *Our Mutual Friend* who fashions out of
rags and refuse her miniature dresses for dolls and who, almost
unheralded, moves gradually to the symbolic center of the novel.
In her position there, she marks the culmination for Dickens of
that fitful and harassed refuge in imagination sought by certain
characters throughout the novels whom a spoiled world seems
increasingly in danger of spoiling. It is a line of declining confidence from Sam Weller in *Pickwick Papers* and Dick Swiveller in
The Old Curiosity Shop through Mrs. Gamp in *Martin Chuzzlewit*
to Wemmick in *Great Expectations*—and beyond, with some
refurbished affirmation, to Jenny Wren. The tag phrase Dickens

uses with formulaic frequency to announce Miss Wren is "the dolls' dressmaker." For Jenny is a maker; she stitches, and binds, and seams, and in so doing tries to repair the chaos of her days. And she sings beautifully, and has had visions. One of the most profoundly moving characters ever brought forth from those inspired Dickensian marriages of gift and craft, Jenny Wren can be seen in her own creative making to act out such a union of vision and device. As in the case of Sam Weller especially, at the other end of the novelist's career, the artistic marvel of Jenny's conception is itself a large part of the significance toward which her whole being tends. She is not only created by, she comes in fact to symbolize, the Dickensian fancy at its most spacious and versatile.

The metaphor of Jenny's "golden bower" is a far cry from idle analogy. Just before her unvoiced address quoted in the epigraph, Jenny and Riah the Jew have met for the first time Miss Abbey Potterson, who has complimented Jenny on her "bower" of exquisite blond hair: " 'Why, what lovely hair!' cried Miss Abbey. 'And enough to make wigs for all the dolls in the world' " (III,2). Already it is hinted that the materials of Jenny's artistry can be somehow self-supplied, here in one sense, later in another. " 'Call *that* a quantity?' returned Miss Wren. 'Poof! What do you say to the rest of it?' As she spoke, she untied a band, and the golden stream fell over herself and over the chair, and flowed down to the ground." In keeping with the idea that the raw matter of her craft can be furnished directly from her own person, the oddly overspecified "herself" in that last sentence (rather than the more likely "her") underscores the reflexive nature of this self-embowerment. The motif of romantic haven is used repeatedly by Dickens both in *Our Mutual Friend* and before, but nowhere else is the symbol so intrinsic. Jenny Wren physically incorporates the retreat she has beaten from the world. She has sought a bower apart from "the weariness, the fever, and the fret" of society, and in searching she has become that bower. In her own proper person she is the Romantic idea she personifies, what Keats (once again, and in another place) called the "bower quiet for us" that art promises to maintain. Yet there is a caustic, an embittered side of her nature also caught in our brief epigraph, that defensive solipsism which forces upon "me" a capital "M," twists "I" into italics,[1] and thereby underlines Jenny's morbid self-consciousness and paranoia. The war between such neurosis and her visionary access is the struggle I will be tracing through *Our Mutual Friend*. But it is important first to note the place of Jenny's "bower" in the development of Dickensian pastoralism.

As we know from the last chapter, the theme is primarily ironic in Dickens, with the pastoral impulse only rarely sanctioned by the narrator. Usually it is a bloodless pretense, a delusion. Mrs. Merdle's fictitious claim of being "pastoral to a degree, by nature" (*L.D.* I, 33) makes her the last and most blatant of the false Arcadians, while in the same novel we find Mrs. Plornish's wholesome "little fiction" of the "perfect pastoral" in her "counterfeit cottage" (II,13). Two novels later we come to Wemmick's moated garrison of imagination at Walworth Castle, an implicit domestic pastoral this time, with its "bower" and that "ornamental lake, on whose margin the bower was raised" (*G.E.*,25). And by the next novel we have arrived at Boffin's Bower in Jenny Wren's own book. The haven of Mr. and Mrs. Boffin is a domestic compromise between her taste for fashion and his for comfort, so that as Mr. Boffin explains, "we have at once, Sociability (I should go melancholy mad without Mrs. Boffin), Fashion, and Comfort" (I,5). Their Bower, of course, is as artificial as Acrasia's in *The Faerie Queene*, but here there is no attempt to seduce us, in any sense, with the illusion. Everything is blatantly "art," and the sympathetic imagination is needed in large doses to make of the "flowery carpet" a terrain of lush "vegetation," a "flowery bed" (I,5). Just as in Wemmick's sanctuary, the art again finds compensation in edible provisions, and "while the flowery land displayed such hollow ornamentation as stuffed birds and waxen fruits under glass shades, there were, in the territory where vegetation ceased, compensatory shelves on which the best part of a large pie and likewise of a cold joint were plainly discernible among other solids" (I,5). The novel's next chapter opens on a description of a tavern called the Six Jolly Fellowship-Porters, the bar of which is, once again, just such a fusion of art and natural bounty, containing "cordial-bottles radiant with fictitious grapes in bunches" and all manner of delectables. Dickens tells us in so many words that the tavern is a "haven" of human warmth and enjoyment "divided from the rough world," indeed a place of "enchanting delusion" (I,6). The convivial joys of the tavern come straight from the Pickwickian world, and have had previous incarnations in The Maypole Inn of *Barnaby Rudge* and The Blue Dragon of *Martin Chuzzlewit*. Yet the ideas of refuge and "enchanting delusion" are new, an index to the darkening world outside the tavern. The enchantment of *Pickwick* is now just that, a spell, an illusion, still delightful but less safe and lasting.

It is no accident that Boffin's Bower and the Fellowship-Porters come back to back in *Our Mutual Friend*. They are both havens from an unsympathetic world, and the parallel is worked out in quiet detail. The Bower is itself "fitted and furnished more like a luxurious amateur tap-room than anything else," and when we adjourn to the professional tap-room in the next chapter, here is what we are told: "The wood forming the chimney-pieces, beams, partitions, floors, and doors, of the Six Jolly Fellowship-Porters, seemed in its old age fraught with confused memories of its youth. In many places it had become gnarled and riven, according to the manner of old trees; knots started out of it; and here and there it seemed to twist itself into some likeness of boughs." The bar is itself a bower, a natural hideaway. "Not without reason was it often asserted by the regular frequenters of the Porters, that when the light shone full upon the grain of certain panels, and particularly upon an old corner cupboard of walnut-wood in the bar, you might trace little forests there, and tiny trees like the parent-tree, in full umbrageous leaf" (I,6). It is also hardly accidental that these two versions of imaginative haven should come together in this particular novel, for in ways that have never been fully noticed *Our Mutual Friend* is Dickens's finest study of imagination, its outlets and repressions. Finally, it can be no coincidence—but rather a rounding out of Dickens's bower motif by a sort of concentric symbolism—that we have recently left Jenny Wren in the inner sanctum of this very bar: the lame artist surrounded by the golden bower of her hair within the enchanted bower of the tavern itself. Miss Abbey Potterson is in fact the proprietor of the Six Jolly Fellowship-Porters, and at her first meeting with Jenny she began by offering the child, just before we entered the scene, a draught of that most pastoral-sounding beverage, "shrub" (III,2).

To appreciate the widest import of Jenny's golden embowerment, we must return now to her first scene and follow her troubled passage through the awesome sprawl and mass of this remarkable book. In the deadening constriction of its atmospheres and the symbolic completeness of their delineation, *Our Mutual Friend* is Dickens's most modern novel, *The Waste Land* of his career as Johnson has put it.[2] Dickens has even anticipated Eliot with a specific image in connection with Jenny Wren. The famous symbol in *Prufrock* for the torpor and insensibility of modern life —the evening "spread out against the sky / Like a patient etherised upon a table"—is much like the description of Jenny's neighborhood in London as it is first approached by Charley Hexam and Bradley Headstone. In a world where the escape motive is so widespread, even the personified city seeks release, appearing "with a deadly kind of repose on it, more as though it had taken laudanum than fallen into a natural rest" (II,1). London itself in this bleak sector seems narcotized upon the landscape, and in the very center of such spiritual desolation Jenny must fight off the inertia of her own crippled body and the enervation that attends everything about her—in order simply to live. On the next page, Bradley and Charley arrive at her lodgings and are taken aback by this "child—a dwarf—a girl—a something." Miss Abbey will later ask, "Child, or woman?" and Riah's reply will be, "Child in years . . . woman in self-reliance and trial" (III,2).

For her two first visitors the matter is less certain. Before Bradley and Charley even discover her occupation, however, they cannot help realizing her rare skill: "The dexterity of her nimble fingers was remarkable" (II,1). Here I think we are being asked to link Jenny's skill, in the abstract, to that of the other precise craftsman in the novel, Mr. Venus. Silas Wegg is, in his mangled readings from Gibbon and his extemporaneous balladeering, the "literary man" as con-artist, the sham poetizer of *Our Mutual Friend*, a one-legged charlatan of art whose own body is partly artificial. The true imaginative man, the true dreamer and romantic in the novel, the passionate lover and, if not a conventional artist, then a most accomplished artisan, is Mr. Venus. He takes an artist's pride in his work, but his beloved Pleasant Riderhood will have nothing to do with the "exquisite neatness" of his craftsmanship, even though he has just sent "a Beauty—a perfect Beauty—to a school of art" (I,7). Venus is no troubadour; he loves like one and pines like one, languishing in true courtly fashion, and he has the perfect name for one, but he does not articulate exactly as a poet does, piecing and shaping words into an organic whole. Mr. Venus is, rather, an "Articulator of human bones" (I,7). This is what has become in Dickens of the articulating imagination. It is the symbolic decline and fall of poetry, and only Jenny's verbal wit seems to have survived the ruin.

As a parodist rather than a parasite, in contrast to Wegg's mercenary versifying, Jenny breaks into her own "impromptu rhyme" after realizing that Charley and Bradley have come to see Lizzie, not her:

> "You one two three,
> My com-pa-nie,
> And don't mind me;" (II,1)

And later, accompanied by a "prodigiously knowing" glance at Lizzie when Eugene visits:

"Who comes here?
A Grenadier.
What does he want?
A pot of beer." (II,2)

This is satire by irrelevance, and she baits Bradley Headstone with
another form of it, a stretch of nonsensical alliterative prose-poetry
she calls "a game of forfeits," when he first tries to guess her occupation: "I love my love with a B because she's Beautiful; I hate
my love with a B because she is Brazen; I took her to the sign of
the Blue Boar, and I treated her with Bonnets; her name's Bouncer,
and she lives in Bedlam.—Now, what do I make with my straw?"
(II,1). Language like this lives on the edge of its own Bedlam, but
under Jenny's control it becomes both the ironist's defense against
insanity and a weapon against dullness.

Jenny can temper playfully with words, as in "Lizzie-Mizzie-
Wizzie" (II,2) and "Humbugshire" (III,10), or she can defiantly
turn a cliché against its wielder, as when her father whines out
"Circumstances over which had no control" and Jenny converts
his empty nouns into punitive verbs: "I'll circumstance you and
control you too" (II,2). Or there is the time when Eugene tries to
extort information about Lizzie's whereabouts, and Jenny retorts
with a pun: "And of course it's on the subject of a doll's dress—
or *address*—whichever you like" (III,10). But nothing places Jenny
more conclusively in the line of Dickens's verbal satirists than her
modified form of the "Wellerism"—"Let me see, said the blind
man" (II,2)—which also takes her back to that possible source for
Sam's own habit in Sancho Panza's ". . . and then we'll see, as one
blind man said to the other."[3] Of necessity, however, Miss Wren's
ironies are far more defensive than Sancho's or Sam's. When it
works, her sardonic wit curtains her from the world, and an entire
career in satiric wariness is summed up when, after a harsh dis-
missal of her drunken father, Dickens shows us Jenny "laughing
satirically to hide that she had been crying" (III,10).

With her spry acerbic wit, Jenny would seem to have no immediate predecessors, to harken back instead to those early men of
ironic volubility like Sam and Dick. Yet there is in fact an intermediate figure to whose style Jenny's talkative satire is heir,
another misshapen character who compensates with imagination
and irony for her physical deprivation. I speak of the incredible
Miss Mowcher in *David Copperfield*, that "volatile" dwarf who is
one of Dickens's most brilliant eccentrics, and who exhibits many
characteristics of the others in her own combustible style. When
she first meets David, she taunts him about his beardlessness with

Quilpian glee: "Face like a peach!...Quite tempting! I'm very fond of peaches" (D.C.,22). Like Dick Swiveller, she inclines to satiric doggerel: "Did he sip every flower, and change every hour, until Polly his passion requited?" (22). Like Dickens himself or Sam Weller, she burlesques parliamentary style: "Upon my life, 'the whole social system' (as the men call it when they make speeches in Parliament) is a system of Prince's nails!" (22). She even plays a "game at forfeits" like the one Dickens will later give to Jenny: "I love my love with an E, because she's enticing; I hate her with an E, because she's engaged." (22). Perhaps most important of all in establishing her credentials as a satirist, she is allowed her own "Wellerism," which is at the same time a mockery of linguistic affectation; these are the words with which she exits from her first scene in the novel: "'Bob swore!'—as the Englishman said for 'Good night,' when he first learnt French, and thought it so like English. 'Bob swore,' my ducks!" (22).

Miss Mowcher hates affectation of all sorts, and calls it by that important Dickensian term "refreshing humbug" (22). In this she supplies a neat contrast to Mr. Micawber. The texture of her speech is a constant travesty of the euphemistic habit, and whereas Micawber pompously carries on, for instance, about the expression "sea-legs" with regard to "conventional impropriety" (52), Miss Mowcher pretends to an ironic uneasiness about the word "garters" in a colloquial exclamation: "Oh my stars and what's-their-names!" (22). Or she treats Steerforth and David to this priggish comedy after climbing to the top of the table: "'If either of you saw my ankles,' she said, when she was safely elevated, 'say so, and I'll go home and destroy myself!'" (22). Miss Mowcher even has a major speech about those euphemisms and periphrases for "rouge" employed by women who contract for her beautician's services, which she offers as "another instance of the refreshing humbug I was speaking of" (22). This ugly and deformed woman makes her living by beautifying the ugliness of others, but she sees through their pretense and sustains herself with "refreshing" laughter at their cosmetic rhetoric.

The incessant bracing ironies by which Jenny Wren tries to invigorate her own life are the next step in this conception. Not merely a parodist, however, Jenny finds other avenues of verbal expression. Like Dickens himself, Jenny Wren is also a tireless coiner of names, ironic and otherwise. Fledgeby becomes "Little Eyes," Riah "Fairy Godmother," and even "Jenny Wren" is her own idea. So we learn soon after meeting her: "Her real name was

Fanny Cleaver; but she had long ago chosen to bestow upon herself the appellation of Miss Jenny Wren" (II,2). She thus offers the perfect foil for the lassitude and slack acceptance of Eugene Wrayburn, who, on the following page of the novel, answers her query, "Mr. Eugene Wrayburn, ain't it?" with "So I am told." *The Oxford Companion to English Literature* leaves much unsaid when it explains its entry "Jenny Wren" simply as the "business name" of Fanny Cleaver. Surely it must deserve space on the roster of allegorical names in Dickens, for she has tried to enroll it there herself. A "jenny" is a female bird in general; the wren is a bird noted for warbling, and we know that Jenny has a lovely voice; the two together, as the *OED* tells us, form the "popular, and especially nursery name for the wren ... sometimes regarded in nursery lore as the wife, bride, or sweetheart of Robin Redbreast," and we know that Jenny waits patiently for the clumsy sweetheart who will one day come courting. The girl who hates children for the fun they have made of her, and yet who has devoted her life to dressing dolls for children, here borrows from the literature of childhood for her own rechristening. Her art and her imagination, by which she has been baptized anew, seem to elevate her beyond her own sad prejudices. With more application and no less conviction, the dolls' dressmaker might well join nurse Gamp in the neat self-assuring formula: "Jenny Wren is my name, and Jenny Wren my nature." Fanny Cleaver has bestowed upon herself a liberating pseudonym, a *nom de plumage* whose assonant lift is meant to carry her fancy above the sordidness of her cares and labors; it is no "business" matter at all, but for Miss Wren a matter of life instead of death. Gnawed at and severely flawed by experience, deprived, coarsened, Jenny has never been numbed. She has spirit still, and she must go vigilantly in order to levitate it against the fatal drag of a world from which all élan has long since vanished.

We are instructed further in the significance of her self-naming later in the novel, in the context of some quiet word play. Jenny at one point explains something about Christian customs to Riah the Jew "in consideration of his professing another faith," as the narrator puts it, and Jenny's first words after this are well timed, for she classifies herself as one of those "Professors who live upon ... our taste and invention" (IV,9). Such is the "faith" she has all along been "professing," and the verbal echo cunningly reminds us that Jenny has, in effect, made a religion of fancy, devoting her spirit to those twin deities "taste" and "invention." It is in the preceding chapter that we hear another oblique play on words from Jenny's own lips in connection with the name Jenny Wren itself, her primary inventive feat. Fascination Fledgeby hopes out loud that he has made no mistake in addressing her as "Miss Jenny," and the dolls' dressmaker has recourse to a suggestive noun: "'Probably you don't mistake, sir,' was Miss Wren's cool answer; 'because you had it on the best authority. Mine, you know' " (IV,8). Her "word" is, of course, not only the best but the only surety, the sole authorization. Since the name Jenny Wren has in fact been self-bestowed, her authority is, in the hinted pun, that of authorship itself. Imaginative invention becomes both source and warrant.

At the end of Jenny's first chapter, the first in Book II, an odd coincidence comes to light. Lizzie explains that she met the poor girl by "chance at first, as it seemed, Charley. But I think it must have been more than chance." Jenny turns out to be the granddaughter of "the terrible drunken old man" on one of the bills in the old Hexam cottage, those notices of drowned people who became the ghoulish inventory of Gaffer Hexam's trade. We first learn of these obituary posters in the scene where Eugene looks in through the window and sees Lizzie "weeping by the rising and falling of the fire," with the pictures of the drowned men on the walls "starting out and receding by turns" (I,13). As a descendant of one man among these oscillating firelit forms, Jenny seems to have come up from Lizzie's past with all the fanciful powers (and more, as we will see) once associated with the Hexam hearth. The domestic myth of fire-gazing has assumed many beneficent shapes on the way to *Our Mutual Friend*, as we know, and Jenny would naturally resent Charley's attempt to cancel its "reality" for Lizzie. Fire-gazing seems to him a childish and dangerous fancy, for "we are looking into the real world now" (II,1). To Jenny, however, it is still an enchanting custom:

'Look in the fire, as I like to hear you tell how you used to do when you lived in that dreary old house that had once been a windmill. Look in the—what was its name when you told fortunes with your brother that I *don't* like?'
    'The hollow down by the flare?'
    'Ah! that's the name! . .'' (II,11)

Miss Wren knows only too well the inevitable fissuring of vision from the daily blankness of routine, and she is instinctively sympathetic to anyone's effort at uniting the real and the ideal. She herself cannot. She must always fluctuate between the remembered beauties of her innocent imagination and the sullied bondage of experience. Yet her energy is so intense that it has brought her a glimpse, for a time only, but sublime, of a departed dream more glorious than any of the fire-conjured "pictures of what is past" in Lizzie's "hollow down by the flare" (I,3). For Jenny Wren has had a revelation.

In this connection, the most interesting comment J. Hillis Miller has made about Dickens he made not in his long and well-known book on the novels, but indirectly, in a lecture on George Eliot to a Comparative Literature Colloquium at Yale on March 4, 1971. He suggested that the history of nineteenth-century fiction can be seen in part as the history of its internalization for individual characters of that Romantic experience previously restricted to the extraordinary imagination of the gifted poet. To document such a history for the novels of Dickens in particular has been one of my chief concerns in this book, and it is a chronicle that naturally comes to rest in the transcendental visions of Jenny Wren and their collapse into the narcotic escapism of John Jasper in the next and last novel.

At one point soon after Jenny's first appearance, revealing by her own imitative drone that ear for phrase which Dickens has shared with her, she asks: "I wonder how it happens that when I am work, work, working here, all alone in the summer-time, I smell flowers" (II,2). (Notice the difference in effect between the comma punctuation of "work, work, working" here and the accelerating hyphenation of the phrase "skip-skip-skipping," used by Jenny in the previous chapter to describe the games of other children.) Eugene Wrayburn "was growing weary of the person of the house" and "suggested languidly" that "As a common-place individual, I should say ... that you smell flowers because you *do* smell flowers." But Jenny's response makes it clear that hers was not at all a commonplace question:

'No, I don't ... this is not a flowery neighborhood. It's anything but that. And yet, as I sit at work, I smell miles of flowers. I smell roses till I think I see the rose-leaves lying in heaps, bushels, on the floor. I smell fallen leaves till I put down my hand—so—and expect to make them rustle. I smell the white and the pink May in the hedges, and all sorts of flowers that I never was among. For I have seen very few flowers indeed, in my life.'

There are no gardens, no "bower," except in her own imagination, as Lizzie realizes. "'Pleasant fancies to have, Jenny dear!' said her friend: with a glance toward Eugene as if she would have asked him whether they were given the child in compensation for her losses." Jenny also tells of the delightful birds she hears at such times: "'Oh!' cried the little creature, holding out her hand and looking upward, 'how they sing!'" And as Jenny continues, her face becomes overspread with a look "quite inspired and beautiful."

Now comes the unfolding of her childhood dream of heaven, the lost but still sponsoring vision to which she seems to owe her recurring pastoral fancies:

'I dare say my birds sing better than other birds, and my flowers smell better than other flowers. For when I was a little child,' in a tone as though it were ages ago, 'the children that I used to see early in the morning were very different from any others that I ever saw. They were not like me: they were not chilled, anxious, ragged, or beaten; they were never in pain. They were not like the children of the neighbours; they never made me tremble all over, by setting up shrill noises, and they never mocked me. Such numbers of them, too! All in white dresses, and with something shining on the borders, and on their heads, that I have never been able to imitate with my work, though I know it so well. They used to come down in long bright slanting rows, and say all together, "Who is this in pain?" When I told them who it was, they answered, "Come and play with us!" When I said, "I never play! I can't play!" they swept about me and took me up, and made me light. Then it was all delicious ease and rest till they laid me down, and said all together, "Have patience, and we will come again." Whenever they came back, I used to know they were coming before I saw the long bright rows, by hearing them ask, all together a long way off, "Who is this in pain?" And I used to cry out, "Oh, my blessed children, it's poor me! Have pity on me! Take me up and make me light!" (II,2)

In the tread and build of this soliloquy, from the tentative "I dare say" through the transfiguring conjunctive rise of "swept about me and took me up, and made me light" to its plaintive, partial re-sounding at the end, this is magnificent writing, a brilliantly inflected prose whose repetitions are spell-binding and incantatory, with no smirch of sentimentality. And no mundane fixities. Ambiguity in the phrases "made me light" and "make me light" is the insignia of a spiritual release, a new freedom and multiplicity. In both tenses, only the transforming verb holds and is stable; the personal pronoun hovers between direct and indirect object, "light" between adjective and noun. After the deadening weight of my life, pleads Jenny, make light my burden and give me bodiless ease at last. After my benighted trials here below, create for me a world of light. And after earthly life, transfigure me to my angelic destiny; in this my vision, make me the very source of vision—a suffering mortal reborn in the image of divine light itself. So powerfully Blakean, this is a breathtaking romantic vision that also becomes Dickens's own "Intimations Ode." Jenny is indeed inland far from her immortal sea, but she has tried to keep safe her imagination of angels, and their long bright slanting rows offer a "fountain-light" (to echo Wordsworth once again) by which, in the arid, blackened wastes of London, her desolation is sometimes bathed, her griefs quenched. When Jenny realizes that Lizzie is heading for trouble with Eugene, she even tries to delegate her fancy as a kind of spiritual support: "Oh my blessed children, come back in the long bright slanting rows, and come for her, not me. She wants help more than I, my blessed children!" (II,11).

Real children mocked the old-fashioned Jenny with "shrill noises," so her fancy comforted her with the blessed unison of cherubs. The initial glory and the dream have gone, but at times Jenny smells flowers and hears a chorus of songbirds. And she has almost achieved what she has dreamed in her own person, despite the bad back and queer legs, for Jenny Wren has named herself a songbird—developing an eye as "bright and watchful as the bird's whose name she had taken" (II,11)—and has grown herself a bower. Her initial vision was not of the world, or for it; it could not be willed or sustained. It came and went as a blessing, a recompense, but it was a divine and ultimately inaccessible beauty which she has "never been able to imitate" in her dolls' dresses. The vision cannot be accommodated, and her art must always remain a partially unsatisfactory mediation between what is ordinary, even wretched, in her life and those surprising splendors of her epiphany.

The latter are short-lived indeed. During her recitation, Jenny's "late ecstatic look returned, and she became quite beautiful" (II,2), yet all too soon, after the return of her drunken father, she reverts to a pitiful and largely pitiless cripple, a victim and yet a victimizer: "As they went on with their supper, Lizzie tried to bring her round to that prettier and better state. But the charm was broken. The person of the house was the person of a house full of sordid shame and cares, with an upper room in which that abased figure was infecting even innocent sleep with sensual brutality and degradation. The dolls' dressmaker had become a little quaint shrew; of the world, worldly; of the earth, earthy" (II,2). This is the recurring tragedy of Jenny's life: that fancy is an unreliable refuge from drudgery, that what is beautiful in her life must inevitably evaporate, the lovely lapsing away into what is mean and demeaning, and that at such times all glory is of the imagination, unimaginable. Robert Garis's uneasiness here is hard to fathom. After quoting the above passage, he objects strenuously that Jenny is "an impressive human being able to choose her own moods and her own expressions."[4] This is just what Dickens has told us she is *not* able to do, her paradisal vision not a matter of choosing, but a descent of grace. Garis insists that "Jenny Wren is not a 'shrew,' quaint, little, or otherwise; there is no significant perspective in the novel from which her feelings can be accused of being 'worldly' or 'earthly.' " Take her or leave her, Jenny Wren can only be what Dickens tells us about her, and the question-begging circularity of Garis's argument is typical of the back-handed compliments he pays Dickens throughout his book. When he complains that the passage in question is "symptomatic of the whole novel in that it almost knowingly disgraces its possibili- ties,"[5] he is missing the large point about Jenny Wren that she is her own worst enemy, that her greatest grief is her own knowing disgrace of finer possibilities.

Jenny's "shrewishness" is kept perfectly in character by Dickens because it is always shrewd, and her insistence that she is the one and only "person of the house" is a just retaliation against her father's abdicated humanity. Her relation with Mr. Dolls is cer- tainly a troubling one for the reader, but no less so for Jenny. She seems driven by adversity almost beyond guilt. There is no doubt about her callous humiliation of Mr. Dolls, and yet there is no way to decide which comes first in his degradation, the unforgiv- able on his part or the unforgiving on hers. The "dire reversal of the places of parent and child" (II,2) is simply the given of their lives. Dickens, too, is at least as hard on Mr. Dolls as his daughter is. The old man's drunken approach to insentience is complete at his death, and the balanced repetitions of Dickens's prose fix the terrible parallel for us when we are told that "in the midst of the dolls with no speculation in their eyes, lay Mr. Dolls with no speculation in his" (IV,9).

With Mr. Dolls reduced to a state no better than that of his namesakes, those wax effigies of human life, a pattern is com- pleted that began in the previous chapter with an intriguing parallel between Jenny herself and one of her dolls. There we heard Miss Wren "trolling in a small sweet voice a mournful little song, which might have been the song of the doll she was dress- ing, bemoaning the brittleness and meltability of wax" (IV,8).

And we may even recall at this point one of the earliest descriptions of Jenny, in which she seemed to be "articulated" like one of her own dolls: "As if her eyes and her chin worked together on the same wires" (II,1). A less obtrusive balance of syntax and sense in "a small sweet voice a mournful little song" performs now a quieter service than in the description of Mr. Dolls. The strange mirroring in this sentence begins mildly when Jenny's song is said to be as "little" as the "small" voice that sings it—and then slides into a curious instance of Dickensian animism enacting here a kind of ingrown allegory by which art bewails its own perishability. In her dual role as artist, Jenny is both a singer and, as Riah put it earlier with his own symmetrical phrasing, "a little dressmaker for little people" (II,5), and the reciprocal littleness now of singer (or voice) and song is matched here again by a second (if indirect) identification between maker and made. Meaning folds over itself once more as the artifact inherits the natural anxiety of the artist and laments the mutability (or "meltability") of its own medium.

Even before his death, Mr. Dolls was blessed with no more speculation than one of his daughter's lifeless dolls, and yet there is a mysterious side of things in this novel where a doll herself (and I use the personifying pronoun advisedly) can indulge in as much speculation about death and ends as anyone in the book. Through a psychic atmosphere thick with such violent imaginative extremes, between slumps of torpor and the reaches of certain miraculous vitalities, the dolls' dressmaker must steer her fancy, must pilot her life. Small wonder that her "betterness" is constantly imperilled. By her earliest raptures Jenny Wren was literally transported, lifted out of her life, borne free. Later came her birds and miles of flowers. Short of this grace, far below it, with her fancy all but chafed away to a cutting edge in satire, falls her defensive wit; yet her imagination, worn thin and harsh, has still managed to hold on, and even her acidity is tonic. What alone deadens is that final phase of her bitterness when even the "better look" is effaced and forgotten, the cruel victory of the everyday that grounds all memories of her transport and grinds them to a halt, like one of her own dreamed birds struck down.

We have to believe Dickens when he tells us that for Jenny Wren there can be no willed maneuvers of renewal. Yet as the prison house closes about her, she must keep guard against a complete walling-up of the apertures to wonder, and Jenny has been able to stake out a limited opening upon transcendence in her unlikely haven on the roof of Pubsey and Co. There we find Jenny and Lizzie seated reading "against no more romantic object than a blackened chimney-stock" (II,5). There are no magnificent "miles of flowers" now, but only a "few boxes of humble flowers." As Riah and Fledgeby join them, Jenny will become the prophet of her own divine vision, with the unimaginative Fledgeby an excommunicate from the fold of true believers. Dickens is implicitly participating here in that scaling and codification of fancy suggested by his eminent fellow Victorian John Ruskin, who saw the "pathetic fallacy" as the result of a temperament "borne away, or over-clouded, or over-dazzled by emotion," and who knew that this "is a more or less noble state, according to the force of the emotion which has induced it."[6] No one could have agreed with Ruskin more completely than did Dickens that "it is no credit to a man that he is not morbid or inaccurate in his perceptions, when he has no strength of feeling to warp them; and it is in general a sign of higher capacity and stand in the ranks of being, that the emotions should be strong enough to vanquish, partly, the intellect, and make it believe what they choose."[7] Fledgeby is a man, as it were, monstrously unwarped, falling at the lower end of Ruskin's fourfold ranking as "the man who perceives rightly, because he does not feel." Jenny Wren is the closest Dickens ever comes to the polar fourth stage. Beyond the first and second orders of poets, Jenny is one of those creatures who "see in a sort untruly, because what they see is inconceivably above them. This last is the usual condition of prophetic inspiration."[8] For the spiritual opposition of Fledgeby and Jenny there is no convergence: he is conducted to her rooftop sanctuary by Riah, "who might have been the leader in some pilgrimage of devotional ascent to a prophet's tomb," but Fledgeby is not at all "troubled by any such weak imagining" (II,5).

Fanny Cleaver, we know, has kept her spirit aloft partly through the invented name Jenny Wren, and the name conferred on Mr. Riah by Eugene Wrayburn seems to elevate him in Jenny's direction as well. Eugene considers Riah a "Patriarch," explaining that "I address him as Mr. Aaron, because it appears to me Hebraic, expressive, appropriate, and complimentary" (III,10). As brother to the prophet Moses and first high priest of the Hebrews, Aaron is a fitting namesake for Jenny's confidant and "high priest," who seems, in his sacred relation to the mysteries she incarnates, to have made good the promise of "divine light" parodied in the etymology of that forename Uriah from *David Copperfield* which may well come to mind when we first meet Mr. Riah.

Jenny soon explains her latest "pleasant fancy" on the roof—how, above the closeness and clamor of the city, "you see the clouds rushing on above the narrow streets, not minding them, and you see the golden arrows pointing at the mountains in the sky from which the wind comes, and you feel as if you were dead." Grammar and definition in the participial phrase "not minding them" are beautifully loosened, as if set free—the normal tethers of reference, both lexical and syntactic, here disengaged. The verb "minding" registers as both "mindful of" and "troubled by,"[9] and, complicated by the ambiguity of its referent, makes for an unusual tri-valent syntax. What or who is "not minding" what? The clouds pay no attention to the streets; neither, therefore, are they troubled by them. And the darkened streets, of course, pay heaven no mind. "You" too are with the clouds, neither worrying over nor even noticing the despoiled place you have climbed free of. When asked by Fledgeby what it feels like "when you are dead," this is Jenny's reply: "'Oh, so tranquil!' cried the little creature, smiling. 'Oh, so peaceful and so thankful!'" The adjective "thankful" answers in near echo to "tranquil" (as restated by "peaceful") in the way that Jenny's profound sense of gratitude follows upon her achieved and private sanctity, a condition of the spirit which she goes on to explain in a serene conjunctive series: "And you hear the people who are alive, crying, and working, and calling to one another down in the close dark streets, and you seem to pity them so! And such a chain has fallen from you, and such a strange good sorrowful happiness comes upon you!" Our interest, in the last clause, is drawn by an incremental rhythm through the unpunctuated chain of pre-nominal adjectives to the strange good paradox at its end, that "sorrowful happiness" which marks Jenny's attempt to wrest elation from the slavish levellings of melancholy. We have recently seen how the doubled adjectives in "small sweet voice" and "mournful little song" helped imply the quiet parallel Dickens had in mind, and here again his habit of multiplied adjectives is turned to special account. As always in his style, Dickens refuses to rest easy in the habitual, pressing it constantly for new yields. As we are about to see, this pre-nominal loading of modifiers can easily be impressed into imitative service.[10]

To pick up the text where I left off, it is important to realize that the "sorrowful happiness" which Jenny recommends when "you feel as if you were dead," this crucial phase of her escape artistry, is in fact subjunctive, an "as if" hypothesis. This has nothing in common with Little Nell's actual death-wishes in *The Old Curiosity Shop*. Like any romantic, Jenny simply dreams of a finer time, remembered or foreseen. Once again, though, her dreaming seems to approach achievement, for she herself appears to Riah like a vision: "the face of the little creature looking down out of a Glory of her long bright radiant hair, and musically repeating to him, like a vision: 'Come up and be dead! Come up and be dead!' " Here the mimetically elongated phrase "long bright radiant hair," describing what is often her bower, here her Glory, seems to echo —to be "musically repeating"—the adjectival cadence of her divine children's "long bright slanting rows," just as Jenny herself approximates in her own person at such moments, "like a vision," the best she has imagined. Mantled in the radiance of her golden hair, Jenny stands revealed as the type or emblem of the miracle only she has witnessed, and that almost far-fetched conditional metaphor of the "prophet's tomb" (to which Riah "might have been" leading Fledgeby) is now doubly actualized. Jenny's vision is not "prophetic" only; her rooftop vantage does in fact become a kind of "tomb," from which we are invited by Jenny, shrouded in the raiment of her Glory, to "Come up and be dead!" Little Nell never knew anything like this. Closely neighbored by the paradox of "sorrowful happiness," the predication "be dead" is all the more clearly an exonerating oxymoron, reminding us that we are now in the presence not of suicidal surrender but of vivifying transcendence, not of death and non-being, but of rebirth.

Jenny's gift for commuting between life and death in no way blinds her to the final reality of the latter. Justifying to Riah her inability "to hire a lot of stupid undertaker's things" for her father's funeral, she says that it would seem "as if I was trying to smuggle 'em out of this world with him, when of course I must break down in the attempt, and bring 'em all back again. As it is, there'll be nothing to bring back but me, and that's quite consistent, for *I* shan't be brought back some day!" (IV,9). In terms not too distantly related to her own transcendental vocabulary, this is the inexorable "consistency" of life's track toward dying: that you can come up and be dead as often as you like, but that one day body will catch up with soul, and then no one, not even yourself, will be able to bring you down and back. Such terms seem deliberately to recur at the book's spiritual nadir, and again they set a terminus. After two false starts and pointless backtrackings,

Bradley Headstone, followed by Riderhood, passes onto the wooden bridge in the direction of the locks where the two men will soon be found dead. It is Bradley's last aimless setting-out in the novel, and there is a proleptic irony in Riderhood's "The Weir's there, and you have to come back, you know" (IV,15). Jenny would of course know better; there is a day for all of us when we do not come back. Riderhood has once before "gone down" into the Thames, into death, and his spirit brought nothing back from that descent. It was his last chance. Having already encountered Jenny on the rooftop, Fascination Fledgeby says to her at their second meeting, "Instead of coming up and being dead, let's come out and look alive" (IV,8). By such reminders along the way, it would seem, we are conditioned to hear a final distorted echo of Jenny's invitation in Headstone's death summons to Riderhood. "I'll hold you living, and I'll hold you dead," he promises, and his last words in the novel are "Come down!" (IV,15). Come down and die, he says, for death is our long-sought mutual friend, and for us there will be only death, not the luxury of "being dead." Death cannot be outfaced or deflected. And only by a miracle of imagination like Jenny's can it be understood, unburdened of its terror, returned into the cycle of the living.

Though we see no one at all mourning the joint death of Headstone and Riderhood, Jenny herself is deeply moved by the frightful passing of her father. Her understatement records anything but indifference: " 'I must have a very short cry, godmother, before I cheer up for good,' said the little creature, coming in. 'Because after all a child is a child, you know' " (IV,9). That last tautological catch phrase is in fact, by Jenny's own eccentric definition, a poignant ambiguity. She has always referred to her father as her bad "child," and a child is a child, however prodigal. But Jenny is herself a child, and may be admitting here to her own vulnerability: I have tried to put away childish things, like dependency, like tears, but after all a daughter *is* a daughter. In the wake of pain, however, there must be restoration, and Jenny later tells Riah that at the height of her mourning, "while I was weeping at my poor boy's grave," she had the inspiration to model clothes for a doll on the clergyman's surplice. The energies of her own craft have in a sense "brought her back" from the grave this time, reclaimed her spirit, as she turns the ceremony of chill finality into one of warmth and continuity. For her clergyman doll will not be found presiding at funerals, but rather "uniting two of my young friends in matrimony" (IV,9).

It is a mordant irony when, two chapters later, the matrimonial and funereal services of a clergyman are in fact reversed in Bradley Headstone's mind. He secretly hopes that Reverend Milvey will be visiting Lizzie in order to preside at Eugene's funeral, and when Milvey realizes what Headstone is getting at in his leading questions, he asks, "You thought I might be going down to bury some one?" (IV,11). Bradley admits the half truth that this "may have been the connexion of ideas, sir, with your clerical character." But like the "clerical character" of the doll's surplice that Jenny has sketched out, the intended professional function is instead matrimonial, and Milvey finally admits to Headstone that he is on his way to "perform the marriage service" at Lizzie's wedding.

While dressing herself in mourning, Jenny eased her grief by imagining what her future sweetheart would think if he were there to see her fine clothes, and later, with her graveside sketch for the clerical surplice, death is again replaced by sexual union in Miss Wren's fancy, burying by the prospect of marrying. Such an imaginative transformation will take place one last time in the novel's next chapter, "The Doll's Dressmaker Discovers a Word." There language moves past mere communication into a sacramental communion, as Jenny manages to understand the one word, "Wife," that may retrieve Eugene from the edge of death where he is muttering it repeatedly. I think Dickens wants us to consider the word "Wife" here as a solitary expression of the ultimate Word, a creative sign that defines one person in terms of another and brings about that true "mutuality" which alone might redeem society. And like the original Word, the noun "Wife" seems to actuate itself by the very act of being spoken and comprehended, becoming the efficient cause of its own fulfillment. As the abstract, passive title to the subsequent chapter implies, no sooner is the word understood and articulately repeated than "Effect is Given to the Dolls' Dressmaker's Discovery." Language has been rendered "effective," creative, in an almost primal sense: a self-effecting decree. By discovering the "Word," and thus bringing Lizzie and Eugene together, Jenny has once again, through her unique powers, transformed mortality into matrimony, Eugene's deathbed into a marriage altar. And when the wedding service is read, a text "so rarely associated with the shadow of death," it is only fitting that Jenny should be in attendance, and that she should at last freely give way to her feelings: "The dolls' dressmaker, with her hands before her face, wept in her golden bower" (IV,11).

The "Word" which complements "Wife" is of course "Husband," and the implications of this entry in Society's lexicon are debated in the final chapter of *Our Mutual Friend*, "The Voice of Society," along with the concomitant definition of "gentleman." The scene at this last Veneering dinner is rife with linguistic sophistry, and even the chauvinistic Podsnap fusses with the vocabulary of definition in a spurt of his characteristic nonsense: " 'We know what Russia means, sir,' says Podsnap; 'we know what France wants; we see what America is up to; but we know what England is. That's enough for us.' " In this broken series, Podsnap moves from "means," meant colloquially for "intends," to a verb of being, "is," used self-definingly. This is the demagogue's faith in words as mere rhetorical fodder which is exposed when Podsnap turns his narrow mind to the debate over Eugene's marriage, with Twemlow objecting to the whole discussion as a private matter which "The Voice of Society" has no business pronouncing judgment upon: " 'I am disposed to think,' says he, 'that this is a question of the feelings of a gentleman." Podsnap snaps back with a sentence whose buried and two-faced premise recalls the use of "honourable gentleman" in *Pickwick's* opening chapter: " 'A gentleman can have no feelings who contracts such a marriage,' flushes Podsnap." Just as the "hon. gent." in *Pickwick* could somehow at the same time be a "humbug,"[11] so now there may be, according to Podsnap, such a creature as a "gentleman" with "no feelings," the implicit definition again robbing the term of its proper understanding. At the same time, Podsnap would deny to Lizzie Hexam the title of "lady" when Twemlow introduces it; Podsnap "echoes" his usage with disdain, and Twemlow returns: "... *you* repeat the word; *I* repeat the word. This lady." Yet Twemlow alone has "discovered" this word in the crucial sense of having found a definition for it. This he makes clear for the analogous case of "gentleman," explaining that he employs the term in its "common sense": "I beg to say, that when I use the word, gentleman, I use it in the sense in which the degree may be attained by any man." He does not apply it in some hermetic "Pickwickian sense," as denoting a social and economic category measured on the scale of "Society," but rather as a "degree" of ethical being which has a meaning available to "the common sense and senses of common people," as Dickens says in the Postscript to *Our Mutual Friend* in connection with the Poor Law.

The first chapter of the first novel Dickens wrote began with a debate over language, and the last chapter of the last book he finished returns to such a format, with the term "gentleman" again the word at issue. Sam Weller entered that first novel as the embodiment of a "gentleman's gentleman," with enough wit and verbal integrity to set language right for a time. Jenny Wren, given a "Wellerism" as if to establish her lineage more clearly, emerges from *Our Mutual Friend,* and from her own defensive wit there, as a major heroine of authentic speech. Whereas Podsnap's response to any aspect of "those vagrants the Arts" which does not mirror his own poor, prejudiced experience is an immediate "excommunication" (I,11), Miss Wren, herself a "vagrant" artist, holds to the redemptive virtues of communication and finally "discovers a Word" that can, by being spoken forth, unite "gentleman" and "lady" and so bind up the rent fabric of society in the private domestic sphere. Refusing to excommunicate language as Podsnap does, she instead elevates it from the de-meaning muddle, so to speak, into which it has slumped.

There is still more to notice about her time as Eugene's nurse. After he has been brutally beaten by Headstone, Jenny is called in at Eugene's request to attend him in his feverish coma. She is "all softened compassion now" (IV,10), and it comes about that through her "close watching (if through no secret sympathy or power) the little creature attained an understanding of him that Lightwood did not possess." Here Dickens's strategic parenthesis is his thesis. Jenny does have a "secret power" that brings her once again into contact with that other world on whose border Eugene is now wandering, "as if she were an interpreter between this sentient world and the insensible man" (IV,10). Her nimbleness and agility, the "natural lightness and delicacy of touch, which had become very refined by practice in her miniature work"—these very skills of her imaginative craft now give her an "absolute certainty of doing right" in dressing wounds, easing ligatures, and adjusting bedclothes. The practical dexterity of Dickens's most visionary character, previously used to approximate those heavenly glimpses in her worldly art, now makes of Jenny Wren the perfect nurse. This is the ministering imagination in its finest hour, and it suggests an important parallel with Lizzie, who was able to save Eugene from the river four chapters earlier only through a skill similarly "refined by practice" in her old life with her father, where the bodies fished from the river were already corpses: "A sure touch of her old practised hand, a sure step of her old practised foot, a sure light balance of her body, and she was in the boat" (IV,6). The past itself has been salvaged for good ends, as Jenny had hoped in another context when asking Riah to "change Is into Was and

Was into Is, and keep them so" (III,2). The thrust of Jenny's visionary energy is like a lone cantilever stabbing into the free space of
imagination; nothing meets it to complete a span, yet there are
staunch reinforcements in the human plane that gird it at its point
of departure. The implied comparison between Lizzie's saving
skills and Jenny's is one of these.

"If there is a word in the dictionary under any letter from A to Z
that I abominate, it is energy." With almost Pickwickian completeness, this was language divorced from reference; Eugene was so
removed from the idea of "energy" that he seemed to respond to it
only as a word, a lexical vexation, and even as such he detested it.
He went on record with this statement in the novel's third chapter,
but now the dolls' dressmaker, described at one point as "rigid from
head to foot with energy" (IV,9), has helped rehabilitate Eugene,
by a kind of psychic osmosis, for a new life of "purpose and
energy" (IV,11). Eugene originally summons Jenny, however, for
another and more astounding sort of osmosis, a transference of
fancy by which he hopes to bring Jenny's visionary solace into the
orbit of his own stricken and fevered brain. When Jenny first arrives, Eugene asks if she has seen "the children," and, puzzled at
first, Jenny finally replies with "that better look" upon her, re-
hearsing for us her visionary history and its gradual domestication
into the pastoral:

'You mean my long bright slanting rows of children, who used to bring
me ease and rest? You mean the children who used to take me up, and
make me light?'
Eugene smiled, 'Yes.'
'I have not seen them since I saw you. I never see them now, but I am
hardly ever in pain now.'
'It was a pretty fancy' said Eugene.
'But I have heard my birds sing,' cried the little creature, 'and I have
smelt my flowers. Yes, indeed I have! And both were most beautiful and
most Divine!'
'Stay and help to nurse me,' said Eugene, quietly. 'I should like to have
the fancy here, before I die.' (IV, 10)

The imagination meets its apotheosis through an act of mercy, in
one of the most perfect and moving scenes Dickens ever wrote. It
is as if Jenny's "most Divine" visions will help guarantee heaven
for Eugene; the limited artist of imagination must now aid in
imagining the limitless, and this is her great ministration. Jenny
has a doll called Mrs. (not Miss) Truth which she has used with
Bradley Headstone as a kind of lie-detector or moral touchstone
(II,11), but the highest Truth she has envisioned she has never been

able to dress her dolls in, never been able to marry with the world. Only now in her own person, selflessly and feelingly, can she become that accommodation which she could not willfully achieve in her art. Just as she became herself "like a vision" on the rooftop in singing out her invitation to come up and be dead, so now she is again her transcendent fancies given flesh within the golden bower of her hair, a personification at Eugene's side of her own dream of heaven, the very vision of her vision.

When Mr. Sloppy first meets Miss Wren at the end of the novel, it is an "event, not grand, but deemed in the house a special one" (IV,16). Her luxuriant blond hair accidentally tumbles down about her shoulders, and when Sloppy marvels, Jenny for the first time drops the defensive and often belligerent periphrasis "my back's bad, and my legs are queer" to admit point-blank, "I am lame." But when Sloppy sees her use her crutch-stick and tells her "that you hardly want it at all," Jenny is obviously touched. A rare thing has happened—a spontaneous exchange of friendship has, without recourse to her visions, brought "that better look upon her." When Jenny next explains to Sloppy the supposedly yet unsolved mystery of "Him, Him, Him" who is coming to court her, Sloppy breaks into such uncontrolled, raucous glee that Jenny finds it irresistible: "At the sight of him laughing in that absurd way, the dolls' dressmaker laughed very heartily indeed. So they both laughed, till they were tired." For the first time in *Our Mutual Friend* Jenny Wren laughs out loud in unembittered, uninhibited good spirits, and the result is a good weariness this time, not ennui or exhaustion. I believe we are encouraged to see the advent of Mr. Sloppy as the Coming of Him, and to notice how imaginatively well matched he and Miss Wren really are. Not only is Sloppy an artisan like herself, an accomplished cabinet maker who also appreciates the fine arts and will consider himself "better paid with a song than with any money" (IV,16) for the work he plans to do on Jenny's crutch, but he will also be able to entertain Jenny in return. For Sloppy's imagination has found play in impersonation, one of the comic novelist's own favorite forms of articulation. As Betty Higden told us early in the novel, "You mightn't think it, but Sloppy is a beautiful reader of a newspaper. He do the Police in different voices" (I,11). Abetting one's suspicions about T. S. Eliot's debt to Dickens and to that "Unreal City" of *Our Mutual Friend*, the recently published drafts of *The Waste Land* unveil "He do the Police in Different Voices" as the joint title of the original two-part format.[12] Like Fresca in a cancelled portion of "The Fire Sermon" (though Dickens was probably not in Eliot's mind here), Jenny Wren's "style is quite her own."[13] "Not quite an adult, and still less a child, / By fate misbred," Miss Wren too might have been "in other time or place" a "lazy laughing Jenny." When the happy laughter Sloppy brings to the close of her story begins to redress fate's imbalance in genuine emotional terms, we leave *Our Mutual Friend* on the eve of a great victory for the theme of imagination in Dickens.

Betty Higden, who praised Sloppy's newspaper recitations, is of course another figure for this theme in the novel. Although there is "abundant place for gentler fancies . . . in her untutored mind" (III,8), when faced with the vastness of the river Betty hears only a suicidal beckoning, "the tender river whispering to many like herself, 'Come to me, come to me! . . . death in my arms is peacefuller than among the pauper-wards. Come to me!'" (III,8). This is death, and it is very different from the transcendence of Jenny's invitation to "Come up and be dead!" Betty finds peace in Lizzie Hexam's arms in the famous death scene at the end of the chapter from which I have been quoting, but Jenny's imagination is much stronger than Betty's "gentler fancies," and she does not have to die. To borrow Dickens's last words about Betty Higden, Jenny's paradisal visions alone "lifted her as high as heaven." When we first met Jenny, she taunted Bradley Headstone with that "game of forfeits." Life for her has been such a game, but she has managed by imagination to cheat destiny, to forfeit as little as possible and to keep much intact. Through the help of her intermittent refuge in fancy, those therapeutic visions for her crippled days, she has, by the time of Sloppy's arrival, almost won the game. Gifted with a fanciful nature "in a double sense," a spirit both "figurative and poetical," both verbal and visionary, Miss Wren returns these chapters to their point of departure, as she becomes perhaps the finest, the most complete "imaginist" in the pages of our most imaginative novelist. After all the waverings, the prevarications, the foul violations of experience, some remarkable "pleasant fancies" have seen Jenny Wren through, safe within her golden bower, to a relief and a leniency.

Epilogue

We have, by the time of *Our Mutual Friend*, come a long way from Dick Swiveller's "Pass the rosy wine!" Here is Silas Wegg, the false artist of the "figurative" imagination, trying to corrupt the truly "poetical" Mr. Venus:

'We'll devote the evening, brother,' exclaimed Wegg, 'to prosecute our friendly move. And afterwards, crushing a flowing wine-cup—which I allude to brewing rum and water—we'll pledge one another. For what says the Poet?

> "And you needn't Mr. Venus be your black bottle,
> For surely I'll be mine,
> And we'll take a glass with a slice of lemon in it to
> which you're partial,
> For auld lang syne." '

This flow of quotation and hospitality in Wegg indicated his observation of some little querulousness on the part of Venus. (III,6)

Wegg's motives are wholly ulterior, his public "flow" of words indicating no internalized fancies. As in the distinction a page earlier between "the words" and "the spirit" of another quotation, both the verbal and the temperamental imagination are once again counterfeited in Wegg's "quotation and hospitality." His fancy is corrupt, one might say—and this may be, ultimately, the only distinction one can draw between the true and false avenues of imagination in Dickens—corrupt because for Silas Wegg and for the many men like him in the novels, fiction-making is more a scheming than a dreaming.

Dickens's perspective on such characters is always bifocal, their imaginative defaults being both moral and psychological. They cheat everyone, including themselves. They have not learned one of Dickens's great lessons: that fancy must be its own reward, and

222

that to use it solely as a means to an end is to lose it as a place of rest, native and invigorating. The Weggs of this world are out to defraud, but whatever it is they hope to gain they must pay for, finally, with their own souls. The vivid fabric of a character's dreams and fancies can, only at his certain peril, be surrendered to a deceiving surface of mere fabrication. Being only outward is, in the end, its own worst reprisal, for the spirit withers beneath a surface that is all "front." While Dick Swiveller finds it inspiriting to *believe* that a glass of gin and water might be distilled by fancy into a "flowing wine-cup," Wegg, with his rum and water, finds it merely useful to *pretend*. Mrs. Plornish and Mr. Wemmick like to fancy themselves as amateur pastoral architects; Mrs. Skewton and Mrs. Merdle, for instance, seem to care only that other people should believe in their Arcadian affinities. The ethic of imagination in Dickens teaches that falsehood is the opposite not of simple truth but of integrity, that there are lies which enliven as well as stifle, that there are Micawbers as well as Pecksniffs, Gamps as well as Skimpoles.

Even as early as *Pickwick Papers*, we meet not only Sam Weller but also Alfred Jingle. What Nabokov has one of his characters say about Professor Pnin, Dickens might well have written, with less irony, against Sam's name: "Our friend . . . employs a nomenclature all his own. His verbal vagaries add a new thrill to life. His mispronunciations are mythopeic. His slips of the tongue are oracular."[1] As with Nabokov, such praise would also be a testimonial to the stylistic art of Dickens himself, but the oneness between character and creator is never quite realized again after Dickens's first novel. And even there Alfred Jingle begins to give wit, word play, and fiction-making a dubious name, calling into question the permissible limits of imagination. The Pickwickian schism, as I have discussed it, exists between the stark facts of experience and a guarded, artificial innocence—a schism bridged, hesitantly and in part, by the end of the book. This is the novel in its Pickwickian aspect, so to speak. But *Pickwick Papers* has another life, whole and saner, a unitary vision mirrored in the included personal life of Sam Weller. Much of Sam's verbal invention he pretends to be quoting, while all of what he says sounds as if it were his author's own voice vicariously ascribed: the Dickensian verbal genius doing its Cockney accent. We sense when we are with Sam that we are at the heart of the novel, and at the heart of the novelist's power. This is never to happen again, except by fits and starts. For there is a wider, deeper schism in Dickens, whose career charts a fall into imaginative division between the author's voice and that of his characters, a cleft in style itself. Redemption, on those rare occasions when it is possible, means a renewal of this closeness between the fiction-maker and his character—a healing of the comic voice itself, as with Dick Swiveller, of visionary power, as with the fire-gazers, or of both, as in the lone case of Jenny Wren.

Dickens tends not to write about writers, about professional artists, about the vocational imagination at all. Nor as a rule does his prose, outside the clearly bounded domains of linguistic parody, take itself as its subject. Yet with a furious and persuasive invention unequalled in our fiction, Dickens's effortless way with words becomes an access back to their source, an exploratory "way" into the poetic impulse itself from which language springs. While Sam Weller was present to embody and give voice to this impulse, the Dickensian narrator was freed primarily to attack inauthentic forms of expression. For the satirist, too, *Pickwick Papers* was a utopian opportunity. Its monumental life occupies a third of these pages with the same disproportion it had for Dickens's career, its sudden and unexampled perfection becoming ever after the measure of his achievement. The change in scale with the fourth chapter of this study, and especially thereafter, follows the necessary division and multiplication of interests in Dickens's own art. His thirteen novels after *Pickwick* can be seen to plot out what I have called the drama of approximation in his writing, that struggle on behalf of his characters to regain for them the imaginative composure of a Sam Weller, the acute beauties of wit and style from which they have been disinherited. Understood in this way, style is a function of sanity; it is anything that gives form to our imaginative content, anything that shapes our fancy. When style fails the men and women of Dickens's novels, as it does repeatedly, it is left to the narrator to revive.

The resulting developments in Dickens's prose, the enriched layering and complication of his syntax, the proliferation of imagery, the augmented variations in tone and shade, have scarcely eluded the notice of critics. I have therefore felt free to treat these developments selectively, to examine style mainly when, with peculiar directness, it oversees or enacts the trials of imagination. I hardly wish to minimize the overall dramatic growth of Dickens's narrative style, but merely to specify a context in which its development may seem more than ever urgent, even mandatory. As it became, from *Oliver Twist* forward, increasingly a prose of the

London industrial metropolis, it was called upon more and more often to offer alternatives. Countering the pull of urban anonymity, the quirks and assertions of its own verbal personality were there constantly to remind us that identity might still vibrantly hold its ground. The flamboyance of this reminder is Dickens's great contribution to the history of prose, and it is for this, as well as for his vision of metropolis, that Dickens fronts on modernity like no other author of the nineteenth century. Few writers can be felt to have changed the nature of writing itself. Yet this we feel with Dickens. Without his whole-hearted, brilliantly driven experiments in language, the extremist vistas of twentieth-century fiction might have settled for nearer horizons, safer terrain. Dickens's faith in language was a faith in style, in its ability to confer form, to make fancy expressive. It was an evangelical faith, and there are characters in every novel who bear it witness, just as there are villains of imagination who warn us against its shams and blasphemies.

Dickens remains the great writer of modern industrial society. Page by page, his fertile language created the idiom needed to describe the new society, while the antic contrivances of his fancy, its dauntless power and caprice, kept viable a way out. The Dickensian style can at any moment turn away from the world, and with a bold agile grace remake it. Dickens wants this option for his characters as well, this aptitude for redrafting the real. Again *Pickwick Papers* sets the ambivalent pattern, for whereas Sam Weller exhibits the poet's healthy power of re-vision, Jingle, no less fanciful, hardly less gifted, goes wrong. My subject here, and Dickens's in novel after novel, has been the fictive capacity of ordinary men and women to rescue themselves from society's toxic indifference, from the corrosive, denaturing routines of getting from day to day. No such fictions can be ignoble. They mobilize the mind against deadness, and they may become saving privacies.

Such befriending dreams are a romantic indemnity, and my crowded fifth chapter was a psychological polling of selected characters in Dickens who must resort to these escapist fancies, deprived men and women who have struggled for imaginative suffrage against the forbidding indifference of society at large. As early as *Pickwick Papers*, bruised and humbled in Fleet Prison, Alfred Jingle marshals what little sarcastic energy he has left for a mock-pastoral tribute to the prison yard as a "pretty" haven, "romantic, but not extensive" (*P.P.*,42). While society as a whole in Dickens grows steadily more imprisoning, every emancipated fancy becomes itself a criminal aberration, and any space for personality that is at all "romantic" or "extensive" can be sought only in the inner landscapes of imagination.

A contrast between the relentless depersonalization of the urban prison and the chance for some kind of romantic reprieve runs with the deepest grain of Dickens's own imagination, and shows its lineaments on the surface of his last novel, the unfinished *Mystery of Edwin Drood*. It has been remarked how beautifully fitting it is that Dickens should have laid down his pen for the last time after writing the phrase "falls to with an appetite" (*E.D.*,23), but for me the quintessential last word comes in the penultimate chapter Dickens had time for, where that central tension in his writing between romantic hope and the antithetical urban society is embodied for the last time. Rosa, Grewgious, and Tartar, in their different ways the most romantic characters in the novel, attempt a major pastoral retreat in their rowing excursion, appeasing their "appetite" not only for food but also for that romantic experience so often denied to city-dwellers as they "stopped to dine in some everlastingly green garden, needing no matter-of-fact identification here" (22). In moving beyond the city, they seem to have journeyed past factual or geographic reality itself (which must be the symbolic point of Dickens's circumlocution about the actual place name) into the landscape of daydream. Yet before long this escapist paradise gives way to the specter of metropolis as if by a dying into modern life, a drifting back irrevocably from the Edenic dream: ". . . all too soon, the great black city cast its shadow on the waters, and its dark bridges spanned them as death spans life, and the everlastingly green garden seemed to be left for everlasting, unregainable and far away." What cannot be regained, however, ought never to be lost sight of in the mind's eye, as Jenny Wren has shown us. The fancy cannot let itself be disenfranchised, its prerogatives usurped, and to guard against this is the task of the true escape artists in Dickens's novels, both the burden and the privilege of their imaginations.

Such fiction-making as the pastoral nostalgia we find in *Edwin Drood* is often strategic in Dickens, a defense against things unpoetic. But when all is said and done, when word and deed have subsided, the fancy must have more to offer than merely its embattled tactics. The imagination is not only the means but the reason to survive. When a character's defenses are down, when peace comes, a true fancy will have left something residual—indeed, a place where the spirit may for a time reside. As far as we are shown, a Jingle or a Pecksniff has hollowed out no place for the dreaming mind, no such interiority. They are all surface fictions, all lies. While a lie is an act of untruth, a fiction may become a habitable structure apart from truth. By telling only lies we resign the imagination's power for widening into dimensioned fancies, for making possible a homing of the spirit. Cast up into a single antithesis, the difference is that between Dick Swiveller, reformed, and Silas Wegg. Wegg's opposite number in *Our Mutual Friend*, whom he never once encounters face to face, is of course Jenny Wren, that visionary girl who knows, just as Dick Swiveller had to learn with his "pleasant fictions" before her, that life's "pleasant fancies" are their own recompense. When Wegg tries instead to make his poetry "pay off," he is in fact selling out his imagination, a worse injury, though he never knows it, than the loss of his leg. It is his spirit's own self-mutilation.

Finally it is with Sam Weller and Miss Wren, however, that we have the most exquisite bracketing of Dickens's career. From the very start, Dickens had an intuitive sense that the imagination alone can anchor our spirit in the drift of anonymity. First Sam Weller, with miraculous ease and finesse, and at the end Jenny Wren, wearied by pain and its remorseless threats of dis-illusionment, ratify this belief with adrenal and improving fancies. By the agency of imagination, and like no other characters in Dickens, they are empowered to know and understand—Sam through his "figurative" Wellerisms, Jenny through her "poetical" visions—the ultimate anonymity of death itself. I will go back to Dick Swiveller now for one last parable. The imagination can be authenticated in Dickens's novels only when it makes an inward space for personality. Fictions that are no more than pretense merely close out the world and forestall its intimidations. But true fancy, as with Mr. Swiveller's "apartments," serves to pluralize reality. It builds alternative places in the mind, fictive chambers like Dickens's own expansive and colorful narrative (there is no better example) where new room is made for the imagination—spacious, airy, and gaily lit.

Appendix
Notes
Index

Appendix

A Note on the Narrative Imagination

Even after the dozens of pages throughout where style has been my immediate subject, there are still a few summary points that cannot be left unmade, and which will, I hope, begin to round out a context for the remarks on narrative language that have gone before. I have already narrowed the field considerably with the term "narrative." We might say, loosely and broadly, that there are two basic types of style in Dickens, or in any writer for that matter: descriptive (or narrative) and ascribed, the difference told simply by noting the boundaries marked by quotation. With the personal styles of Dickens's characters, as they articulate their individual fancies, I have necessarily been most concerned. Yet treatment of the narrative or descriptive voice itself has often accompanied such concern, especially during moments of silent inwardness on the part of these "imaginists," or in those feverish scenes where certain imaginations have been struck dumb.

Or in the psychoanalyzed rhetoric of the Pickwickian style and its superfluous fluency with which I began. When Sam Weller makes sarcastic capital of Mr. Muzzle's own ossified honorific metaphor, "flow of ideas," in criticizing Magistrate Nupkins's "style of speaking"—saying of such "ideas" that "they come's a-pouring out, knocking each other's heads so fast that they seems to stun one another; you hardly know what he's arter, do you?" (*P.P.*, 25)—Sam is sitting in for Dickens as a dissenting voice against this self-concussive, dunderheaded rhetoric, which "stuns" in the unlooked-for sense not only the speaker, but, if he is not careful, the listener as well. Elsewhere Sam, like Dickens, enters his dissent more slyly with a deadpan adoption of this same stupid eloquence, part of that generalized comic assault discussed in the early chapters of this book as the impersonal satiric style and which, on the unwitting part of the Pickwickian editor, was used to bracket and decontaminate the "impersonatorial" excesses of the inset stories. The fun of this satire lasts through to Dickens's final book, *The Mystery of Edwin Drood*, where the oppressive orator Honeythunder, last of rhetoric's naughty company, is a man drugged by the sound of his own thunderous voice, who treats Crisparkle as merely "an official person to be addressed, or a kind of human peg to hang his oratorical hat on" (*E.D.*,6). Honeythunder admits that "I never see a joke. . . A joke is wasted upon me, sir," and would therefore fail to understand Dickens's satiric comedy in using his own pompously inflated style against him when Honeythunder accidentally sits on Joe the coachman's hand: "The driver instituted, with the palms of his hands, a superficial perquisition into the state of his skeleton, which seemed to have made him anxious" (6).

I began to diagnose this sort of lunatic high style in the first chapter, and such egregious language was then contrasted in the second with that hurried, heated prose of the "impersonatorial" mode, which, like the demented imaginations to which it gave voice, had either to be warded off or inoculated against by the main body of *Pickwick's* narrative. Beginning with the delirium tremens of the dying clown and the ravings of Heyling, Dickens puts such trials of the mind under frequent observation in his novels with a narrative style that becomes at times almost encephalographic. ⌐Fevers bring, unbidden, the most extreme energies of imagination, and their scrutiny by style itself is part of Dickens's continuing study in human fancy, in mentalities tenanted both by invited and by involuntary imaginings.⌐ One of the most famously melodramatic stretches of narrative in Dickens, the flight from Dijon of Carker the Manager in *Dombey and Son*, exemplifies this "fever style" at its most ambitious, where for page after page straightforward description is at every turn turned inward, while the external scene is simultaneously invaded by the neurotic imagination before which the landscape unfolds in "a fevered vision of things past and present all confounded together" (*D.S.*,55). Outside reality reflects and enforces Carker's obsessive rage, as the "clatter and commotion" of his coach "echoed to the hurry and discordance of the fugitive's ideas" (55). Dickens's style is empowered to respond to this mental echoing within even the smallest compass,[1] and the syntactic balance of the sentence immediately following this sets up an unnerving parallel between the scenic and the psychic: "Nothing clear without, and nothing clear within." One more sentence, and fragmentation, parataxis, and the fast shift from present to past participles have all become synchronized to the rapid passing of the scene, as they mark the transition from objects to distraught observation: "Objects flitting past, merging into one another, dimly descried, confusedly lost sight of, gone!" From the more or less objective first phrase, we move to the impression of "merging," which is what objective reality here (the world of "objects") seems to (i.e., is seen to) be doing; the objective and the subjective are themselves "merging," and when we turn from active to passive voice for the past participles "descried" and "lost sight of," with their important adverbs "dimly" and "confusedly," we have stepped into the realm of disturbed perception only, until objective reality and observation merge once again in the monosyllabic finality of "gone!" The transference from scenic to psychic monotony, the intersection of "without" and "within," dictates even the plan of analogy in this sentence a few pages later, where the metaphor "wheel," as an image of painful psychic revolution, is borrowed from the immediate external scene, from the coach in which Carker is making his escape: "The monotonous ringing of the bells and tramping of the horses; the monotony of his anxiety, and useless rage; the monotonous wheel of fear, regret, and passion, he kept turning round and round; made his journey like a vision, in which nothing was quite real but his own torment." Repeated three times here in different forms, the word "monotony" becomes an obsessive refrain in the episode as a whole, where, as this sentence spells out, the subjective has dislodged the objective literally by *subjecting* it to feverish and demented pressures.

One of the most important uses of fever as the projection of an internal distemper of spirit comes not for a single villain like Carker, but for society at large in *Barnaby Rudge* and *A Tale of Two Cities*, those two historical novels in which the mass imagination itself is the protagonist that falls ill. In the *Tale*, the "leprosy of unreality" (II,7) which infects France during the Revolution is interpreted repeatedly as a feverish disturbance in the body politic which deforms the consciousness of an entire nation: "Every pulse and heart in Saint Antoine was on high-fever strain and at high-fever heat" (II,21), and without the ordinary rhythms of waking and sleeping, time is again violently distorted, all alleviation hopeless: "There was no pause, no pity, no peace, no interval of relenting rest, no measurement of time. Though days and nights circled as regularly as when time was young, and the evening and the morning were the first day, other count of time there was none. Hold of it was lost in the raging fever of a nation, as it is in the fever of one patient" (III,4). Beginning in stiff, regularized parataxis and alliteration—a sort of prose relentlessness—that last summary gives way to biblical echoes which remind us that in these revolutionary cataclysms apocalypse is near: it is the best of times, it is the worst of times, it threatens the end of time.

Style repeatedly conditions our response to the aimless and maniacal frenzy of the Terror, and we are to respond, I think, primarily to the mental atmospherics of the scene—to the engagement of imagination with hysteria. Dickens's oddly opaque preface is an attempt to suggest this. After saying that he "conceived the main idea of this story" while acting in a Wilkie Collins drama, he explains that a "strong desire was upon me then, to embody it in my own person." This is puzzling enough. Does he mean by "embody" to play the lead, take all the parts, or somehow incorporate and enact the spirit of the novel? There follows the most awkward, involuted, and downright difficult statement I have come upon in Dickens, scarcely clarifying the matter: ". . . and I traced out in my fancy, the state of mind of which it [the main idea of the story] would necessitate the presentation to an observant spectator, with particular care and interest." Decode this as best we can, and Dickens seems to be saying that his "main idea," whatever it may be, requires primarily the accurate presentation of a certain "state of mind," as plotted out in Dickens's imagination. By "state of mind" he surely means the feverish excitement of the Revolution, and the presentation of this is necessitated by his main idea (here the odd circularity of this explanation is coming to light) because it *is* the main idea. As we saw for *Pickwick*, subjectivity is also the subject of the *Tale*, the mass imagination gone horribly wrong and contaminating an entire nation, without possibility of quarantine.

The presentation of this terrorized subjectivity is conducted with every available resource of Dickens's narrative prose. It is "embodied" in his "own person" in the sense that it is impersonated by the style's propellant repetitions, the dizzying monotony of its iterated imagery, the wild, improbable elongations of its motifs. To simulate nightmare and fever, Dickens's own narrative personality must somehow assimilate their intensities, and Dickens insists in his preface that the idea "has had complete possession of me; I have so far verified what is done and suffered in these pages, as that I have certainly done and suffered it all my-self." What is this overmastering possession by a single idea if not an admission of monomania? Taine wrote, largely in criticism of this side of Dickens's artistry, that the "imagination of Dickens is like that of monomaniacs," an imagination which at its most ex-cessive produces a "style of sickness rather than of health,"[2] indeed the prose of "feverish rapture."[3] Forster discusses this critique of Dickens's style along with the even less complimentary remarks by G. H. Lewes about the prose of "hallucination," and defends Dickens by claiming that when "he imagined a street, a house, a room, a figure, he saw it not in the vague schematic way of ordi-nary imagination, but in the sharp definition of actual perception, all the salient details obtruding themselves on his attention."[4]

That last phrase might have been written by Dickens himself about the spectator on the roof of Todgers's, when the salient ani-mation of the scene, as in hallucination, begins to grate on his nerves, to usurp and fluster his attention, to possess him with dis-proportionate and monomaniacal assertiveness.[5] Dickens was there examining the power of his own imagination as it became irritated into feverish ill-health, yet short of this neurotic excess, the meta-phor of "monomania" seems just right to describe those famous overtures to Dickens's later novels, like the fixated repetitions of "fog" in Bleak House or "stare" in Little Dorrit. At such times we notice "the salient details obtruding themselves" in an obsessive manner which is altered hardly at all for the opening of Edwin Drood, but which is there manifestly revealed as hallucinatory imitation, with the drugged iterations of "Tower" and "spike" re-producing the "scattered consciousness" of John Jasper as it "fan-tastically pieced itself together."

Thinking to strengthen his case against the opposition, Forster quotes from a letter Dickens sent to him which actually corrobo-rates the "hallucination" theory. Dickens writes that when "I sit down to my book, some beneficent power shows it all to me, and tempts me to be interested, and I don't invent it—really do not, but see it, and write it down."[6] Dickens ends by alluding to the toll taken by this release of imagination: "It is only when it all fades away and is gone, that I begin to suspect that its momentary relief has cost me something." On the next page of the Life, in a decep-tively new context, Forster quotes a letter from Dickens to Bulwer-Lytton which makes the point in another way, Dickens suggesting that it is his "infirmity" to "perceive relations in things which are not apparent generally."[7] The imagination costs the mind, the

exercise of hallucinatory vividness taxes consciousness to a sometimes unhealthy extent, and it is this "infirmity" that is warned of
on Todgers's roof, and from which Tom Pinch is granted immunity. Taine admitted that Dickens was "admirable in the depicture
of hallucinations. We sense that he feels himself those of his characters, that he is engrossed by their ideas, that he enters into their
madness."[8] He enters into: here again is the idea of impersonation,
of inhabiting and acting out traumatic states of mind. It is an effort
of imagination, an effort of style, and it has its liabilities.

Picking up *A Tale of Two Cities* again, we find beyond the
preface two internal studies of this same narrative phenomenon.
Just after Miss Pross has said about herself to Mr. Lorry, "Never
imagine anything. Have no imagination at all," she begins her account of Dr. Manette's sleepless nights in a style whose unflinched
repetitions remind us of Dickens's own heightened narrative in the
surrounding story: "Sometimes, he gets up in the dead of the night,
and will be heard, by us overhead there, *walking up and down,
walking up and down,* in his old prison. She hurries to him, and
they go on together, *walking up and down, walking up and down,*
until he is composed... In silence they go *walking up and down
together, walking up and down together,* till her love and company
have brought him to himself" (II,6;italics mine). Dickens cannot
resist making the point explicit: "Notwithstanding Miss Pross's
denial of her own imagination, there was a perception of the pain
of being monotonously haunted by one sad idea, in her repetition
of the phrase ... which testified to her possessing such a thing." It
is as if Miss Pross herself has latched upon precisely "the state of
mind of which it would necessitate the presentation to an observant spectator," and there is nothing at all "curious," as Sylvère
Monod thinks,[9] about this identification between repetitive style
and imaginative insight.

It is an indirect tribute, not too modestly veiled, to Dickens's
own empathetic style, and a similar point is later made with Dr.
Manette's letter, whose repetitions Monod finds "scandalous"[10] in
their obsessive overuse. Yet like Miss Pross, Dr. Manette is a
Dickensian narrator by proxy, and the rhythms of his account are
meant, almost involuntarily, to call up the young woman's feverish repetitions in the story he relates. The doctor's "memory is circumstantial and unshaken," he claims, but it is not altogether
calmly that, after ten years, he envisions the details of his story "as
I saw them all that night" (III,10). This disturbing immediacy, including the anguished monotony and repetition of the original

scene, cannot help but occupy and control the prose of his account. Monomania is at times a communicable infirmity; style is its carrier, and yet often its only relief.

This is certainly true for Mr. Peggotty during his narrative of Emily's flight and fever in *David Copperfield*, led off by a series of monotonous repetitions about the disfigurement of time: "Likewise the fire was afore her eyes, and the roarings in her ears; and there was no to-day, nor yesterday, nor yet to-morrow; but everything in her life as ever had been, or as ever could be, and everything as never had been, and as never could be, was a-crowding on her all at once, and nothing clear nor welcome" (*D.C.*,51). Here, long before Miss Pross or Dr. Manette, and modified by the same calm deliberation in the telling, is the power of impersonation in the hands of a simple and sincere man caught up in the fearful drift of his own story, as if hallucinated by it, and finding it necessary to stop soon after that last description, "as if for relief from the terrors of his own narrative," terrors which are all the more acute for the slow, steady lucidity with which they are recounted.

David comments on the intensity and immediacy of Mr. Peggotty's narrative in a most revealing manner, using the word "earnestness" so often applied by David, and by Dickens elsewhere, to his own craft as a writer: "He saw everything he related. It passed before him, as he spoke, so vividly, that, in the intensity of his earnestness, he presented what he described to me, with greater distinctness than I can express. I can hardly believe, writing now long afterwards, but that I was actually present in these scenes; they are impressed upon me with such an astonishing air of fidelity" (51). We might call Mr. Peggotty's story another communicable hallucination, a powerful story of fever that can, despite its own strongly willed coherence, call forth feverish impressions at third hand. In this remarkable concentricity, vividness within vividness, we have one of the most interesting studies in Dickens of language as impersonation, style as "infirmity," a fascination with the narrative imagination itself, its strengths and its dangers, that dates back to the portraits of Dismal Jemmy and Jack Bamber in the first novel and that is always very much on Dickens's own mind as a story-teller.

What I want to consider now is the Dickensian style in another major capacity, a version of narrative experiment which runs in every way counter to the headlong imperative surges of the "fever style," yet which, and perhaps nowhere more beautifully than in *David Copperfield*, performs side by side with it. Such dramatic,

nervous alternations of style, such restless tensile variations, inform us about the motor nerves of Dickens's prose. As we know
from the first chapter, the comedy of Dickens's phrases is often
owed to discrepancy, to ironic contrast. And as early as *Pickwick
Papers*, too, Dickens's contrapuntal set of mind was evidenced by
that vital tension between the impersonal satiric manner and the
impersonatorial mode. Even in the absence of quarantine, the
habit persists. One is enticed by widespread and various evidence
to call it almost the essential genius of Dickens's prose to go forward through contrastive patterns of tone and registration. What
I therefore wish to treat now is the development of yet a third
mode, a kind of lyric counterpoint both to satire and to manic
simulation, a quiet, lucid prose that increases greatly the potential
for that alternating momentum which is the very life of Dickens's
style.

The metaphor in *David Copperfield* for the retrospective imagination as "a half-sleeping and half-waking dream" finds unusual
dramatization early in the novel, where Mr. Mell's anything but
mellifluous flute lulls the young David into that "middle state
between sleeping and waking" (*D.C.*,5). The episode, accompanied
by the mellow chords of that new prose which becomes available
at such times, is one of the most undiluted romantic moments in
Dickens—an almost Keatsian waking-dream during which Mr.
Mell's flute supplies the intoxicating song of the nightingale. A
sort of melancholy fit has fallen upon the young David, as "the
influence of the strain upon me was, first, to make me think of all
my sorrows, and then to take away my appetite; and lastly to make
me so sleepy that I couldn't keep my eyes open." And the act of
recollection itself recovers the sensation: "They begin to close
again, and I begin to nod, as the recollection rises fresh before me."
We are immediately transported into the present tense, and "Once
more the little room . . . fades before me, and I nod, and sleep." As
in a Keatsian surrender of ego, identity itself lapses away on the
waves of this "secret prose": "I wake with a start, and the flute has
come back again, and the Master at Salem House is sitting with his
legs crossed, playing it dolefully, while the old woman of the house
looks on delighted. She fades in her turn, and he fades, and all
fades, and there is no flute, no Master, no Salem House, no David
Copperfield, no anything but heavy sleep" (5).

The phrase "secret prose" is of course Graham Greene's, his
well-known label for "that sense of a mind speaking to itself with
no one there to listen,"[11] the Dickensian prose of "delicate and

exact poetic cadences, the music of memory."[12] In the scene of Mr. Mell's flute-playing, the music of memory is overheard by the mind until the mind itself drifts away on the paratactic iterations "no flute, no Master, no Salem House, no David Copperfield . . . ," and is no longer awake to listen. This diffusion of ego is the opposite of hazarded identity in fever, and such quiet inward prose energizes reserves of Dickens's verbal powers that are left dormant during his more frenetic exercises in psychic reproduction. This "secret prose" also has the same capacities for reinstating past impressions as does the prose of fever; the quiet times of imagination, as well as its neuroses, can be communicated at second hand, revived in a sort of beneficent rather than painful hallucination.

Even earlier in *David Copperfield* there is a single sentence of superb dreamlike immediacy: "I never hear the name, or read the name, of Yarmouth, but I am reminded of a certain Sunday morning on the beach, the bells ringing for church, little Em'ly leaning on my shoulder, Ham lazily dropping stones into the water, and the sun, away at sea, just breaking through the heavy mist, and showing us the ships, like their own shadows" (3).[13] Reality is here a waking-dream: like a shadow of itself. Yet such a moment is the opposite of nightmare, of the feverish torments of memory, its prose the opposite of the driven impersonatorial mode. Instead of grinding, rushing, relentless verb phrases there is a long, lazy row of absolute constructions in which nonfinite participles serve to fix, to immortalize, the memory, each absolute longer than the last in a widening expansion across the surface of imagination, as if in imitation of the concentric ripples on the water which would be sent out from Ham's stones. Held before us in the simplest and most transparent diction, the timeless moment has widened out perceptually from the sound of church bells in the ear to the feel of Emily upon David's shoulder, to the sight of Ham at the water's edge, and finally to the vision of sun and ships away at sea.

I have mentioned Keats twice. There is an even greater musician of memory whose most complete orchestration, *The Prelude*, appeared for the first time in 1850, the year of *David Copperfield's* publication. Two years later Dickens began publishing his next novel, the first that could actually have been influenced by Wordsworth's poem, and in *Bleak House* there does seem to be a deliberate allusion to the renowned "spots of time." As it happens, the scene is a premonition of Esther's fever and disfigurement, the great change that is soon to come upon her. Esther has ventured out on a "cold, wild night" in which the afterglow of the sunset

appears—in an operative definition of the Wordsworthian sublime
—"both beautiful and awful" (31). There is also a "lurid glare" in
the direction of London, which "engendered" a "fancy," itself perhaps a warning of the coming fever, "of an unearthly fire." Just
before that passage on the Yarmouth beach, David had mused: "I
don't know why one slight set of impressions should be more particularly associated with a place than another, though I believe
this obtains with most people." In this later scene from *Bleak
House,* Esther Summerson makes a similar comment on the odd
workings of memory: "I had no thought that night—none, I am
quite sure—of what was soon to happen to me. But I have always
remembered since that when we had stopped at the garden-gate to
look up at the sky, and when we went upon our way, I had for a
moment an undefinable impression of myself as being something
different from what I was then. I know it was then and there that
I had it" (31). And again, as in *Copperfield,* the "secret prose" of
private nostalgia completes the meditation in a wide radius of
remembered sensations, here with what appears to be a direct echo
of Wordsworth (my italics): "I have ever since connected the feeling
with that *spot and time* and with everything associated with that
spot and time, to the distant voices in the town, the barking of a
dog, and the sound of wheels coming down the miry hill."[14]

Without this new kind of prose response—it should by now be
clear—Dickens's increasing reliance on romantic experience and
consolation for his figures of imagination would have been beyond
honest portrayal, lost in discursiveness. In the absence of spoken
wit, this lyric inwardness of style is what makes possible those
beautifully private moments of self-recognition and reunion in the
later novels. As with none but our greatest writers, style grew with
psychology, developing to meet the needs of theme. Like the drastic impersonations of the fever style, Dickens's secret prose lies at
the core of his resources as a dramatic symbolist. I wanted simply
to get this straight, and to get it down. Together with his brilliant
satiric prose, any truly comprehensive analysis of these abutted
and reinforcing styles would be the work of another book.

Notes

PROLOGUE

1. All quotations are from the *New Oxford Illustrated Dickens* (London, Oxford University Press, 1948–1958), but references in parentheses follow standard practice with Dickens by pointing simply to chapter and, where applicable, to book, in order to make location easier in the many widely available editions. For standard novelists other than Dickens I have quoted from recent paperback editions, and given page references in the notes. The following abbreviations are used for Dickens's novels: *P.P.* for *Pickwick Papers; O.T.* for *Oliver Twist; N.N.* for *Nicholas Nickleby; O.C.S.* for *The Old Curiosity Shop; B.R.* for *Barnaby Rudge; M.C.* for *Martin Chuzzlewit; C.C.* for *A Christmas Carol; D.S.* for *Dombey and Son; D.C.* for *David Copperfield; B.H.* for *Bleak House; H.T.* for *Hard Times; L.D.* for *Little Dorrit; T.T.C.* for *A Tale of Two Cities; G.E.* for *Great Expectations; O.M.F.* for *Our Mutual Friend; E.D.* for *The Mystery of Edwin Drood.*

2. George H. Ford, *Dickens and His Readers: Aspects of Novel-Criticism Since 1836* (Princeton, N.J., Princeton University Press, 1955), p. 117.

3. Steven Marcus, "Dickens After One Hundred Years," *The New York Times Book Review,* June 7, 1970, p. 49.

4. Sigurd Burckhardt, *Shakespearean Meanings* (Princeton, N.J., Princeton University Press, 1968), p. 93.

5. Jane Austen, *Emma,* ed. Lionell Trilling (Boston, Mass., Houghton Mifflin, 1957), p. 261.

6. Charles Dickens, "Preliminary Word," *Household Words,* 1 (1850).

7. Wallace Stevens, "Imagination as Value," *English Institute Essays 1948* (New York, Columbia University Press, 1949); rpt. in Stevens, *The Necessary Angel: Essays on Reality and the Imagination* (New York, Vintage Books, 1951), pp. 138–39.

CHAPTER 1. THE PICKWICK CASE: DIAGNOSIS

1. Miguel de Cervantes, *The Adventures of Don Quixote,* II, trans. J. M. Cohen (Baltimore, Md., Penguin Books, 1950), p. 741.

2. Steven Marcus, "Language into Structure: Pickwick Revisited," *Daedalus* (Winter 1972), p. 187.

3. *Ibid.*, p. 194.

4. *Ibid.*, p. 189.

5. George Gissing, *Charles Dickens: A Critical Study* (London, 1898), p. 185.

6. Angus Wilson, *The World of Charles Dickens* (New York, Stein and Day, 1970), p. 118.

7. Henry Fielding, *Joseph Andrews*, ed. Martin C. Battestin (Boston, Mass., Houghton Mifflin, 1961), p. 11.

8. Ibid., p. 7.

9. Otto Jespersen, *Growth and Structure of the English Language*, 9th ed. (Oxford, Basil Blackwell, 1948), pp. 126–27.

10. Laurence Sterne, *The Life and Opinions of Tristram Shandy, Gentleman*, ed. James A. Work (New York, Odyssey, 1940), p. 164.

11. Ibid., p. 200.

12. Ibid., pp. 26–27.

13. Fielding, *Joseph Andrews*, p. 8.

14. Ibid., p. 199.

15. Sterne, *Tristram Shandy*, p. 320.

16. "Politics and the English Language," *A Collection of Essays by George Orwell* (Garden City, N.Y., Doubleday, Anchor Books, 1954), p. 173.

17. *North British Review*, 3 (May 1845), 76. Quoted in part by Ford, *Dickens and His Readers*, p. 114. Ford's section on "The Artist" provides a good rapid sampling of contemporary remarks about Dickens's style, some of which I have quoted here at greater length from the original sources.

18. Vladimir, Nabokov, *Lolita* (New York, G. P. Putnam's Sons, 1955), p. 39.

19. Ibid., p. 41.

20. Rpt. from *Household Words*, 18 (1858) as lead article in *The English Language: Essays by Linguists and Men of Letters, Volume II, 1858–1964*, ed. W. F. Bolton and D. Crystal (Cambridge, Eng., Cambridge University Press, 1969), pp. 1–2.

21. W. K. Wimsatt, Jr., *Philosophic Words: A Study of Style and Meaning in the "Rambler" and the "Dictionary" of Samuel Johnson* (New Haven, Conn., Yale University Press, 1948).

22. Ibid., p. 1.

23. Ibid., p. x.

24. Ibid., p. 117.

25. George Meredith, "An Essay on Comedy," *Comedy*, ed. Wylie Sypher (Garden City, N.Y., Doubleday, Anchor Books, 1956), p. 34.

26. Fielding, *Joseph Andrews*, p. 168.

27. Ibid., p. 116.

28. Nabokov, *Lolita*, p. 296.

29. G. L. Brook, *The Language of Dickens* (London, André Deutsch, 1970), p. 52.

30. H. P. Sucksmith, *The Narrative Art of Charles Dickens: The Rhetoric of Sympathy and Irony in his Novels* (Oxford, Clarendon Press, 1970), pp. 41–69.

31. *The Morning Post* (March 12, 1836), quoted in a different connection by Walter Dexter, "The Reception of Dickens's First Book," *The Dickensian*, 32 (1936), p. 48.

32. Stephen C. Gill, "*Pickwick Papers* and the 'Chroniclers by the Line': A Note on Style," *Modern Language Review*, 63 (1968), 33–36.

33. W. K. Wimsatt, Jr., *The Prose Style of Samuel Johnson* (New Haven, Conn., Yale University Press, 1941). See his discussion of parallelism, pp. 15–37.

34. Ralph Waldo Emerson, *Nature*, ch. IV, "Language," *Works*, I (Boston, 1884), 35.

35. *The Saturday Review* (May 8, 1858), p. 474.

36. See Walter Jackson Bate, *The Achievement of Samuel Johnson* (New York, Oxford University Press, 1955), pp. 14–16.

37. Miriam Allott, *Novelists on the Novel* (New York, Columbia University Press, 1959), p. 318.

38. Alice Meynell, "Charles Dickens as a Man of Letters," *Atlantic Monthly*,

January 1903; rpt. in *The Dickens Critics*, ed. George H. Ford and Lauriat Lane (Ithaca, N.Y., Cornell University Press, 1961), p. 96.

39. *The Saturday Review*, pp. 474–75. Again quoted partially by Ford (p. 114), who seems to agree that, as satire, the style is proceeding "unconsciously." Given Dickens's agreement with Saxonist standards, this is scarcely probable.

40. Sterne, *Tristram Shandy*, p. 38.

41. Brook, p. 169.

42. Sylvia Manning, *Dickens as Satirist* (New Haven, Yale University Press, 1971), p. 42.

43. George Meredith, *The Egoist*, ed. Lionel Stevenson (Boston, Houghton Mifflin, 1958). The "artist in phrases" (p. 252) is Mrs. Mountstuart Jenkinson, and the "meanings" (p. 177) belong to Clara Middleton.

44. The "Pickwickian sense" here is distantly akin to "the Roman style" that was "affected" by Lovelace and Belford in *Clarissa*, as explained in Richardson's footnote to the letter of March 13th: "it was an agreed rule with them, to take in good part whatever freedoms they treated each other with, if the passage were written in that style." Samuel Richardson, *Clarissa Harlowe*, ed. John Angus Burrell (New York, 1950), p. 81.

45. Marcus, "Language into Structure," p. 190.

46. Ibid., p. 191.

47. See Eric Partridge, *Name into Word: A Discursive Dictionary* (London, Secker and Warburg, 1949), p. 340.

CHAPTER 2.   QUARANTINE

1. Quoted by Steven Marcus, *Dickens: from Pickwick to Dombey* (New York, Basic Books, 1965), p. 13.

2. In his newest essay on the novel, Marcus has also heard inverted Miltonic echoes, though in the first rather than the second chapter. The novel's opening he takes to be "a parody of a scene in heaven, a fanciful rendering of an unwritten episode of *Paradise Lost*. These comic-epic, immortally foolish creatures are going to visit the earth and report in their correspondence on what they see" ("Language into Structure," p. 188). What Marcus's interpretation and mine have in common, apart from Milton, is the sense that Dickens is consciously engaged at the beginning of *Pickwick Papers*, in various ways and places, upon the creation of a comic myth.

3. J. Hillis Miller, *Charles Dickens: The World of His Novels* (Cambridge, Mass., Harvard University Press, 1958), p. 4.

4. Ibid., p. 15.

5. W. H. Auden, "Dingley Dell and the Fleet," *The Dyer's Hand* (New York, Random House, 1962); rpt. in Martin Price, ed., *Dickens: A Collection of Critical Essays*. Twentieth Century Views (Englewood Cliffs, N. J., Prentice-Hall, 1967), p. 71.

CHAPTER 3.   RELEASE

1. Vladimir Nabokov, *Nikolai Gogol* (Norfolk, Conn., New Directions, 1944; corrected ed., 1961), p. 142.

2. This resembles the idea of "rootless burlesque" or "directionless parody" so often mentioned by William F. Axton, *Circle of Fire: Dickens' Vision and Style and the Popular Victorian Theater* (Lexington, University of Kentucky Press, 1966). Axton is pointing out that disproportionate wording in Dickens which is ridiculous without direct ridicule, a "burlesque play with the grand style—an incongruous inflation of diction and images which just misses being arch" (p. 211).

3. Northrop Frye, "Dickens and the Comedy of Humors," *Experience in the Novel: Selected Papers from the English Institute* (New York, Columbia University Press, 1968), p. 58.

4. Jonas Barish, *Ben Jonson and the Language of Prose Comedy* (Cambridge, Mass., Harvard University Press, 1960), pp. 295–96. Barish himself does not discuss Mr. Pickwick.

5. This is what one presumes Charles Kent to have been suggesting in his essay on "Wellerisms" when he noted, during his discussion of the Cambridge "Exam Paper" on *Pickwick* and its frequent reference to the Wellers, that "it is especially worth bearing in remembrance . . . that the First Prize taken under that Paper was won by Mr. Walter Besant, the novelist, and the Second Prize by Mr. Walter Skeat, the philologist." What Kent was apparently hinting at is the conjunction in Sam Weller of creative fancy and verbal preoccupation, of the novelist's together with the linguist's imagination. See Kent, "Introduction," *Wellerisms from "Pickwick" and "Master Humphrey's Clock,"* selected by Charles F. Rideal, ed. Charles Kent (London, 1886), xxi. For the "Exam Paper" see Charles Stuart Calverley, *Complete Works* (London, 1901), pp. 115–117.

6. Indexed by Wimsatt, *Philosophic Words*, p. 131. "Ebullition" also appears later in chaps. 41 and 51, and is used by Joyce in the phrase "phenomenon of ebullition" eight pages into his own parody of "philosophic" jargon and argument in the "Ithaca" phase of *Ulysses* (New York, Modern Library, 1961), p. 673.

7. See above, p. 8.

8. Marcus, "Language into Structure," p. 199.

9. Wilson, *The World of Charles Dickens*, p. 121.

10. Marcus, *Dickens*, p. 239.

11. See Sam's play on "drift" (Ch. 42) and "change" (Ch. 45), again couched in "Wellerisms." In the recent Broadway musical "Pickwick," an attempt was made both to update and to "spice up" Sam's characteristic gimmick, but the result, with its even more frequent puns and double-entendres, tended merely to cheapen the original into something like the vaudevillian's stock one-liner. Instead of "out with it, as the father said to the child wen he swallowed a farden" (12), the stage Sam has it, as it were, backward: "It came out all right in the end, as the man said when the baby had swallowed the button." Sam is a bit too arch and self-conscious throughout the production, singing a song called "Talk Your Way Out of It," or, when asked by Pickwick for a reference ("Can you get a character?"), replying "I *am* a character!" This is information Dickens's Sam would surely have left for us to discover.

12. James Joyce, *Ulysses*, p. 328.

13. Ibid., p. 332.

14. See above, pp. 10–11.

15. It is interesting to note the marked falling off in the relation between master and man in John Fowles's novel *The French Lieutenant's Woman* (Boston, Mass., Little, Brown, 1969), where we meet a Cockney servant called Sam Farrow, a "Sancho Panza" figure (p. 43) who had not read *Pickwick Papers* but who "knew of Sam Weller . . . from a stage version of it" (p. 41). The novel is set only thirty-one years after the writing of Dickens's famous book, but things have changed drastically. There is still the comedy of circumlocution associated with the master, Charles, when he glorifies an idea like "as you say" in speaking with his Sam: "You may have been, as you so frequently asseverate, born in a gin palace" (p. 40). But we soon hear that whereas Sam Weller "was happy with his role," Sam Farrow merely "suffered it" (p. 43). Mr. Pickwick's man took a real joy in language, and Fowles's surprising inversion is that now it is the master who keeps Sam Farrow around as a daily audience for his effete word play, "his characteristic . . . and deplorable fondness for labored puns and innuendoes: a humor based, with a singularly revolting purity, on educational privilege" (p. 43).

16. Lola L. Szladits, ed., *Charles Dickens 1812–1870: An Anthology* (New York, Arno Press, 1970), p. 117.

17. Cervantes, *Don Quixote*, I, 204.

18. Fielding, *Joseph Andrews*, p. 19.

19. Ibid., p. 255. Win Jenkins in Smollett's *Humphry Clinker*, one of Dickens's favorite novels, is heavily indebted to Fielding's Mrs. Slipslop, and among her dozens of accidental puns—including "deify the devil" (letter of Oct. 4) and a letter signed "with true infection" (June 3)—there is even a Weller-like turn with legal jargon in her personification of "habeas corpus" as "Apius Korkus, who lives with the ould bailliff, and is, they say, five hundred years old" (June 14).

20. Sterne, *Tristram Shandy*, p. 563.

21. Daiches, "Misunderstanding as Humour: An Aspect of the English Comic Tradition," *More Literary Essays* (Chicago, Ill., University of Chicago Press, 1968), p. 40.

22. Madeline House and Graham Storey, eds., "Appendix A. Dickens's Diary," *The Letters of Charles Dickens, I, 1820–1839* (Oxford, Clarendon Press, 1965), p. 639.

23. See Ford, *Dickens and His Readers*, p. 5.

CHAPTER 4.   THE PIVOTAL SWIVELLER

1. Eberhart, *Selected Poems, 1930–1965* (New York, New Directions, 1965), p. 98.

2. James R. Kincaid, *Dickens and the Rhetoric of Laughter* (New York, Oxford University Press, 1971), p. 99.

3. Ibid., p. 95.

4. Ibid.

5. Ibid., p. 82.

6. J. Redding Ware in *Passing English of the Victorian Era: A Dictionary of Heterodox English, Slang, and Phrase* (London, 1909) explains this jargon as a "fine figure of speech" for drunk: "Drink and hot sun both produce red face. Good example of *double entendre*, or rather perhaps of direct satire by indirect means. 'I see you've been in the sun, Tom!' " (p. 236). Dick's usage is in fact cited as example by John S. Farmer and W. E. Henley, comp. and ed., *Slang and its Analogues Past and Present* (London, 1904; rpt. New York, Kraus Reprint Corp., 1965), p. 27.

7. J. B. Priestley, *The English Comic Characters* (London, John Lane, The Bodley Head, 1925), p. 225.

8. Ibid., p. 226.

9. Etymology teaches us that "swivel" is also related at its root to the obsolete form "swive," meaning "to copulate." Certainly Dick Swiveller, in his low companionship with the shiftless rake Trent, is one of the likeliest candidates in Dickens for a young man, as the *OED* has it, "given to sexual indulgence."

10. G. K. Chesterton, *Appreciations and Criticism of the Works of Charles Dickens* (London, 1911), p. 24.

11. We are not forced to guess at her age in drawing parallels with Little Nell, as Jack Lindsay does when he says that the Marchioness is "around eleven or twelve" when she first appears. See Lindsay, *Charles Dickens: A Biographical and Critical Study* (New York, Philosophical Library, 1950), p. 194.

CHAPTER 5.   APOLLO AND THE NAUGHTY COMPANY

1. See above, pp. 20–21.

2. Northrop Frye, "Dickens and the Comedy of Humors," p. 59.

3. Marcus, *Dickens: from Pickwick to Dombey*, p. 239.

4. Chesterton, *Charles Dickens: A Critical Study* (New York, 1906), p. 231.

5. Chesterton, *Appreciations and Criticisms*, p. 101.

6. Ibid.

7. George Eliot, *Middlemarch*, ed. Gordon S. Haight (Boston, Mass., Houghton Mifflin, 1956), p. 63.

8. Marcus, *Dickens*, p. 214.

9. Ibid., p. 217.

10. Ibid., p. 217.

11. Barish, *Ben Jonson*, p. 295.

12. Brook, *The Language of Dickens*, p. 214.

13. Manning, *Dickens as Satirist*, p. 242.

14. Ibid., p. 243.

15. Frye, "Dickens and the Comedy of Humors," p. 61.

16. Ibid., p. 64.

17. Barish, *Ben Jonson*, p. 203.

18. Ibid., p. 199.

19. Philip Roth, *Portnoy's Complaint* (New York, Bantam Books, 1970), p. 81.

20. Fielding, *Joseph Andrews*, pp. 138-39.

21. Meynell, in Ford and Lane, *The Dickens Critics*, p. 99.

22. Robert Lewis Taylor, *W. C. Fields: His Follies and Fortunes* (New York, Doubleday, 1949), p. 113.

23. Kenneth Tynan, "Three Individualists," *Curtains* (New York, Atheneum, 1961), p. 356.

24. Ibid., p. 355.

25. Schwartz, "The Genius of W. C. Fields," *The Nation* (Feb. 11, 1950); rpt. in Donald A. Dike and David H. Zucker, ed., *Selected Essays of Delmore Schwartz* (Chicago, Ill., University of Chicago Press, 1970), p. 435.

26. Ibid., p. 436.

27. Ibid., p. 433.

28. Ibid., p. 434.

29. Priestley, *The English Comic Characters*, p. 273.

30. Randolph Quirk, *Charles Dickens and Appropriate Language* (Durham, Eng., University of Durham, 1959), p. 21.

CHAPTER 6. ESCAPE ARTISTS

1. William H. Gass, *Fiction and the Figures of Life* (New York, Vintage Books, 1972), p. 148. See also p. 51.

2. This is a quality of Dickens's style that is often noted in criticism, now and then in the pages behind us here. Martin Price, for instance, has compared the stylistic atmosphere of a Dickens novel to that of an Augustan satire, observing that "style is itself the touchstone by which we test the falsity or rigidity of what it describes." See Price, "Introduction," *Dickens: A Collection of Critical Essays*, p. 12. Sylvia Manning writes in *Dickens as Satirist* that "Dickens's own energy" is a standard of value communicated by his prose: "The flexibility and above all the enormous vitality of the satiric style constitute an ever-present contrast to the joylessness of automatism and repression" (p. 41).

3. In "Fettered Fancy in 'Hard Times,' " *PMLA*, 84 (1969), David Sonstroem mentions the "fairy palaces" simile, along with the analogy whereby "Machines become elephants" and other such metaphors, to instance "the zestful and defiantly imaginative narrative personality, who uses Fancy against Fact in several direct and very effective ways" (p. 521). In his study of "The Rhetoric of Sympathy and Irony" in Dickens, Sucksmith sees too much sympathy and too little irony in the simile, and thus makes my point for me by making the very mis-

take I think Dickens is warning us against; Sucksmith writes that the narrator "criticizes Coketown harshly in *Hard Times* and yet by also seeing the lighted mill by night as a 'fairy palace' suggests the factory has more to it than dirt, monotony, and oppression." See Sucksmith, *The Narrative Art of Charles Dickens*, p. 343.

4. D. H. Lawrence, *The Rainbow* (New York, Viking, 1961), p. 28.

5. Ibid., p. 37.

6. Angus Wilson, *The Middle Age of Mrs. Eliot* (London, Seeker and Warburg, 1958), p. 278.

7. This is the example cited by Fowler as "the most familiar and violent instance" of *nominativus pendens*, a form of anacoluthon, in *A Dictionary of Modern English Usage*, 2nd ed., revised by Sir Ernest Gowers (London, Oxford University Press, 1965), p. 393. In his appendix to *The Language of Dickens* on "Substandard Grammar," Brook draws three out of his four examples of this usage from Mrs. Gamp (p. 246, items 94 and 95).

8. Dorothy Van Ghent, "The Dickens World: A View from Todgers's," *Sewanee Review*, 58 (1950); rpt. in Price, p. 29.

9. C. S. Cooper, *The Outdoor Monuments of London* (London, The Homeland Association, Ltd., 1928), pp. 35–6; photograph, p. 153.

10. Van Ghent, p. 29.

11. Ibid.

12. See Appendix, p. 236.

13. Ibid., pp. 237–240.

14. Angus Wilson, "Dickens on Children and Childhood," *Dickens 1970*, ed. Michael Slater (New York, Stein and Day, 1970), pp. 225–26.

15. The episode from which I quote is found in *Jane Eyre*, ed. Mark Shorer (Boston, Mass., Houghton Mifflin, 1959), pp. 321–22.

16. See Appendix, pp. 234–37.

17. On this complex and fascinating issue see especially Julian Moynahan, "The Hero's Guilt: The Case of *Great Expectations*," *Essays in Criticism*, vol. X, no. 1 (1960), pp. 60–79.

18. Evelyn Waugh, *A Handful of Dust* (New York, Dell, 1959), p. 202.

19. Ibid., p. 203.

CHAPTER 7. THE GOLDEN BOWER OF "OUR MUTUAL FRIEND"

1. To adapt to the present case a pocket of latter-day Dickensian word play from Vladimir Nabokov's *Transparent Things* (New York, McGraw-Hill, 1972), one might say that the italicized "characters" here (both Jenny herself and the pronoun that proclaims her, as Nabokov distinguishes between "personae" and "signs") are protectively self-"inclined" (see p. 92).

2. Edgar Johnson, *Charles Dickens: His Tragedy and Triumph*, II (New York, Simon and Schuster, 1952), p. 1043.

3. See above, pp. 73–74.

4. Robert Garis, *The Dickens Theatre: A Reassessment of the Novels* (Oxford, Clarendon Press, 1965), p. 252.

5. Ibid.

6. Ruskin, "The Pathetic Fallacy," from *Modern Painters*, III (1856); rpt. in Harold Bloom, ed., *The Literary Criticism of John Ruskin* (New York, Doubleday, Anchor Books, 1965), pp. 65–66.

7. Ibid., p. 66.

8. Ibid., p. 67.

9. Jane Austen had already exploited the comic potential of this pun on "mind" when she had Mr. Bennet answer his wife's wistful comment "I should not mind any thing at all" with a satiric misunderstanding based on another,

unintended definition of her verb: "Let us be thankful that you are preserved from a state of such insensibility." See Mark Shorer, ed., *Pride and Prejudice* (Boston, Mass., Houghton Mifflin, 1956), p. 99.

10. The most histrionic use of frontal adjectives in these mimetic jam-ups is Dickens's thudding bravura when describing Lady Tippins, with her "immense obtuse drab oblong face, like a face in a tablespoon" (*O.M.F.* I,2).

11. See also p. 109 above.

12. T. S. Eliot, *The Waste Land: A Facsimile and Transcript of the Original Drafts Including the Annotations of Ezra Pound*, ed. Valerie Eliot (New York, Harcourt Brace Jovanovich, 1971). Calling her father a "swipey old child," Jenny says at one point that he is "fit for nothing but to be preserved in the liquor that destroys him" (III,10), conjuring up an image of the preserved and bottled "children" in Mr. Venus's shop, those "hydrocephalic" babies (III,14). To die by "water on the brain" is a fitting end in a symbolic drama many of whose cast, from the title character John Harmon on down, are threatened with or succumb to "Death by Water," including Gaffer Hexam, Rogue Riderhood, Bradley Headstone, and Eugene Wrayburn. Surely the section of Eliot's poem bearing this title does not resist such associations, and there is that especially curious mention of an "infant hydrocephalous" in a passage Eliot himself subsequently struck from the "Death by Water" manuscript (p. 75).

13. Ibid., p. 27. All the brief quotations here are from this page of the manuscript.

EPILOGUE

1. Nabokov, *Pnin* (New York, Avon, 1959). p. 164.

APPENDIX

1. In *Circle of Fire* Axton devotes eighteen pages (234–52) to the governing rhythms, measures, and motifs of Carker's flight, with a detailed emphasis on broad syntactic patterning and repetition. For the present, however, my interest is with the narrowest range at which Dickens can perform his stylistic simulation.

2. H. A. Taine, *History of English Literature*, II. trans. H. Van Laun (New York, 1871), p. 344.

3. Ibid., p. 347.

4. John Forster, *The Life of Charles Dickens*, ed. J. W. T. Ley (London, Cecil Palmer, 1928), pp. 717–18.

5. See above, pp. 174–77.

6. Forster, p. 720.

7. Ibid., p. 721.

8. Taine, p. 344.

9. Sylvère Monod, "Some Stylistic Devices in *A Tale of Two Cities*," *Dickens the Craftsman*, ed. Robert B. Partlow, Jr. (Carbondale and Edwardsville, Ill., Southern Illinois University Press, 1970), p. 175.

10. Ibid., p. 174.

11. Greene, "The Young Dickens," *The Lost Childhood and Other Essays* (London, Eyre and Spottiswoode, 1951); rpt. in Ford and Lane, *The Dickens Critics*, p. 247.

12. Ibid., pp. 345–46.

13. To comment on these lines in connection with Greene's theory about Dickensian lyric prose, as Ford does, by observing merely that "such a passage has its own glow" is not even to scratch the surface of such a complex verbal

effect. See George H. Ford, "Dickens and the Voices of Time," *Nineteenth-Century Fiction*, Dickens Centenniel Issue, 24 (March 1970), p. 430.

14. Esther's compound wording of "then and there" and "spot and time" seems to imply a compromise on Dickens's part about that very question Hartman believes to arise from Wordsworth's phrase: "It is hard to decide whether the first or the second member of the partitive construction 'spots of time' should be emphasized." See Geoffrey H. Hartman, *Wordsworth's Poetry 1787–1814* (New Haven, Conn., Yale University Press, 1964), p. 212.

Index